TRANSITIVITY
Grammatical Relations in
Government-Binding Theory

Linguistic Models

The publications in this series tackle crucial
problems, both empirical and conceptual, within the
context of progressive research programs. In
particular, Linguistic Models will address the
development of formal methods in the study of
language with special reference to the interaction
of grammatical components.

Series Editors:
Teun Hoekstra
Harry van der Hulst
Michael Moortgat

TRANSITIVITY
Grammatical Relations in Government-Binding Theory

Teun Hoekstra
University of Leiden

1984
FORIS PUBLICATIONS
Dordrecht - Holland/Cinnaminson - U.S.A.

Published by:
Foris Publications Holland
P.O. Box 509
3300 AM Dordrecht, The Netherlands

Sole distributor for the U.S.A. and Canada:
Foris Publications U.S.A.
P.O. Box C-50
Cinnaminson N.J. 08077
U.S.A.

CIP

Hoekstra, Teun

Transitivity: grammatical relations in government-binding theory / Teun Hoekstra. – Dordrecht
[etc.]: Foris Publications. – (Linguistic Models; no. 6) – With references.
ISBN 90-6765-014-5 bound
ISBN 90-6765-013-7 pbk.
SISO 805.1   UDC 801.5
Subject heading: general linguistics; grammar.

ISBN 90 6765 014 5 (Bound)
ISBN 90 6765 013 7 (Paper)

Printed in the Netherlands by ICG Printing, Dordrecht.

for Sonja

Table of Contents

Acknowledgements

The research project which has led to the present book was started in 1978, directly after I finished my studies of Dutch Language and Literature. The title of the project was "Derived Grammatical Relations". The idea behind the project was that the nature of grammatical relations could most sensibly be studied from the point of view of processes which affect grammatical relations in some way or other. My aim was to provide a reasoned classification of various types of such processes (e.g. passive, tough-movement etc.) as well as an inventory of elements (verbs, adjectives) which trigger these rules.

The project was embedded within the ongoing discussion between generative grammar and relational grammar. It was my naive assumption that a decision in these matters could be obtained and that, once such a decision had been made, a detailed. description was the next relevant step. I soon realized that this undertaking was indeed naive. Fortunately, various circumstances enabled me to attain a more solid linguistic background before carrying out the project.

First of all, I had the opportunity to visit the Salzburg Summer Institutes in 1979 and 1982, the first of which was organized in combination with the Summer Institute of the LSA. I would like to thank my teachers Joseph Aoun, Frank Heny, Richard Kayne, Ed Keenan, Robert Lees, David Lightfoot, Luigi Rizzi, Thomas Roeper and Thomas Wasow for their stimulating courses and the Netherlands Organization for the Advancement of Pure Research (ZWO) for sponsoring my attendance of these courses. My personal development owes much to the GLOW conferences, which are always a pleasure to attend.

I owe a great intellectual debt to Michael Moortgat. He taught me the value of the philosophy of science, and his critical attitude showed me that I was too easily satisfied with my own work. In 1979 we both became interested in lexical theory. A number of publications resulted from this joint interest. My real love for linguistics can be traced back to Harry van der Hulst. Our deep and long-lasting friendship and partnership in linguistics has contributed greatly to my own development. We have always had a similar attitude towards our linguistic activities, even though my primary interest is in syntax and his is in phonology. I hope that I can contribute as much to his work as he has done to mine.

Of the people in the Faculty of Letters in Leiden, Erica García, Berend Hoff, Jan Kooij, Bob Rigter, Ariane van Santen, Sjef Schoorl and Jan de Vries have done a lot to encourage and support me, for which I am grateful. Frits Beukema has helped me enormously. He read the entire manuscript several times and suggested many improvements, both of form and of content. Without his help the book would probably be unreadable.

I would also like to thank the staff of the Dutch Lexicological Institute for their hospitality and for guiding me through the wonderful world of optical readers, word processors and printers with which I have prepared the copy for this book.

Finally, it is only fair to apologize in public to my wife Sonja for all the things she had to put up with during my work on this book, for the countless conversations I interrupted to ask her a question relating to the form of what she said, where the contents deserved my undivided attention, for all those times that I was either absent or absent-minded, and for so many other things. The dedication of this book to her is a small token of my gratitude for her tolerance and support.

Abstract

The status of grammatical relations is different in the various theoretical frameworks that are available at present. The research presented here aims at providing an argument to support the conception of grammatical relations in generative grammar. According to this conception, grammatical relations are not to be regarded as primitive, but rather as notions that are defined in structural terms.

In chapter 1, this conception of grammatical relations in generative grammar is compared with the position taken by other frameworks which maintain the assumption that grammatical relations should be regarded as primitives. Arguments are presented in support of the a priori supriority of the generative approach.

Chapter 2 introduces the central notions of the recent Government and Binding framework proposed in Chomsky (1981). Assuming that neither complement selection nor complement ordering can be explained in terms of phrase-structure rules, we propose and define a number of principles in terms of which these aspects of phrase structure can be accounted for. Specifically, it is argued that the central notion of the Government and Binding framework, viz. the notion of government, should be conceived of as a unidirectional notion. Furthermore, a distinction is made between structural government and thematic government. It is further proposed that a second principle, the Unlike Category Condition, excludes from the possible complement types of a lexical category those types that are non-distinct from this lexical category in syntactic feature content. Various differences between Dutch and English can thus be attributed to a single difference at a more abstract level of principles. At the same time, some recalcitrant problems in the grammar of Dutch are given a straighforward solution, specifically the treatment of the two different types of infinitival complements.

Grammatical relations are crucially involved in the statement of relation-changing rules such as passive. Chapter 3 presents a historical overview of the different analyses of the passive that have been put forward in various frameworks. We then proceed with a discussion of other construction types that are related to passives and we argue that this relatedness can be accounted for in terms of the properties shared by the derivation of these constructions, which is determined by general principles. The central question is whether these properties refer to primitive notions like subject and object or whether the structural notions defined in chapter 2 are sufficient. We argue that the latter option is not only feasible, but in fact superior to the former. More specifically, it is shown that in the case of passive the class of NP's that become the subject at the level of S-structure can be characterized in terms of the structural notion of government and that there is no viable semantic characterization which would select the relevant set of NP's. Moreover, the range of passive constructions found in Dutch differs from the range of passive constructions found in English in a way that is predictable on the basis of the differential orientation of government in the two languages.

Chapter 3 also elaborates on the so-called unaccusative analysis, which has been proposed by Perlmutter. This analysis is first extended to cover a wider range of constructions and it is then recast in terms of the Government and Binding framework. Furthermore, it is argued that the class of intransitives which are analyzed as unaccusatives share a number of significant properties with passives, whereas the other intransitives share a number of relevant properties with transitives. On the basis of these clusters of properties, we propose a new classification of verbs in terms of the feature transitivity. The interpretation of this feature differs from the traditional interpretation, however. Within this conception, passive may be regarded as a rule mapping members of the transitive class into the class of intransitives. Interestingly, in turns out that each type of transitive verb has a corresponding intransitive type.

Chapter 4 discusses in some detail the so-called small-clause analysis. This analysis has important repercussions for the concept of subject. We provide a number of arguments in favour of this analysis, one of which involves the analysis of synthetic compounds. Finally, we investigate whether the perfective construction can be analyzed as involving a matrix verb taking a small-clause complement. It turns out that the traditional perfective auxiliaries have to be treated as categories in their own right, i.e. that a reduction to matrix verbs is not possible.

Chapter 1

Grammatical Relations

Grammatical relations like subject and object function as intermediary concepts in the formulation of the mapping between semantically and phonologically relevant representations of linguistic expressions. According to definitions in traditional grammar, grammatical relations are interpreted in an essentialist way. This is evident from such formulations as "the object is that constituent that undergoes the action performed by the subject". Although grammatical relations are thus basically defined in a semantic manner, they are used to express regularities in the formal manifestation of various categories in the language and they figure also in relation-changing rules. Thus, we may find statements like "the direct object is expressed with accusative case" and "in passive sentences, the direct object is the subject of the clause".

Various efforts have been made to reduce grammatical relations as intermediary concepts to either formal (e.g. morphological) categories or semantic categories such as agent etc. Such efforts are very obvious if one deals with a language like e.g. Finnish, which has a large set of morphological cases. Alternatively, if a language does not display any alternations such as active versus passive sentences, the idea might be harboured that in that language grammatical relations do not play a role. However, such an approach reflects an empiricist attitude towards linguistic theory.

What we are interested in is the nature of grammatical relations in a general theory of natural language. A rationalist approach to linguistic theory requires that one assumes that all languages are variations on a common theme that is determined by general laws and principles governing their organization. We shall adhere to the basic assumption of generative grammar that these laws and principles are formal in nature and hence determine the notion of a possible grammar of a natural language. It is only within this context that questions like the ones we are interested in can sensibly be asked. Furthermore, we shall assume a mentalistic interpretation of these laws and principles; if they are denied that interpretation, there is no rational criterion to distinguish between alternative proposals. As linguistics is an empirical science, a truth claim must be involved beyond a mere correspondence with the data[1].

A well-known criticism, levelled mainly by structuralist grammarians, is that grammatical relations are defined in such a way that formal and semantic notions are conflated. Such a conflation is of course what one would expect given the intermediary nature of these concepts. However, this piece of criticism is more principled in nature: concepts like subject and object are argued to derive from aristotelian logic: they are motivated in terms of the logical analysis of propositions and as such are alien to linguistics. Although this criticism may turn out to be right, we think that the strongest assumption is that there is an isomorphy between syntactic analysis and logico-semantic analysis of linguistic expressions. We furthermore assume that it is a fruitful hypothesis that logico-semantic structures are invariant across languages. From these assumptions it follows that syntactic structures must be assumed to be invariant across languages as well. At first sight, this claim is blatantly wrong. Nevertheless, at a more abstract level languages might be much more similar than would appear from their superficial differences. To the extent, then, that languages can be shown to be similar at an abstract level, there might indeed be a correspondence between syntactic and logico-semantic structures. The variations between languages might be accounted for in terms of alternative fixings of parameters provided by Universal Grammar. It is for instance conceivable that logico-semantic structures are not linearly ordered and that ordering differences of constituents among languages derive from the implementation of principles of the X'-syntax in different ways. It should of course be kept in mind that much variation among languages is unsystematic, in that it results from historical accident. This variation cannot and should not be accounted for by principles of Universal Grammar. On the other hand, it is not possible to know in advance which part of the variation can be explained in a principled fashion, although some cases are clearer than others.

Having outlined some of the background assumptions that we adopt, we now turn to a closer examination of the way in which grammatical relations are treated in a number of different frameworks, in order to highlight the issues that are relevant for the rest of the book. It will be clear that concepts such as subject and object do not have any content outside the frame of reference of the theory in which they are exploited. As is the case with all concepts whose existence and properties cannot be determined through direct perception, the justification of grammatical relations depends on the relative success of the theory that exploits them. Basically, then, it is impossible to compare the grammatical relations used in theory A with the grammatical relations used in theory B without comparing theory A and theory B as well. Nevertheless, to some extent this is what we shall do. We shall focus on the question whether grammatical relations should be given the status of primitives, i.e. irreducible notions provided by Universal Grammar, or whether they can be defined in terms of other primitives. The former interpretation is accepted in Relational Grammar and frameworks that are in many respects similar to it, whereas Generative Grammar proper has always held on to the position that grammatical relations are derivative concepts. We shall start the overview with a discussion of Relational Grammar (1.1.), after which we turn to Functional Grammar (1.2.). Finally, we return to Generative Grammar in section 1.3.

1.1. Relational Grammar

Relational Grammar arose in the first half of the seventies as an offshoot of standard transformational grammar. Since its conception was based on criticism directed at transformational theory, one may, with the advantage of retrospect, investigate to what extent the original motivation for it is still valid. It turns out that the changes which have occurred in the Extended Standard Theory have undercut the basis for the criticisms that gave rise to Relational Grammar.

Relational Grammar (henceforth RG) was heavily involved within the derivational paradigm and with what is now called the construction-specific approach. In these earlier versions of transformational grammar, "there was almost a one-to-one relation between transformations and construction types" (Lightfoot 1979a:58). Lightfoot cites Dougherty (1975) who "has argued that this practice reflected a perpetuation of Harrisian taxonomic transformations into research on generative grammars". This construction-specific approach is essentially taken over and further developed by RG. Because it is assumed that a truly explanatory theory of language should generalize over different languages, transformational theory must be regarded as unsuccessful. In a structural description of the

passive transformation for English, all sorts of elements had to figure that are
irrelevant to the phenomenon of passive, but are required in order to allow for a
proper factorization of the input strings. Other, equally irrelevant, material
has to be referred to in the structural description of the passive transformation
of a different language. This prevents the relevant generalizations. Perlmutter
(to appear:4) states this as follows: "transformations stated in terms of linear
order of constituents made it necessary to formulate distinct rules for languages
with different word orders for what could be characterized in relational terms as
the same phenomenon cross-linguistically". Heny (1981:2-3), in his appraisal of
the Government and Binding theory, discusses the same problematic feature of
earlier transformational grammar. He notices that the grammatical transformations determine as significant the structural units that appear in them. However,
one could ask in what sense these units are significant. "The theory did not tell
us. It incorporated no claims to the effect that certain sequences were more
"natural", others "impossible" ;... it is not surprising that attempts to ask
questions about the cross-linguistic significance of transformations made little
headway while the classical transformation formed the core of grammatical theory"
(Heny, loc.cit).

    While the work of Chomsky and his followers eventually led to the abandonment
of this construction-specific approach, RG carried it on and since the criticism
against an entirely structural way of formulating the construction-specific
rules seemed valid, primitive notions were adopted in order to overcome these
problems. Thus Chomsky's (1965) claim was rejected that grammatical relations are
irrelevant to the formulation of grammatical rules, because independently motivated phrase markers supply sufficient information.

    A different kind of motivation for the RG framework does not derive from
problems regarding cross-linguistic generalizations, but from considerations
pertaining to rule ordering. As we noted above, RG was conceived in a period in
which derivational aspects were of crucial interest. Relevant issues were rule
ordering, the cycle, rule typology etc. Proponents of RG argued that the entire
set of grammatical rules might be partitioned into two subsets, one of which
includes the rules that affect grammatical relations (e.g. passive) and the other
the rules that do not refer to grammatical relations. The former were considered
to be cyclic, unlike the latter, which in turn all involve an essential variable
in their formulations and were therefore able to create unbounded dependencies
(e.g. question formation)[2]. This typology would have some explanatory power if it
is assumed that all and only relation-changing rules operate in the cycle, while
all other rules are postcyclic. The former set could then be formulated in terms

of primitive grammatical relations, whereas the remainder could be regarded as
proper transformations. This would resolve a lot of ordering stipulations.

Again, we may wonder whether this piece of motivation is still relevant. It is
worth noticing that the classification of rules proposed in RG is captured by the
distinction between MOVE NP and MOVE WH in the framework of Chomsky (1977)[3].
Therefore, the classification itself may be regarded as expressing a genuine
distinction. However, the idea that instances of WH-movement, i.e. rules that may
give rise to long distance dependencies, can be regarded as postcyclic seems to
be incorrect[4]. The only valid criterion for the proposed classification, therefore, is that some rules involve grammatical relations while others do not. The
basic question, then, is whether the instances of NP-movement should be formulated in terms of grammatical relations rather than in terms of structural
notions. The fact that instances of WH-movement do not alter grammatical relations follows automatically from the fact that the landing site of these rules is
a non-argument position, viz. COMP. The intrinsic ordering of instances of WH-
movement versus NP-movement may be a genuine issue (cf. van Riemsdijk & Williams
1981, van Riemsdijk 1981b for discussion), but a motivation for the adoption of
RG can no longer be derived from it.

Let us now focus on the grammatical relations themselves. In what sense are we
to understand the claim that they are primitives? It should first be noted that it
is difficult to regard the grammatical relations distinguished by RG as homogeneous concepts. Compare this with the notion of subject in the standard theory of
generative grammar. Subject is defined as the NP which bears a specific structural relation to the predicate at a given level. NP's that are subject at
distinct levels share this structural property, i.e. if NP_i is the subject of a
clause at the level of D-structure and NP_j is the subject of the same clause at
the level of S-structure, both are the sister of VP at that level. In this sense,
the content of the notion subject is homogeneous within the standard theory.
Within RG, on the other hand, there is no unified content, as the notion of
subject is not defined, but is indeed primitive. The relevant question is what
the motivation is to use the same label in both cases, i.e. to assume that they
actually bear the same relation at these different levels.We would like to argue
that only the same label is involved.

Let us concentrate first on final-stratum relations, i.e. relations borne by
nominal dependents at the level of what we may, perhaps somewhat misleadingly,
call surface structure. The question of why a specific grammatical relation is
assigned to some nominal dependent at the final level has nothing to do per se
with the assignment of these relations at other levels, but is determined by

behaviour shared with nominal dependents in other sentences. Thus, in English
clauses one constituent may be said to be the final subject of the clause, since
there is always an NP that determines the agreement on the verb. To express this
common trait of NP's in different clauses, they are all said to bear the subject
relation in the final stratum. Let us assume that this is the way in which final
subjecthood is determined. One might say, then, that subjecthood is in some sense
defined, rather than primitive (i.e. defined in terms of agreement), but this
would be misleading because agreement itself is stated in terms of the relation
between the finite verb and the subject. The same is true for other phenomena that
are accounted for in terms of the notion of final subject. Since subjecthood is
not derived, therefore, from anything, it may be said to be primitive.

Initial grammatical relations on the other hand have a different status.
Although not much discussion has been devoted to this issue, it appears that
initial grammatical relations are assumed to be determined by semantic functions
like agent etc. (cf. Perlmutter 1979:278, 1981:322). If we assume, for the sake
of the argument, that semantic notions such as agent can be given a clear enough
content, we may conclude that initial grammatical relations are in some sense
defined. This bears out our claim that in RG there is no homogeneous content for
the notion of e.g. subject since there are no properties that initial subjects
and final subjects have in common[5].

The strategy of assigning different levels of representation to clauses is of
course motivated in the same way as the traditional distinction between deep
structure and surface structure in standard transformational grammar, i.e. to
allow the statement of generalizations. Some of these concern the notion of
possible derivation. The variation of possible derivations is limited in RG in
terms of universal laws and universal characterizations of rules. It is of course
especially with respect to these universal laws and characterizations that
grammatical relations are primitive.The problem with this approach is that it
leaves the universals relatively unexplained.

Let me illustrate this briefly. Keenan & Comrie (1977,1979) present evidence
in favour of the so-called accessibility hierarchy of nominals with respect to
relativization. The hierarchy is defined in terms of grammatical relations and
embodies a number of implicational universals, such as "if a nominal A bearing a
certain grammatical relation X is accessible for relativization strategy 1, then
each nominal bearing a grammatical relation Y, such that Y outranks X on the
hierarchy can be relativized with strategy 1 as well". Malay is cited as an
example of a language in which the major relativization strategy is limited to
subjects and objects. Let us assume that it is possible for this language to

determine what a subject is and what a direct object and let us also assume that
the claim made by Keenan & Comrie is correct. What we would like to know is why the
claim is true; in other words, why e.g. an indirect object, if this is a definable
category in Malay, cannot be relativized in the same way. It would seem that the
answer which is provided is that the nominal bearing the indirect object relation
is inaccessible because it bears the indirect object relation, i.e. because it is
assigned a specific name. This failure of indirect objects can only be related to
the behaviour of indirect objects in other respects by virtue of this name. Chung
(1976) mentions five object characteristics, one of which is the accessibility to
the major relativization strategy (**yang**-relativization)[6]. The other are passivizability, **diri**-reflexivization, object preposing and the possibility of functioning as equi-trigger, i.e. the capacity of functioning as the antecedent of a
null complement subject. To this, we could add as a sixth characteristic the fact
that subjects and direct objects are realized as NP's, unlike all other grammatical relations. Starting with this last characteristic, we note that direct
object may be defined as the NP dominated by VP. Assuming furthermore that Malay
does not allow preposition stranding, several of the characteristics mentioned by
Chung may be explained in terms of structural properties: passive is applicable
to direct objects only, since movement of the indirect object NP to subject
position would yield a structure with a stranded preposition; the same may be
said for object preposing. The fact that **diri**-reflexivization is restricted to
direct objects may be related to this, since **diri** appears to be a clitic which
must be attached to the verb. Generating **diri** in a PP would either require an
extraction from PP or result in a situation in which **diri** is not attached to the
verb.

I do not pretend to give a full and motivated analysis here; the discussion
only serves an illustrative purpose. It shows that taking indirect objecthood as
a primitive leaves the differential properties of direct and indirect objects
unexplained, or explained only to the extent that the generalization involves the
same label. A structural approach, on the other hand, relates the explanation of
these differential properties to existing configurational differences. It will
be clear that the failure of indirect objects to undergo **yang**-relativization can
be explained along similar lines (see Cinque 1981 for a similar argument).

In the following chapters (specifically in chapter three), a more elaborate
example of the same kind of reasoning will be given. I trust that the above
discussion suffices to demonstrate the advantage of the structural approach over
the RG approach to grammatical relations.

1.2. Functional Grammar

Functional Grammar, as developed in Dik (1978,1981,1983) and in several papers in Hoekstra, Moortgat & Van der Hulst (1981) and Bolkestein et al. (1981), resembles Fillmore's (1968) Case Grammar in taking semantic functions as the primary notions in terms of which linguistic expressions are analyzed. The syntactic functions subject and object are additional in that they are invoked only to account for differences in expression of what is taken to be one and the same underlying predication. Only these two syntactic functions are assumed to be relevant and their interpretation differs from the usual syntactic interpretation; rather, they are interpreted as specifying which argument is selected to represent the primary resp. secondary vantage point from which the predication is described.

The effect of assigning a syntactic function to a particular argument is a neutralization of the way in which the argument is expressed. Thus, in English, an agent argument is expressed in a **by**-phrase, unless it is assigned the syntactic subject function. Similarly, a recipient argument is expressed in a **to**-phrase, unless it is assigned either the subject or the object function. Languages are supposed to be different with respect to the number and nature of semantic arguments that can receive a syntactic function. Thus, it is assumed that object assignment in Bantu languages is much freer than in English. In Chi-Mwi:ni, object assignment may take place for instruments, benificiaries, recipients and goals (cf. Dik 1978:102). The reader is referred to Hoekstra & Dimmendaal (1983) for a different view on the relevant phenomena in Bantu languages.

Dik's claim that two syntactic functions suffice for the purposes of accounting for the differential expressions of predications across languages tallies with the observation that usually a basic clause in a language contains no more than two relatively unmarked constituents. The statement needs further qualification, but I assume that the essential point is clear. Moreover it is generally assumed that these two classes of unmarked constituents (Relational Grammar's final subject and object) do not constitute semantically homogeneous classes, i.e. do not have independent semantic content, as opposed to instruments, locatives, benefactives (cf. Johnson 1977:153). We notice, then, that this is a consequence of the fact that in Functional Grammar these syntactic functions may be assigned to arguments with different semantic functions, with the result that their formal manifestation is neutralized. The functions subject and object are

indeed additional. It is even possible that they are irrelevant for a specific
language. For the syntactic function subject this would be the case if it may only
be assigned to the agent argument. Object assignment would equally be irrelevant
if it is restricted to goal arguments (cf. Dik 1981). In Dik & Gvozdanović (1981)
and De Groot (1981) it is claimed that subject assignment is indeed irrelevant
for Serbo-Croatian and Hungarian respectively, because these languages do not
exhibit anything that is comparable to passive. It would seem that there is a flaw
in this reasoning. It should first of all be noted that assignment of a syntactic
function may be optional in a particular language. This is necessary for object
assignment in Dutch, as can be seen from the following argument. A recipient
argument to which no syntactic function is assigned is expressed by a PP with the
preposition **aan,** whereas it appears as a bare NP if it is assigned the object
function. So, in (1a) the recipient **Marie** has not been assigned the object
function, unlike the recipient argument in (1b). It can be claimed that in (1b)
the object function is assigned to the goal argument, but in (2b), the goal
argument has received the subject function. Nevertheless, the recipient argument
is expressed in a PP with **aan.** This is possible only if assignment of the object
function is optional.

(1) a. dat Jan aan Marie een boek geeft
       that John to Marie a book gives

    b. dat Jan Marie een boek geeft
       that John Mary a book gives

(2) a. dat het boek Marie door Jan gegeven werd
       that the book Mary by John given was

    b. dat het boek aan Marie door Jan gegeven was
       that the book to Mary by John given was

Theoretically, then, there might be a language in which assignment of the
syntactic object function is optional, but restricted to goal arguments. The
effect of assigning vs. not assigning the syntactic function would be a difference in formal manifestation of the goal argument, e.g. it would be realized in
some sort of PP if object function is not assigned, but as a bare NP if this
function is assigned. However, no such language seems to exist. What is worse is
that there does not seem to be a language in which assignment of the object

function to the goal constituent has any effect on the way it is expressed. In (1b) above, it is not possible to determine whether the object function has been assigned to **het boek** or not.

What this suggests is that there is a tight relation between goal and object. To a certain extent, this is expressed by the fact that object assignment to the goal argument is the unmarked case. In Relational Grammar, this would be captured by assuming that the simplest derivation is that the initial object is also the final object, since in that case, no relation-changing rule has applied. However, if the claim that subject and object do not constitute semantically homogeneous classes of arguments is correct, the idea that initial direct object in Relational Grammar is identical to a class of arguments that can be characterized as goal in Functional Grammar appears to be dubious.

More or less the same issue is discussed in Perlmutter (1981) with respect to the notion subject. In Dik (1978), it is claimed that agreement in Achenese is determined by the agent argument, rather than by the argument to which the subject function is assigned, although subject assignment is relevant in Achenese. The analysis of Achenese agreement in Lawler (1977) is formulated in terms of initial subject, a notion that cannot be equated with agent in Functional Grammar, for the obvious reason that the notion of initial subject does not cover a semantically homogeneous class in Relational Grammar. According to Dik, agents only appear in action predications. His claim that agreement in Achenese is determined by the agent argument predicts therefore that agreement will only be found in action predications. Perlmutter (1981) convincingly shows that this prediction is incorrect. Perlmutter concludes from this that Lawler's original formulation in terms of initial subject must be maintained and hence that Functional Grammar is not capable of providing an adequate analysis of this and similar phenomena that are dealt with in terms of initial subject in Relational Grammar. What is needed therefore in Functional Grammar is some unifying concept beyond the notion of syntactic subject which is employed already.

The need for such a concept is also clearly illustrated in a paper by De Groot (1981). As mentioned above, De Groot claims that in Hungarian the notion of subject is irrelevant. Agreement in this language presents Functional Grammar with a similar problem as agreement in Achenese: the verb not only agrees with agent arguments, but with arguments having a different semantic function as well. This is illustrated by the following examples, taken from De Groot (1981:150).

(3) a. Péter hisz
       Peter believes

b. A szél fúj

The wind blows

c. A levél leesik

The leaf falls

d. A fa áll a kertben

The tree stands in the garden

All verbs in (3) show agreement with the sentence-initial NP, which is a Positioner, a Force, a Processed and a Zero function argument respectively. De Groot seeks to solve this problem by introducing a new concept, the concept of "initial argument". It should be noted that the arguments of a predicate are unordered according to Functional Grammar. The notion "initial" refers either to the ordering of arguments on the semantic function hierarchy, or some ordering with respect to the kind of predication that is expressed by a particular predicate. Thus, the agent argument is initial in an action predication, as it is the most central argument. The notion of initial argument is defined as follows: "The first argument in a nuclear predicate-frame is, depending on the state of affairs, the argument with the function Agent, Positioner, Processed, Force or Zero" (De Groot 1981:153). The notion of initial argument, then, covers a semantically heterogeneous set of arguments and may be considered to have the same extension as the notion of initial subject in Relational Grammar.

We could ask at this point whether Functional Grammar also needs a notion of "second argument" that can be considered as the counterpart of the notion initial direct object in Relational Grammar. This appears to be the case. De Groot (1981) claims that the syntactic function of direct object is of no relevance for Hungarian either. The phenomenon that would traditionally be described as object agreement in this language should be then formulated in terms of semantic functions, for which the function Goal is the most obvious candidate. According to Dik (1978:37), a Goal argument appears in three types of predications, viz. as second argument in action predications which "typically designates the entity to which the Action is applied by the Agent", in position predications, if these are three-place predications as in "John held the thing in place", where **John** is the Positioner and **the thing** is the Goal, and finally in process predications with two arguments, where the Goal function is assigned to the second argument. It is important to observe that the first argument in a state predication like "the thing is on the table" cannot be assumed to have the Goal function, just like

the thing in the previous example, but rather the zero function. The reason for
this is that **the thing** in the state predication triggers agreement as a first
argument, while it triggers object agreement in three-place position predications. It is hard to find any intrinsically semantic considerations, however, to
justify the assignment of distinct semantic functions to **the thing** in these two
examples, given the close semantic similarity (cf. John caused the thing to be on
the table).

Turning to object agreement in Hungarian, then, we see that some concept like
second argument seems to be needed. The discussion in De Groot is not entirely
clear on this point, however. First, he concludes that this agreement cannot be
handled by formulating a notion of second argument since "the semantic functions
of second arguments are too various" (p.154)' In spite of this claim concerning
the variety of semantic functions borne by the arguments that trigger the
relevant agreement, the agreement rule is formulated in terms of the semantic
function Goal. But this conclusion cannot be correct, as shown by the following
example, taken from De Groot (1981:155 (his example (23))).

(4) a. Péter azt   akarja,   hogy én   vezessek
       Peter that-ACC wants-2f that I-NOM drive-1sg
       "Peter wants that I drive"

    b. Péter engem   akar   , hogy   vezessek
       Peter me-ACC   want-1f that   drive-1sg
       "Peter wants me to drive"

The verbs show an alternation between the first and second form. This alternation
is determined by the relevant agreement rule. De Groot himself points out that
engem 'me' in (4b) does not have the Goal function, but rather the Agent function.
It is clear, therefore, that the relevant agreement rule cannot be formulated in
terms of the semantic Goal function. Therefore, it must be concluded that
Functional Grammar needs some concept which covers a set of semantically heterogeneous arguments. The paradox, however, is that object is assumed not to be
relevant for Hungarian.

What the above discussion has shown is that concepts comparable to the
initial grammatical relations of Relational Grammar are needed in Functional
Grammar as well. Notions like first and second argument do appear to play a role
in a wide variety of languages to cover the two relatively unmarked arguments,
irrespective of voice alternations like active and passive . The difficulty with

the conception of syntactic functions in Functional Grammar is that these functions are motivated only for cases of voice alternations. The preceding discussion illustrates, however, that even in languages where voice alternations do not
seem to occur, generalizations over two relatively unmarked constituents appear
to hold as well.

1.3. Generative Grammar

It was mentioned above that in generative grammar grammatical relations are
not primitives, but are rather configurationally defined notions. According to
Aspects (Chomsky 1965), subject can be defined as [NP,S] and object as [NP,VP].
There have always been various problems for this approach. Thus, with bitransitive verbs it is possible to have two NP's dominated by VP. Moreover, a VP may
contain NP's with adverbial functions, cf. the examples in (5).

    (5) a. I gave Mary a bunch of flowers
        b. He dropped the rope five feet
        c. He remained the whole day in bed

Similar problems are created by constructions with secondary predicates as in
(6).

    (6) a. He called John a liar
        b. He ate the meat raw
        c. I considered John foolish
        d. John struck Mary as incompetent

If the definitions of subject and object are generalized to other languages,
still other problems arise. How can the definition of direct object be maintained
for e.g. VSO languages, which do not seem to have a VP, at least not at first
sight? And if these languages do not have a VP, how can the object be distinguished from the subject? It was claimed in **Aspects** that grammatical relations
should not be defined in terms of an interaction of both configurational and
linear properties.

    There are several ways to overcome the problems of the types mentioned above.

For instance, a difference can be made in terms of the level of attachment. Thus, adverbial adjuncts can be assumed to be generated at the level of V", whereas complements are generated at the V' level within an X'-system such as Jackendoff's (1977). Direct object can then be defined not as [NP,VP], but rather as [NP,V']. A similar strategy is suggested in Chomsky (1965) to deal with the two interpretations of "They decided on the boat". Adopting X'-terminology, we can define the prepositional object as [PP,V'] and assume that **on the boat** is generated as [PP,V"] in the reading where the decision is taken while on the boat. The problem with secondary predicates can be solved by adopting the small-clause analysis, which will be discussed in chapter 4. Within the recent Government & Binding framework of Chomsky (1981), two sets of functions are assumed which can be used to differentiate between various constituents, viz. the thematic functions or θ-roles and the Case functions. Various proposals that solve the problems mentioned will be considered in great detail in the present study.

It was mentioned in the introduction of this chapter that grammatical relations were interpreted in an essentialist way in traditional grammar. The kind of definition of grammatical relations found in traditional grammars has to a large extent been justly criticized by structuralists for its conflation of semantic and formal characteristics, but nevertheless, a certain amount of this traditional essentialist approach has survived in generative grammar. To a large extent, this is understandable since the correlation between object as a formally defined notion and such semantic notions as Theme or Goal appears to be widespread both within and across languages. If an instrument is expressed as an NP object, as is the case in various Bantu languages, this is regarded as deviant. We therefore find descriptions of these states of affairs in which some sort of promotion rule is invoked that applies to an underlying structure in which the object is realized in a PP with an "instrumental" preposition. This traditional conception can also be regarded as the initial motivation of such relation-changing rules as passive. It is of course possible to motivate the rule of passive in purely distributional terms (cf. Chomsky 1955,1957), but the construction-specific approach to account for these distributional regularities cannot but have been inspired by traditional concepts like passive. Consider the following example by way of illustration.

The example in (7) exhibits a number of properties that we may collectively take as defining the phenomenon of passive. The verbal part shows "passive morphology", the logical subject is realized in a **by**-phrase and the logical object functions as the syntactic subject.

(7) The girl was kissed by John

(8) It was said by many people that such
experiments are dangerous

(9) It was rumoured that such experiments
are dangerous

From a functional point of view, we may say that the phenomenon of passive can be
characterized as a way of demoting or backgrounding the logical subject, thereby
giving it a less prominent position relative to its active counterpart. In (8),
we find a subset of the characteristics in (7) and there is a functional identity,
viz. of demoting the logical subject. However, in spite of these similarities
there is also a difference: the logical object functions as the syntactic subject
in (7), but not in (8). The question we must ask, then, is whether there is a
formal identity in the grammar with respect to the way in which these sentences
are generated. The standard answer has always been that there is indeed such a
formal identity, viz. that both are generated by means of one and the same rule,
passive. This passive rule was even assumed to be involved in the derivation of
(9), not because any distributional similarity with a corresponding active could
be expressed in this way, but because of the functional similarity to (8), and
hence to (7).

Within this essentialist, or perhaps we should say functional approach, there
was no reason to assume a formal similarity with the derivation of other construction types. Rather, what is to be expected, given the universal claims that
were made, is the occurrence of similarities in a formal sense between the
passive rules of various languages. As was discussed in relation to the framework
of Relational Grammar, this expectation is not borne out.

In chapter 3, we shall argue that various recent analyses of passive and
related construction types still operate from a certain essentialist angle. We
shall defend the claim, however, that the passive phenomenon in Dutch does not
warrant this position. Rather, we shall demonstrate that the constructions
regarded as passive are generated by rules that are insensitive to functional or
thematic properties[7].

1.4. Summary

This introductory chapter serves to set the stage for the three chapters that follow. In chapter 2, we examine the various modules of the recent Government and Binding framework. Here we shall define a particular notion of government. Two aspects of this definition of government are relevant. First, it will be argued that the head of a phrase only governs those phrases that are contained in the first-order projection of this head, excluding those phrases that fall within the government domain of a different head. This means that the specifier of an adjacent projection may be governed, but not the complement of the head of an adjacent projection. A second relevant aspect is that government is assumed to be unidirectional. The choice of direction is a parameter of UG that has to be fixed for each category in each language on the basis of positive evidence.

This relation between governor and governee is regarded as a configurational property that is in general insensitive to functional or semantic relations that exist between them. The government relation is central to the Government & Binding system: Case assignment, the domains relevant for the Binding Theory and the Empty Category Principle are defined in terms of this relation. To some extent, a further central principle of the Government & Binding theory depends on the notion of government, viz. the θ-criterion. It is required that all θ-roles, apart from the external θ-role, are assigned to phrases that are governed by the head that assigns these roles.

In the third chapter, a discussion is presented of passive. This chapter first provides a historical overview of different analyses that have been proposed to deal with passive. We then argue that most of these analyses are misguided in that they assume that passive is in a sense a homogeneous phenomenon. It will be shown that the blind structural relation of government interacts with the subtheories that are in large measure defined in terms of this relation to generate the required sentences. A relevant role in this demonstration is played by the notion of unaccusativity, which is perhaps better known under the name ergativity, although the latter term is more liable to cause confusion than the former.

In the final chapter, we provide detailed motivation for the notion of small clause that is used throughout the other chapters. We shall also have occasion to discuss the analysis of synthetic compounds. The final part of that chapter is devoted to an analysis of the distribution of the two perfective auxiliaries in Dutch, **hebben** and **zijn**.

The present study may be somewhat redundant for those who are well informed about the framework of Government and Binding and the recent history of generative grammar. However, I have tried to provide enough information to make the results of my research accessible to a larger audience. Specifically, chapter 2 presents a rather detailed overview of the most central concepts and principles of recent generative grammar, while chapter 3 contains a historical overview of the major changes within the framework during the seventies. I trust that these overviews are helpful to the reader.

The title of this study may come as a surprise after this short survey of its content. However, once the book is read, a little reflection will suffice to see the reason for its title.

Chapter 2

A Government and Binding Approach to Asymmetries between Dutch and English

In this chapter, a survey is presented of the central principles of the theory of Government and Binding (henceforth GB-theory), as outlined in Chomsky (1981) and references cited there.At the same time, I shall discuss the syntax of Dutch and a number of asymmetries between Dutch and English. As these languages have had only a relatively short period of independent development, it is worthwhile exploring whether various overt differences between these languages can be traced to a small number of differences in the abstract principles of grammar.

The discussion of these differences is used to motivate a number of changes in the definition of the central principles of the GB-theory. Specifically, it is argued that the notion of government contains a parameter concerning the direction in which government holds. Government in a particular grammar, then, is unidirectional. In this respect, government of the category verb in Dutch differs in orientation from that of the verb in English. This difference of orientation is shown to have many consequences in the languages, some of which involve aspects of the languages that are not likely to be learned on the basis of positive evidence.

This chapter also provides an outline of the structure of Dutch which will be helpful for the discussion in the rest of the book. This will make the book more accessible to readers not familiar with Dutch.

2.1. Introductory remarks on GB-theory.

The introduction of the GB-framework has had important repercussions for the

study of grammar in general and for the study of comparative syntax in particular. In the development of generative theory, the initial focus was placed on
formulating various rule types and their interaction in order to attain sufficient expressive power to formulate the required generalizations, until it was
realized that this undertaking, although rather successful from an empirical or
descriptive point of view, had the conceptual disadvantage of leading away from
the explanatory task rather than coming to grips with it. This led to the
conceptual shift in the research program of aiming at reducing the expressive
power of the rule systems employed rather than enlarging the stock of empirical
tools whenever empirical data seemed to require this. As was to be expected, this
change brought with it a temporary reduction of the empirical coverage, as
several phenomena previously accounted for were dismissed either as not belonging
to the domain of sentence grammar or as not falling under the scope of core
grammar or as matters supposedly dealt with by other components of the system,
the proper functioning or even contents of which were left totally obscure (see
Drachmann 1981). However, it should be kept in mind that the justification of
such abstractions is not an a priori matter, but is determined by the ultimate
success attained under these abstractions, compared to the success of competing
theories. I think that from this perspective, GB-theory compares favourably with
its competitors.

Even though inquiry during the seventies was directed toward the more direct
explanatory goal of restricting the expressive power of the theory by imposing
all sorts of constraints on the form and functioning of rules, the framework was
relatively unsuitable as an explanatory theory in the domain of comparative
syntax. Differences between languages could easily be accounted for in a variety
of ways, e.g. in terms of statements to the effect that a particular rule was
absent in the grammar of one language, but present in the grammar of another
language, without it being clear why this should be so. Moreover, as long as the
conception of transformations was grafted on specific construction types, there
did not seem to be a way in which various differences in transformational
behaviour could be related to each other. A simple example illustrates this.
Consider the difference between French and English with repect to the complement
structure of verbs like **donner, give**. In English, such verbs can be followed by
the sequence NP-**to**-NP, comparable to French NP-à-NP, but whereas English also
has the possibility of NP NP, this alternative is lacking in French. In principle, the theory allows for various ways to account for this difference, for
instance by assuming that English has a transformational rule of Dative Movement
(cf. Fillmore 1965, Jackendoff & Culicover 1971, Emonds 1972), whereas such a

rule is absent in the grammar of French. Why this should be the case is left
entirely unexplained, nor is this difference between the languages relatable to
other differences between them, such as the fact that English has infinitival
complement clauses with a lexical subject (as in **I believe John to be a hero**)
which are lacking in French, English has preposition stranding which is lacking
in French and English has particles, which are also absent in French (cf. Kayne
1981c, 1982b).

As long as the explanatory principles of the theory were related to the
systems of rules, this situation remains unchanged in principle. The abandonment
of the construction- specific approach to transformations in favour of a formulation of the transformational component in the format MOVE α proposed in Chomsky
(1977) is desirable as it opens the way to account for the presence or absence of
clusters of construction types in terms of a single parameter, e.g. the value
that α in this format may take. In itself, however, this step is not the most
principled shift in the conceptual development towards the theory of Government
and Binding. The major innovation leading to the framework presented in Chomsky
(1981) is found in Chomsky & Lasnik's (1977) paper "Filters and Control". Here
the concept of wellformedness conditions on syntactic representations was first
introduced.

This innovation led to a shift away from the emphasis on rule systems to an
emphasis on systems of abstract principles determining wellformedness conditions
on various levels of representation. Rule systems can now be kept fairly simple
and general,as all the more specific features of the relations expressed by the
rules are now accounted for in terms of a difference at the more abstract level of
universal principles. The generalizing effect of these wellformedness conditions
is that they place conditions on both derived and non-derived structures, i.e.
structures affected by movement operations and structures which are not affected
by movement. Language-particular fixing of parameters contained in these abstract principles may lead to large-scale differences between the languages
without any actual difference in the rules employed in the grammars of these
languages. A good illustration in the domain of WH-extractions is presented in
Rizzi (1982:ch.2) who argues that differences between English and Italian with
respect to possibilities of WH-extractions are not a consequence of the extraction rules employed, but rather of a different fixing of the set of bounding nodes
for subjacency. Below, I shall have occasion to go into this matter in some
detail. Another illustration is provided in various articles by Kayne (esp.
1981c) where it is demonstrated that some of the differences between English and
French mentioned above follow from a single more abstract difference concerning

the set of structural governors. Yet another example is the account of the
distinction between languages that require or do not require the pronominal
realization of subjects (PRO-drop vs. non-PRO-drop languages), which is given in
Rizzi's work (1982:ch.4), Chomsky (1981) and the references cited there. Each way
of fixing the so-called PRO-drop parameter is argued to have various consequences
for the actual shape of the languages, the need of expressing pronominal subjects
being only one of them. In section 2.7.2., I shall discuss the exact nature of the
PRO-drop parameter.

These examples are mentioned here to demonstrate that the conceptual shift
discussed above has inspired fruitful work in the field of comparative syntax
within the framework of GB-theory. The analyses of differences between Dutch and
English presented in this book are to be considered in the same vein.

Before the various components and principles of GB-theory are discussed in
some detail, an outline of the total organization of the system is presented. I
shall assume as my point of departure the so-called T-model, introduced in
Chomsky & Lasnik (1977) and further developed by Rouveret & Vergnaud (1980),
Chomsky (1981) and references cited there. Each component of the grammar generates a distinct representation for a given sentence of the language. The components are organized as in figure (1). The syntax generates two syntactic representations, D-structure and S-structure, the former being the output of the Base
Component, the latter derived from D-structure by the application of the transformational component which is of the format MOVE α. S-structure feeds into the
two interpretive components that derive a phonetic form and a logical form from
it. These representations can be regarded as the respective representations of
the form and the structure relevant for the meaning of the sentence . The ultimate
semantic interpretation is assumed to be established on the basis of the logical
form[8] . I shall not have much to say about either of these interpretive components
or the representations generated by them.

(1)   The T-model

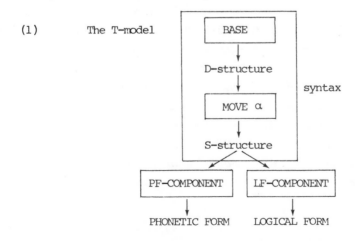

The next two sections present a discussion of the two syntactic subcomponents, the Base and MOVE α.

2.2. The Base Component

Since Chomsky (1965), the Base Component of the grammar has been assumed to consist of two parts: a phrase structure component and a lexicon. Until the introduction of the X'-theory of phrase structure rules and the lexicalist hypothesis, both in Chomsky's (1970) **Remarks on Nominalization**, the Base Component played a rather insignificant role as far as explanation was concerned. The real explanatory capacities of generative grammar were assumed to be concentrated in the transformational component. Newmeyer (1980:118) writes: "...phrase structural and lexical solutions were devoid of interest, and the transformational component was the **explanatory** component of the grammar". During the seventies, much work was devoted to the development of an explanatory theory of phrase structure, specifically by Jackendoff (1977), Emonds (1976). It is thus rather surprising to find that about ten years after the introduction of the X'-theory Stowell (1981:50) writes: ".. the theory of phrase structure is largely redundant, offers no real depth of explanation, and provides little more than an arbitrary collection of generalizations about each phrasal category". Nevertheless, Stowell is right in pointing out a number of important problems concerning the role of PS-rules.

In **Aspects** little more was said about PS-rules than that they were supposed to be of the context-free variety and limited to expanding a single node into one or more daughter nodes. The X'-theory of PS-rules was a great improvement, as the set of possible PS-rules was severely restricted by it. The most generally adopted version of X'-theory was formulated in Jackendoff (1977:36).

$$(2) \quad X^n \longrightarrow (C_1)\ldots.(C_j) - X^{n-1} - (C_{j+1}) \, ..(C_k)$$

where $1 \leq n \leq 3$ and for all C_i, either C_i is Y^3 for some lexical category Y, or C_i is a specified grammatical formative.

The X'-theory formulated in (2) embodies the following claims with respect to phrase structure:

(3)   i. every phrasal category is endocentric

      ii. every lexical category projects three levels of
          superstructure

     iii. the head of a phrase is always one bar-level lower
          than the phrase node immediately dominating it

      iv. only maximal projections may appear as specifiers
          and complements, except for some non-head terms
          that are selected in terms of a specified grammatical
          formative

       v. specifiers will always occur peripheral to the complements
          of the lexical head of a phrase

In Chomsky (1970) and Jackendoff (1977) the terms 'complement' and 'specifier' are used to refer to material following the head and material preceding the head, respectively. This has the undesirable consequence, as noted by Jackendoff (1977:37) that under this approach a phrase bearing a particular grammatical relation to the head will sometimes be called a specifier (e.g. the object in an OV-language) and sometimes a complement. I shall therefore use the term complement to refer to phrases subcategorizing the lexical head and the term specifier to refer to modifiers of various sorts (restrictive and non-restrictive), following a convention familiar by now.

It should be observed that the claims made in (3) follow directly from the formulation given in (2). This implies that these claims are the result of the stipulation which is given in (2). Here we arrive at the first conceptual problem with the theory of PS-rules. First of all, as was pointed out in Heny (1979) there is a large amount of redundancy in the grammar with respect to the determination of the complement structure, in that phrase structure rules essentially repeat information already contained in the lexical entries of the heads of phrases about the nature, number and ordering of complements. This redundancy is also recognized in Chomsky (1981:31), who observes, however, that it would be misleading to describe the categorial component as a specification of redundancy rules over the lexicon, i.e. as an explicit formulation of the class of subcategorization frames that are found in the lexicon. A second problem with PS-rules as traditionally formulated is that they imply the existence of phrases that do not actually occur. It was noted in Hoekstra (1978a:62) that the V' expansion rule in (4), proposed in Jackendoff (1977:69) implies the existence of V' structures in which the head is followed by five complements. Such phrases do not seem to occur and it is unlikely that this is a coincidence.

$$(4) \quad V' \rightarrow \quad V \ (NP)(Prt)(\begin{bmatrix} -obj \\ -det \end{bmatrix}^{\text{"}'}) (PP)(\begin{bmatrix} +obj \\ +comp \end{bmatrix}^{\text{""}})$$

The same point is made in Stowell (1981).Therefore, as PS-rules like the one in (4) are in fact the result of collapsing the options to be found in the complement structure of different verbs, each of which selects only a proper subpart of the total expansion provided by the rule, the rules suffer from overgeneration, since no item selects the total set of complements made available by the rule. A third point concerns the ordering of complements imposed by rules like (4). As the ordering of various complement types is crudely stipulated, no real explanation is offered for the specific ordering imposed by the rule. As long as principles determining the impossibility of other orderings are lacking, no insight is attained or expressed by a rule such as (4). This is one of the main criticisms made in Stowell (1981). It should be noted that, even if we accept that the order of complements (and specifiers) is determined by the PS-rules at the level of D-structure, this in itself does not even suffice as a descriptive account of the ordering of phrases found at S-structure. The freely operating process MOVE α may alter the entire ordering established at the level of D-structure, unless there is a set of principles P that forbids some orderings while accepting others. But in that case, it is the set of principles P rather than the PS-rules that accounts for the orderings found at S-structure. Therefore, apart from being uninteresting from an explanatory point of view, PS-rules are even devoid of descriptive potential with respect to the ordering of complements. Consequently, unless clear evidence in favour of this position is put forward, the idea that PS-rules generate ordered sets can be abandoned, a conclusion that has been advocated by many linguists (see Gazdar & Pullum 1981 who defend the position that PS-rules should generate unordered sets, the ordering being imposed by separate linear precedence rules. In footnote 1. they list a large number of predecessors in this idea). This decision requires, however, that research should be directed to finding principles of the kind referred to above that determine the ordering of phrases at S-structure in an illuminating way. Below I shall go into such principles quite extensively.

In order to illustrate the point made above more concretely and to start the discussion of the syntax of Dutch phrases, I shall examine the complementation to heads of different categories, restricting myself to the complement structure of the major lexical categories V, N, A and P. The discussion in this section necessarily anticipates on various aspects that will be dealt with later. Let us start by listing a number of relevant A'-phrases in Dutch[9].

(5) a. (dat hij) $\begin{cases} \text{verliefd op zijn moeder} \\ \text{op zijn moeder verliefd} \end{cases}$ is

      that he $\begin{cases} \text{in love with his mother} \\ \text{with his mother in love} \end{cases}$ is

b. (dat hij) $\begin{cases} \text{gek op zijn vrouw} \\ \text{op zijn vrouw gek} \end{cases}$ is

      that he $\begin{cases} \text{crazy about his wife} \\ \text{about his wife crazy} \end{cases}$ is

c. (dat hij) $\begin{cases} \text{dat gezeur moe} \\ \text{*moe dat gezeur} \end{cases}$ is

      that he $\begin{cases} \text{that drivel weary-of} \\ \text{weary-of that drivel} \end{cases}$ is

d. (dat hij) $\begin{cases} \text{bang om op te vallen} \\ \text{*om op te vallen bang} \end{cases}$ is

      that he $\begin{cases} \text{afraid to attract attention} \\ \text{to attract attention afraid} \end{cases}$ is

e. (dat hij) $\begin{cases} \text{?zeker dat dat zal gebeuren} \\ \text{*dat dat zal gebeuren zeker} \end{cases}$ is

      that he $\begin{cases} \text{certain that that will happen} \\ \text{that that will happen certain} \end{cases}$ is

      dat hij zeker is dat dat zal gebeuren
      that he certain is that that will happen

This list is not intended to cover all complement possibilities, but the following remarks can be made concerning the structure of A' in view of the examples in (5). First, an adjective can take a PP complement that may follow the head and sometimes precede it. The latter option depends on lexical selection, as far as I can see. Secondly, the adjective may take an NP complement that always occurs to its left. Thirdly, it may take a clausal complement, infinitival as in (5d) or

finite as in (5e). This clausal complement may never precede the head and is
preferably extraposed to postverbal position if it is finite. These observations
could be captured by formulating the rule in (6).

(6) A' -> (NP) (PP) A$^{\circ}$ (PP) (S')

However, as the preceding discussion has revealed, a rule like (6) suffers from
several problems. No adjective will take four complements. In fact, it is
difficult to find adjectives that select more than two complements. Moreover, no
explanation is offered for the particular order stipulated in (6). Therefore, it
offers little more than a descriptive generalization over the phenomena in (5).
There are various problems with AP's that we shall return to later.

We turn now to an illustration of complement structures to verbal heads. In
(7), a number of relevant examples are listed[10]. The so-called V-raising complements are left out. Discussion of these structures is deferred until section 2.7.

(7) a. (dat hij) lacht
       that he laughs
    b. (dat hij) een fout maakte
       that he a mistake made
    c. (dat hij) zijn zuster een cadeautje gaf
       that he his sister a   present gave
    d. (dat hij) op zijn vader wachtte
       that he for his father waited
    e. (dat hij) zijn broer van verraad beschuldigde
       that he his brother of treason accused
    f. (dat hij) aan zijn zus over het boek vertelde
       that he to his sister about the book told
    g. (dat hij) verwachtte dat dat zou gebeuren
       that he expected that that would happen
    h. (dat hij) zijn moeder vroeg of hij snoep kreeg
       that he his mother asked whether he candy got
    i. (dat hij) aan Piet vertelde dat hij rijk was
       that he to Peter told   that he rich was
    j. (dat hij) ziek was
       that he ill was
    k. (dat hij) zijn broer aardig vond
       that he his brother nice found

Again, this list of examples is not intended to be exhaustive. Specifically, no examples are given with particles. I have nothing particular to say about particles in Dutch. For the purpose of this study, they may be thought of as being part of a complex verb. For an elaborate discussion of their status, the reader is referred to Van Riemsdijk (1978a). The examples in (7) illustrate that a verb may take either no complement, a single NP, two NP's, a single PP, an NP and a PP, two PP's, a single S', a combination of either an NP or a PP and an S' and finally a single AP or a combination of an NP and an AP. NP's and AP's always precede the head. So, (7b') and (7j') are ungrammatical.

(7) b'.*(dat hij) maakte een fout
         that he made   a mistake
    j'.*(dat hij) was ziek
         that he was ill

In a combination of NP and AP, the NP must precede the AP. Similarly, the NP complement precedes the PP complement in the unmarked case. So, (7e') is highly marked and (7k') is ungrammatical.

(7) e'.?(dat hij) van verraad zijn broer beschuldigde
         that he of treason his brother accused
    k'.*(dat hij) aardig zijn broer vond
         that he nice his brother found

Clausal complements, with the exception of V-raising structures, obligatorily follow the verb. It is generally assumed among Dutch generative linguists that clausal complements are generated in preverbal position, from where they are moved to postverbal position by the rule of extraposition[11]. We shall discuss this matter extensively in this chapter. For the moment, we shall follow this assumption and place the S' expansion option in preverbal position accordingly. More or less the same holds for the position of PP's. They can always precede the head and in most cases they may occur in postverbal position as well. In order to account for this, it is generally assumed that PP's, too, are generated in preverbal position. An optional rule of PP-over-V, proposed in Koster (1973), moves this PP to postverbal position. Again, these observations can be expressed by means of the following expansion rule for V, assuming PP-over-V and extraposition.

(8) V' -> (NP) (NP) (PP) (PP) (S') V^{o}

It will be obvious that rule (8) meets with the same problems as rules (4) and (6) above. It could be argued that given strong enough conventions, some of the options in (8) and rules like it could be collapsed, but it is hard to see how such an undertaking could be relevant, unless one assumes that such notational conventions are part of the intrinsic knowledge determined by UG. The problem with respect to the order of complements is especially evident in the case of (8). With the transformational component having been generalized to the format MOVE α, it is no longer possible to formulate category- specific rules such as PP—over-V. This implies that the transformational component may not only move PP complements to the other side of the verb, but NP's and AP's as well. Therefore, some principle(s) is/are needed to account for the obligatory preverbal position of these categories, as well as for the obligatory postverbal position of clausal complements. This matter will be addressed below.

Turning next to N', we find examples like the ones in (9).

(9) a. (een) verhaal over vogels
         a   story   about birds

    b. (een) bericht dat we moesten komen
         a   message that we had to come

    c. (de) mededeling over Piet dat hij ziek was
        the announcement about Peter that he ill was

    d. (de) verwoesting van de stad
        the destruction of the city

    e. (de) mededeling aan zijn zus over de bruiloft
        the announcement to his sister about the wedding

The category N cannot take NP complements[12]. The only complement types that we find are the categories PP and S' and they have to follow the head. Not only are NP complements impossible, then, but so are AP's . Next to a V' like (10a), there is no possible N' like (10b).

(10) a. (dat hij) het document geldig verklaart
         that he the document valid declares

b.*(zijn) verklaring van het document geldig
   his   declaration of the document valid

We are not yet in a position to explain why structures like (10b) are impossible. An explanation will be offered in section 2.7.3. It will be evident,
however, that the fact that no AP option is present in an expansion rule like (11)
can hardly be considered a principled explanation.

(11) N' -> N^O (PP) (PP) (S')

The fact that at S-structure no NP complements are found has received an explanation in recent literature. It is assumed that all lexical NP's must receive Case
and that nouns, unlike verbs, do not assign Case to a complement. This Case
solution will be reconsidered below. This account explains why complements to
nouns that correspond to NP complements of verbs are preceded by a preposition,
van in Dutch, **of** in English.

The final category to be considered is the category of prepositions. The
examples in (12) illustrate that P's can take NP, PP and S' complements. It will
be seen later in this chapter that the category of PP's has to be partitioned into
two subcategories, with consequences both for the external distribution and the
internal structure, i.e. the complement types that are allowed.

(12) a. voor de maaltijd
      before the meal

    b. voor na de maaltijd
       for after the meal

    c. voor dat de maaltijd begint
       before that the meal starts

The possibilities of complements to prepositions can again be expressed in an
expansion rule like (13). The other expansion rules that we arrived at in the
previous discussion are repeated here.

(6) A' -> (NP) (PP) A^O (PP) (S')

(8) V' -> (NP) (NP) (PP) (PP) (AP) (S') V^O

(11) N' -> N^{O} (PP) (PP) (S')

(13) P' -> P^{O} (NP) (PP) (S')

If these expansion rules for the grammar of Dutch are compared with the rules for expanding these categories in English, there appears to be a remarkable difference: whereas the complements in Dutch sometimes precede and sometimes follow the head, they consistently follow the head in English. In this respect, Dutch is also surprising from a typological point of view. As noted by Greenberg (1963) in his universal 4, OV languages tend to have postpositions, rather than prepositions like Dutch has. It should be noted that rule (8) is misleading to a certain extent in that, as we noted above, S' always follows the head at S-structure, whereas PP's -usually- may follow the head as well as precede it. Rule (8) abstracts away from these aspects. Similarly, it might be argued that the PP and S' options in rule (6) should be placed in pre-head position by the same token. In that case, A and V cluster together as opposed to N and P.

Before we proceed, it may be useful to introduce the feature system of categories generally assumed in generative grammar. I shall adopt Chomsky's system that defines the lexical categories in terms of the features V and N in the following way.

(14) The feature system of major categories

	+V	-V
+N	Adj	Noun
-N	Verb	Prep

The purpose of a feature system is to define natural classes of categories, as in phonology[13]. The categories V and P cluster together as opposed to N and A in that the former, but not the latter assign Case to an NP they govern. In terms of these features we can now state the following generalization.

(15) In Dutch, [+V] categories follow their complements

[-V] categories precede their complements

The statement in (15) has no theoretical significance as its content will be derived from other considerations below. Summarizing the main point of the

discussion up to now, we have seen that the approach of specifying order of
complements by means of PS-rules is non-explanatory. The same is true with
respect to explaining the non-occurrence of certain types of complements for
certain categories.

Another question that was raised in the preceding discussion relates to the
nature and number of complements that a specific element of a certain category
selects. Evidently, this is not a matter that can be dealt with by means of PS-
rules, since individual items differ in their choice of complements[14]. PS-rules
can only be seen as expressing the potential choices the individual members of a
certain category have. Ever since **Aspects** it has been assumed that subcategorization is a matter of the lexicon. Each lexical element is assumed to have a
subcategorization feature in its lexical representation. In the most generally
adopted alternative considered in **Aspects**, this feature is taken to be the
structural description of the context into which the lexical item in question may
be entered by lexical insertion, which is itself regarded as a transformational
operation[15]. As such, the elements of a subcategorization feature are ordered
among themselves in a way that reflects the order defined by the PS-rule introducing the category. The redundancy introduced in this way is fairly obvious (cf.
above).

The number of complements selected by a particular lexical item is evidently
not entirely arbitrary; it is related to the 'scenario' described by a phrase,
hence by the semantics of the item in question. The nature of the complements is
determined in large part by the kinds of expressions fit to denote certain kinds
of what we may loosely call entities, which we may think of as persons, objects,
events etc. A verb referring to a scenario of selling will more or less predictably select both a complement to express the object of selling and a complement
to express the purchaser. NP's are more likely candidates for the expression
denoting the purchaser than e.g. S', the latter being more suitable to refer to
propositions. We may say, then, that the number and kind of complements selected
by a particular lexical item are in large measure determined by the semantics of
the item and the categorial value of different categorial types. Let us call the
description of the participants involved in the scenario denoted by a phrase
headed by a specific lexical item, the semantic valence of this item, and the
description of the syntactic context in which the item may occur its syntactic
valence. We may say, then, rephrasing our earlier remarks, that there is a non-
arbitrary relation between the semantic and the syntactic valence of a specific
lexical item. If the lexical representation of a lexical item is to include both a
specification of its semantic and its syntactic valence, another kind of redun-

dancy is introduced in the grammar, although of a different nature than the
redundancy between PS-rules and subcategorization features.

The relevance of semantic valence within the framework of generative grammar
has repeatedly been the subject of controversy. It figures in the proposals by
Gruber (1965), Fillmore (1968) and Jackendoff (1972,1976). More recently, within
GB-theory, the concept of θ-grid has been used to refer to more or less the same
notion. A θ-grid is the description of the thematic roles (henceforth θ-roles)
assigned by the head of a phrase to its arguments. It is unclear, however, how
precisely this θ-grid is assumed to be associated with the subcategorization
frame. No generally accepted formulation is available at present of the way in
which θ-roles are assigned to syntactic phrases or to the content of certain
positions in phrase markers, although various suggestions can be found in the
literature (cf. Williams 1981a).

In this study, I shall adopt the following mechanism for the representation
of the θ-grid of a lexical item and the association of θ-roles and syntactic
phrases. First of all, I shall follow Chomsky (1981) in assuming that a lexical
item is not subcategorized for its subject, i.e. I shall assume that subcategorization is restricted to the X'-domain which I shall henceforth refer to as the
head domain. Lexical representations include both a subcategorization feature in
the traditional sense and an associated θ-grid. This association is given
directly in the lexicon for reasons that will be made clear in the following
discussion. As for the θ-role that is assigned to the subject of the phrase, I
shall assume that the θ-grid may contain at most one unassociated θ-role that
is assigned to the syntactically defined subject under the proviso to be made in
section 3.3[16]. The verb **tell** as used in (16), then, will be represented lexically
as in (17).

(16) John told Mary that it was late

(17) morphophonological form   tell
     categorial type   [+V,-N]
     subcategory feature   [-- NP S']
     θ-grid   ↑   ↑ ↑
                            θ1   θ2 θ3

The unconnected arrow represents the unassociated θ-role that will be assigned to the subject as stated above. All other θ-roles must be associated, as is the case in (17). As for the numbers assigned to the different θ-roles, they are used merely to be able to discriminate between them. I take the position, however, that there is no need to distinguish θ-roles such as theme, recipient, agent etc. I assume that the specific content of these notions may be relevant for the ultimate semantic representation, but not for the purposes of sentence grammar. The content of a θ-role is a compositional function, and may therefore vary according to the particular lexicalization. In this, I follow Keenan (1979), Marantz (1980). Thus, **John** in (18a) and (18b) has two distinct θ-roles.

(18) a. John cut the loan
     b. John cut the meat

(see also Hoekstra 1981a). This decision has an important repercussion, in that it excludes the possibility of writing rules that refer to specific θ-roles. A number of such rules, in fact a complete theory of such rules has been proposed in the recent literature (cf. Wasow 1980, Williams 1981a among others). In section 3.3.3., this issue will be dealt with more extensively.

Let us now return to the redundancy that was argued to be introduced in the lexicon by representing in the lexicon both the semantic and the syntactic valence of a lexical item. This redundancy is twofold. First with respect to the categorial nature of the complements and secondly with respect to the number of complements. I shall comment on these issues separately. The relevant question of course is whether these redundancies are real or merely apparent and in the former case, whether the redundancy can be avoided.

As we suggested above, it might be argued that some θ-roles will always be assigned to phrases of the same categorial type. The role of what may be called (without attaching any theoretical significance to this term) recipient for instance will never be assigned to an S'. However, this role can be expressed either by a bare NP or by a PP, headed by **to** in English and by **aan** in Dutch. Note that I do not claim that constructions with a bare NP are in all respects identical to constructions with the recipient expressed by a PP. It is well-known by now that the relationship between the two different frames into which a verb like **give** can appear does not hold for all verbs (cf. Oehrle 1976). In fact, the lexically governed nature of this relationship has been used as an argument to capture the rule in terms of a lexical redundancy rule, rather than a transformational operation (cf. Oehrle 1976, Bresnan 1978, Dowty 1978). There-

fore, the choice of complement type in this case is not entirely predictable and
hence must be listed in the lexicon. Grimshaw (1979) has revealed that it would be
oversimplifying in general to assume that the relation between θ-role and phrase
type is always constant. Consider the following example. Both the verb **ask** and
the verb **inquire** semantically select questions , but whereas this role can be
expressed both by an NP and an S' in the case of **ask**, the verb **inquire** does not
take an NP complement. The examples in (19) illustrate this.

(19) a. John asked the time/what the time was
     b. John inquired *the time/what the time was

Semantically, the NP **the time** in these examples expresses what Baker (1970) calls
a concealed question, as Grimshaw convincingly demonstrates. The fact that **ask,**
but not **inquire** can take an NP to express a concealed question is a matter of pure
stipulation as far as our present knowledge goes. Grimshaw therefore correctly
concludes that "it is impossible to reduce the syntactic categories to the
semantic types or the semantic types to the syntactic categories" (Grimshaw
1979:317). This is not to say, however, that there are no tendencies in selecting
particular phrases, but merely that these tendencies do not have the status of
exception-free rules. It is even true that within a certain categorial type some
expressions are more suitable to express or bear a particular role than others.
This could of course be handled in terms of an elaborate system of selectional
restrictions, but I shall adopt the position that such an undertaking is not part
of sentence grammar. We can conclude that as far as the first type of redundancy
is concerned, it is only apparent.

Let us turn next to the other aspect of redundancy, i.e. the number of complements in the subcategorization frame and the number of θ-roles in the θ-grid.
Clearly, leaving the θ-role that is assigned to the subject position aside, the
number of complements may not exceed the number of θ-roles, disregarding idiom
chunks for the moment. It seems that this type of redundancy, then, is genuine.
However, the requirement that the number of complements must not exceed the
number of available θ-roles follows from a wellformedness condition in GB-
theory, viz. the thematic criterion (henceforth θ-criterion). Informally, the
θ-criterion states that each referential expression bears a unique θ-role and
that each θ-role is assigned to a unique argument (cf. Chomsky 1981:36). A more
elaborate definition of the θ-criterion will be given later. The θ-criterion
not only requires that the number of complements does not exceed the number of
available θ-roles, it also requires that the number of complements is equal to

the number of θ-roles minus the θ-role that is assigned to the subject. Notice that from this requirement it follows that in the case of optional complements the θ-grid should be changed by the deleting the θ-role that is assigned to the complement if it is present. This raises the question of what kinds of operations are possible on the θ-grid. This matter will be dealt with in section 3.3.3. Clearly, then, the θ-criterion captures the redundancy regarding the number of complements.

The θ-criterion has other consequences as well. Notice that since the θ-criterion requires that each referential expression has a θ-role, lexical insertion can be kept context-free, i.e. it is no longer necessary to invoke a local transformation as proposed in **Aspects**. If the number of complements in the phrase marker in which a certain item is entered does not match the number of complements in the subcategorization frame, the θ-criterion will be violated. D-structure, then, will obey all subcategorizational requirements of the lexicon by virtue of the θ-criterion. The Projection Principle generalizes this require-ment to all other levels of representation (cf. Chomsky 1981:29 ff.). This also has the consequence of drastically limiting the number of operations possible by the transformational component. Consider for instance a rule like subject-to-object raising defended in Postal (1974). This operation of moving the subject of an embedded clause into matrix object position is excluded. Suppose that the object position is present at D-structure. Then a θ-role should be assigned to this position or else a violation of the θ-criterion at D-structure would result. Therefore, movement to this position is impossible since it is unsuitable as a landing site. Suppose alternatively that the position is not present at D-structure. If the position of matrix object is created by MOVE α at S-structure, the Projection Principle is violated at S-structure or at D-structure, since the context of the matrix verb differs at these two levels.

The preceding discussion also illustrates that there is no need for the elements of a subcategorization frame to be ordered. The subcategorization frame no longer functions as the structural description of an insertion transformation. We shall assume, therefore, that a subcategorization feature is an unordered list of phrase types, each of which is directly associated with its own θ-role in the grid.

Returning now to the PS-rules in (6), (8), (11) and (13) above, we observe that the specification of the kind and number of phrases surrounding the head in the expansion of these rules is superfluous, as is their order. We can therefore reduce these rules to the following two statements.

(20) i. each head domain has a head

     ii. in Dutch, [+V] heads follow their complements
        while [-V] heads precede them.

Statement (20 i) follows of course from the X'-theory in (2). It turns out, however, that this part of X'-theory is itself unnecessary in that it follows independently from the θ-criterion, since obviously a head is required to θ-mark its complements. As the discussion develops further, we shall see that in fact all claims embodied in the X'-theory as specified in (3) follow from other principles independently, at least in as far as the claims are correct. Thus, it will turn out that X'-theory can be dispensed with as a principle.

The statement in (20 ii) is language particular and needs to be supplemented by principles that determine the order of complements among each other. It will be seen that given these principles, a statement like (20 ii) is superfluous as well.

2.3. The transformational component

After the steady reduction of its expressive power, the theoretical status of the transformational component is much better at present than that of the base component. The transformational component itself is reduced to the format MOVE α where the value of α in the grammar of particular languages may be subject to parametric variation[17].

The rule of MOVE α may operate freely, thus leading to vast overgeneration. The strategy developed during the seventies is to filter out this overgenerating effect, not by increasing the expressive power of the individual rules or of the transformational component as a whole, but rather by the imposition of wellformedness conditions on syntactic representations. These wellformedness conditions, like the Binding Theory, the theory of abstract Case, the Empty Category Principle and the Projection Principle will be discussed below.

In their effect, transformations fall into two kinds of formal operations, viz. adjunction and substitution. I shall assume that adjunction is always Chomsky-adjunction. Whether a particular application of MOVE α is an instance of substitution or of adjunction is not determined by some property of the rule itself, but rather by the kind of relationship that exists between the extraction site and the landing site. In the case of substitution, e.g. as in subject-to-subject raising, the empty category left behind, an NP-trace, is regarded as an anaphor in the sense of the Binding Theory, more specifically an argument-anaphor since its antecedent is in an A(rgument) position. An empty category resulting from adjunction will be defined as a variable or, as we shall document below, as an A'-anaphor , since its antecedent is not in an argument position.

One of the relevant wellformedness conditions has already been introduced in the preceding discussion, viz. the Θ-criterion. A number of consequences of this principle, in combination with the Projection Principle, have already been mentioned. Another consequence is the theory that movement operations leave a trace behind in their extraction site. To see this, consider the possibility that no trace is left behind. In that case, a category would appear somewhere in D-structure as required by the Θ-criterion, but its position is irrecoverable at S-structure. This means that at S-structure the subcategorizational properties are no longer obeyed, in violation of the Projection Principle.

Still another consequence is that the Projection Principle drastically limits the number of possible substitutions to those substitutions that involve a position to which no Θ-role is assigned at D-structure, i.e. a so-called Θ'-position. Since complements can never be Θ'-positions because of the Θ-criterion, the only substitutions possible are operations that move a category into subject position, provided that this subject position is a Θ'-position, since otherwise the moved phrase would end up having two Θ-roles. This follows from the fact that a moved constituent always originates in a Θ-position,i.e. either a complement position or a subject position to which a Θ-role is assigned.

Other modules of the system prevent different tpes of overgeneration. These modules are largely motivated independently, i.e. they function beyond the domain of structures to which MOVE α has applied. There is a single module of the system that is restricted in its scope to MOVE α, viz. the Bounding Theory i.e. subjacency, introduced in Chomsky (1973). The subjacency condition has long been regarded as one of the most outstanding explanatory principles of the system. It subsumed various empirical generalizations, such as the island constraints of Ross (1967), under one abstract principle that is not an empirical generalization itself, as it is in conflict with observable data. In spite of its high prestige, the principle has given rise to some controversy (see Koster 1978a), More recently, the introduction of other principles into the theory has led to a situation in which the empirical domain of subjacency can be reduced to these new principles. Therefore, the question arises whether the subjacency principle, restricted as it is to MOVE α only, can be dispensed with altogether. In section

2.6., I argue that this can indeed be done. First, however, the other principles referred to have to be presented.

It should be noted that if the conclusion that subjacency can be dispensed with can be sustained, the conceptual status of MOVE α becomes problematic itself. In previous debates, Chomsky has stressed that the distinction between trace and PRO should be maintained, because traces have properties different from PRO in that the relation with their antecedents is subject to subjacency. If the locality effects of subjacency can be derived independently, one could wonder whether there is still enough motivation to assume MOVE α. A reductionist point of view would require that movement be regarded as a mere metaphor, i.e. given the functional definition of empty categories, D-structure is in fact a property of S-structure independently from the question as to whether this property of S-structure results from actual movement or not. However, at present I do not see what the empirical consequences of this difference in interpretation of MOVE α would be, although I assume that there will be such consequences[18]. Until some clarity in this is arrived at, I shall continue to adopt the non-metaphoric interpretation of MOVE α without attaching much relevance to it.

2.4. The theory of Binding and the notion of Government

A very important step in the search for conceptual reduction of the transformational component has been the identification of traces left behind by movement with lexical anaphors. As a consequence, the effect of transformational operations is filtered by the independently motivated mechanism that constrains possible antecedent-anaphor relations.

Within the framework of GB-theory, this mechanism is the theory of Binding (henceforth BT) that replaces the former opacity conditions in Chomsky (1973) i.e. the Specified Subject Condition (SSC) and the Tensed Sentence Constraint as well as their later versions in Chomsky (1980), i.e. the Nominative Island Constraint (NIC) and the opacity condition. The BT is formulated in (21).

(21) Binding Theory

A. An anaphor must be bound in its governing
category

       B. A pronominal must be free in its governing
          category
       C. A name must be free

The notions bound and free as used in (21) are defined in (22):

    (22) α is bound if it is coindexed with a c-commanding
        category. If α is not bound, it is free.

The language learner, equipped with the BT, has to find out which expressions in the language count as anaphors in the sense of the BT and which elements as pronominals. Only very limited evidence is required in order to establish this. For English and Dutch, reflexives and reciprocals are anaphors and personal pronouns are pronominals. The BT thus accounts quite straightforwardly for the fact that a personal pronoun is disjoint in reference from the NP with which an anaphor in the same position is coreferential and that an anaphor is excluded in positions where pronominals can be referential. The facts in (23) illustrate this[19].

    (23) a. dat **Jan zichzelf** /***hem** martelt
        that John himself/him tortures

      b. dat **Jan** dacht dat **hij/*zichzelf** moest komen
        that John thought that he/himself had to come

      c. dat Jan_i dacht dat Piet_j $\text{hem}_i/\text{zichzelf}_j$ wilde martelen
        that John thought that Peter him/himself   wanted torture

The BT interrelates crucially with the theory of government in that the relevant domains in which elements must be either free or bound are dependent on government relations, viz. are formulated as governing categories. The theory of government is relevant beyond the BT, however. We shall see below that it is central for the theory of abstract Case and for the ECP as well. The notion of government in GB-theory is in fact a more elaborate version of the traditional notion that certain elements, verbs and prepositions, govern their complements. This traditional notion is relevant only in a prototypical sense. The theoretically more elaborate notion extends this traditional one so as to cover other relations between expressions as well. In recent literature, various distinct definitions of the notion government have been considered (Aoun & Sportiche 1981,

Safir 1982 and references cited there). Here I cite the most generally adopted definition given by Aoun & Sportiche. Later in this chapter, this definition will be replaced.

(24) x, a member of the set $\{ \ [\underline{+}V,\underline{+}N]^{O} \ ,\text{TENSE}\}$ governs y

iff for all F, F a maximal projection, F dominates x

iff F dominates y

Informally, (24) states that x governs y if both x and y are contained in the minimal maximal projection of x and there is no maximal projection that contains y without also containing x, where x is either a lexical category or TENSE. The notion of governing category has been subject to a significant change. The initial formulation was as in (25).

(25) A is the governing category for B iff A is the minimal
      · category containing B and a governor of B,

where A = S or NP

(Chomsky 1981:188). There are various problems with this definition of governing category. On the conceptual side, it is unclear why S and NP rather than any other set of categories would be the only candidates for A. The motivation to select S rather than S' rests on cases like those in (26) involving **for...to** complements. In these examples, the anaphors **each other** and **himself** are bound outside both the minimal S and the minimal S' containing them, but they are bound in the matrix S. Suppose that S' is selected as the possible governing category, then given the definition in (25), the embedded S' would count as the governing category of these anaphors as these anaphors are governed by **for**. The embedded S' does not contain an antecedent for the anaphors, however, so principle A of the binding theory should reject these examples, but they are acceptable.

(26) a. $[_{S'}$ $[_{S}$ they would prefer $[_{S'}$ for $_{S}[$each other to win$]]]]$

b. $[_{S'}[_{S}$he would be happy $[_{S'}$ for $[_{S}$ himself to win$]]]]$

The BT is saved, however, if only S and not S' is a possible governing category. A similar problem would arise in the case of traces left behind by WH-movement if S' was a possible governing category. It is assumed in Chomsky (1981) that such traces must be free, like names, i.e. that these traces are subject to principle C

of the BT. If S' were a possible candidate, WH-traces would always be bound in
their governing category in violation of principle C of the BT. On the empirical
level, the definition of governing category in (25) meets with problems as well.
Consider the example in (27). The anaphor **each other** is governed by the preposition **of**. Both **of** and the anaphor are contained in the NP subject of the embedded
clause. Hence both the NP and the clause containing it are possible candidates
for the governing category of the anaphor. Nevertheless, the anaphor is bound
outside the embedded clause.

(27) They would hate it [$_S$,for [$_S$[pictures of each other]   to be on sale]]

Under the opacity condition and the NIC in Chomsky (1980), (27) did not create any
problem, since the anaphor is neither marked with nominative Case, nor is it in
the domain of a subject. So, both conditions are inapplicable. This suggests the
way to solve the problem (cf. Chomsky 1981:211 ff).

The problem with the definition in (25) is that the possible governing
categories are merely stipulated, but it turns out that whether or not a particular category functions as a local domain for the Binding Theory is a relative,
rather than an absolute matter. This is evident from the well-known examples in
(28).

(28) a. We heard **their** stories about **each other**
     b. **We** heard some stories about **each other**

(28a) and (28b) are structurally on a par. The governing category in (28a) is the
NP **their stories about each other**. There cannot be a binding relationship between
we and **each other** in (28a), which is in keeping with the definition of governing
category in (25). However, **we** can be the antecedent for **each other** in (28b).
Therefore, (25) is replaced by the definition of governing category in (29) where
the notion of governing category is not defined in terms of a stipulated set of
categories, but rather in terms of categories with a certain property.

(29) A is the governing category for B if and only if A is
     the minimal category containing B, a governor of B and
     a SUBJECT accessible to B

(Chomsky 1981:220). If **their** in (28a) can qualify as an accessible SUBJECT for
each other, but **some** or any other element contained in the NP **some pictures of**

each other in (28b) cannot, the difference in possibility of establishing a binding relationship between **we** and the anaphor **each other** would be explained. Moreover, if it is assumed that S but not S' may have an accessible SUBJECT, the choice of S instead of S' would fall out automatically. In the examples in (26), the embedded S does not have a SUBJECT accessible to the anaphors in subject position, hence the embedded S cannot count as a governing category for these anaphors.

The crucial question, of course, is how we are to understand this notion of accessible SUBJECT. Obviously, the notion may not coincide with the traditional notion of subject, since in that case there would be no possibility of accounting for the difference in grammaticality of (26a) and an example like (30).

(30) *They would hate it that each other won the race

So, what is the governing category for the anaphor **each other** in this example? If the Binding Theory is to explain the ungrammaticality of (30), the governing category for the anaphor may not be the matrix clause, since in that domain the anaphor can find a suitable antecedent. How can we differentiate, then, between (26) and (30) in such a way that this difference is captured in terms of the notion of accessible SUBJECT?

Traditionally, the difference in grammaticality between (26) and (30) was accounted for by the Propositional Island Constraint, PIC (Chomsky 1976), a reformulation of the Tensed-S-constraint. In Chomsky (1981), it is argued that the rule for the expansion of S is as follows: S-> NP⌢INFL⌢VP. INFL (inflection) obligatorily contains AGR (agreement) if it contains TENSE. This expresses the fact that agreement is found only in tensed clauses. Agreement itself is considered to be nominal in nature as it possesses features like number and person. In (30), then, the presence of AGR provides an accessible SUBJECT for the anaphor in subject position, but such an accessible SUBJECT is absent in (26), because the embedded clause is tenseless in that case. Therefore, the embedded clause counts as a governing category for **each other** in (30) because the embedded clause contains the anaphor, a governor of the anaphor (TENSE) and a SUBJECT accessible to the anaphor (AGR). Within this domain of the embedded clause, however, there is no antecedent for the anaphor. Therefore, (30) is ungrammatical because it violates principle A of the Binding Theory.

According to Chomsky, we can think of an accessible SUBJECT of a certain domain as the most prominent nominal element in that domain. I would like to propose to change this conception slightly by characterizing accessible SUBJECT

as a possible identifier. This way of characterizing this notion will be relevant
below when we consider WH-movement. We can think of the notion of identifier in
the following way. An anaphor must be identified in a way that is intuitively
clear: the anaphor has no direct reference itself, but only via another expression with which it is coindexed, its antecedent. The syntactic subject position
can always contain an antecedent, i.e. an identifier, for each anaphor in its
domain. In this sense, the syntactic subject position of a clause is always an
accessible SUBJECT for an anaphor in its domain. Notice that I make a distinction
between a position in terms of which the notion of accessible SUBJECT is defined,
and possible fillers of this position. Thus, the subject position is an accessible SUBJECT, not because of the particular content it happens to have, but
because it can always have some content that properly identifies an anaphor in
its domain. Similarly, AGR can be regarded as an identifier of the subject. This
is especially clear in the so-called PRO-drop languages, to which we return
below, where the subject can be left empty, given that it is properly identified
by AGR. Similarly, the specifier position of NP can host an antecedent expression
for an anaphor in one of the complements of the nominal head, as in (28a). The
difference between AGR and specifier of NP on the one hand and subject of a clause
on the other is that the latter is always present as a position, due to the
Extended Projection Principle (cf. Chomsky 1982), whereas the former may either
be absent (as in the case of AGR in tenseless clauses) or be unsuitable to
function as an identifier (as in the case of a determiner as specifier of NP
instead of a genitive NP or a possessive pronoun). This means that anaphors in the
subject position of a clause or in the complement of a noun may have distinct
choices for their governing categories, depending on the presence of AGR or a
suitable specifier respectively, but that anaphors in other positions always have
the same governing category, determined by the presence of a structural subject
of that domain. The relevance of defining accessible SUBJECT in this way will be
further clarified in section 2.6.

A final problem relates to cases like (31). The complement clause contains
TENSE, hence AGR. Therefore, even though the subject NP itself does not qualify
as a governing category because the specifier position does not qualify as an
accessible SUBJECT, the AGR of the embedded clause should define the embedded
clause as the governing category for the anaphor contained in this domain. This
would yield the undesirable result that the anaphor should find an antecedent
within the embedded clause because of principle A of the Binding Theory. This
problem can be solved by slightly modifying the definition of accessible SUBJECT.
Let us assume that AGR and the nominative subject that it identifies are coin-

dexed. Then, the structure of the embedded clause in (31) would be as in (32).

(31) They thought that pictures of each other would be on sale

(32) $[_{S'}$ that $[_S$ $[_{NP}$ pictures of each other$_i]$ AGR$_i$ VP $]]$

Now consider what would happen if **each other** and AGR were coindexed as well. The resulting structure would be such that the entire subject NP would have an index identical to a subpart of it, given transitivity of indexing. Such a situation is always impossible, and this is accounted for by the i-inside-i constraint formulated in (33).

(33) * $[_\gamma \ldots \delta \ldots\ldots]$, where γ and δ bear the same index.

(cf.Chomsky 1981:212). The notion of accessible SUBJECT that is relevant, then, can be formulated as in (34).

(34) A is an accessible SUBJECT for B iff A is a position that may
      contain a possible identifier for B and B is in the
      c-command domain of A, where coindexing A and B
      would not violate the i-inside-i constraint

The definitions of government and governing category given in the preceding discussion suffice for the present moment. For a more elaborate discussion of these notions, the reader is referred to Chomsky (1981), on which most of the preceding presentation was based. As we proceed, many of the issues will be considered again and some of the definitions will be changed.

      Before turning to the relevance of the theory of Binding for the domain of movement operations, I shall discuss the theory of abstract Case.

2.5. The theory of Case

The theory of Binding discussed in the previous subsection partitions the total class of NP type expressions into three distinct subsets in terms of their binding requirements. These binding requirements determine the distribution of these three subsets as a function of the relation with c-commanding NP's. The discussion of the Binding Theory was deliberately limited to visible anaphors and pronouns, i.e. to those elements that are phonetically realized. The distribution of such overt expressions is also determined by the theory of Case, developed in Rouveret & Vergnaud (1980), Chomsky (1980,1981). This device may be regarded as a means to partition the class of NP positions into a subset that accepts NP's with phonetic content and a subset of NP positions that do not allow an NP with phonetic content at S-structure. The former subset comprises those positions to which Case is assigned, whereas the latter subset fails to receive Case. Whether or not a particular position receives Case is a function of its governor. Therefore, the theory of Case is embedded in the theory of government, just like the theory of Binding. Specifically, NP's that are governed by a [-N] category receive Case, as well as the NP governed by TENSE, i.e. the subject NP of a TENSED clause, whereas NP's that are ungoverned or governed by a [+N] governor do not receive Case. This is illustrated in the following examples.

(35) a. John fears the dog
     b.*John's fear the dog
     c.*John is afraid the dog

John in the a- and c-examples receives nominative Case from TENSE. In b. it receives Case in a different way that is irrelevant for our present purposes. The NP **the dog** only receives Case in the a-example, from the verb,which is [-N] , but not in the other examples since nouns and adjectives are [+N] categories. There is a strategy both in Dutch and English to insert a preposition in front of the NP in the complement of the [+N] categories, **of** in English, **van** in Dutch.

(36) a. (John's) fear of the dog
     b. (John is) afraid of the dog.

Prepositions share the [-N] feature with verbs. The assumptions made above account for the fact that in general finite clauses have lexical subjects, whereas non-finite clauses have non-lexical subjects.

(37) a. Piet zei dat hij zou komen
        Peter said that he would come

     b. Piet zei   te zullen komen
        Peter said   to will   come

A relevant question might be whether the two [-N] categories, V and P, assign
the same Case or not. It has been proposed that prepositions assign oblique Case,
while verbs assign objective Case (cf. Hornstein & Weinberg 1981, Lightfoot 1980,
Chomsky 1980), but whether this claim is correct is a matter of dispute (cf.
Kayne 1981c). Furthermore, there might be categories that determine what is
called inherent Case. The core instances of Case assignment can be formulated as
in (38).

> (38)   i. TENSE assigns nominative Case to a governed NP
>   ii. [-N] categories assign objective (oblique) Case to a governed NP
>   iii. Specific categories may assign inherent Case to their
>   complements.

The assignment of Case interacts with a wellformedness constraint which applies
at S-structure, the Case-filter, formulated in (39).

> (39) *NP if NP has phonetic features but no Case

While it is clear that the Case-filter restricts the distribution of lexical expressions to positions that receive Case, it is not clear whether it also limits
the distribution of invisible elements to positions to which no Case is assigned.
Notice that this would imply that invisible categories are in complementary
distribution with visible categories. In order to be able to answer this question, it is of course necessary to determine what is to count as an invisible
category. Obviously, empty positions created by deletion processes do not fall
under the scope of the notion relevant to us. It is standardly assumed that
deletions operate in the so-called left-hand component of the grammar that
relates S-structure to phonetic form. The Case Filter, on the other hand, is
assumed to apply to S-structure itself, hence the empty categories resulting from
operations applying after S-structure are irrelevant to the matter under discussion. Let us limit the discussion, therefore, to base-generated empty categories
and empty categories that result from MOVE α.

     As for PRO, it is assumed that PRO must be ungoverned. This requirement
follows from the Binding Theory given the characterization of PRO as a pronominal
anaphor. This implies that PRO should both be free and bound in its governing
category, a requirement that can only be fulfilled if there is no governing
category, hence no governor for PRO. Let us accept for the moment that this so-
called PRO-theorem is correct. It then follows that PRO is also limited to
positions to which no Case is assigned, because Case is assigned under govern-

ment.

Concerning trace, then, it should be noted that the situation is more complicated. Traditionally, i.e. since Chomsky (1977), a distinction has been made between the two major instances of MOVE α, viz. MOVE NP and MOVE WH. Similarly, a distinction can be made between the traces left behind by the former and the traces left behind by the latter. The two types are exemplified in (40a) and (40b) respectively.

(40)   a. John seems t to have left
       b. What did you buy t?

The trace of **John** in (40a) occupies the subject position of a tenseless clause. Hence, no nominative Case is assigned by TENSE. Therefore, the trace occupies a position that does not receive Case. The moved constituent, on the other hand, occupies the subject position of the tensed matrix clause at S-structure and hence receives Case in this position. The trace of the WH-phrase in (40b), on the other hand, is governed by the verb **buy** and therefore is in a position to which Case is assigned. Its antecedent expression **what,** however, is moved to a position to which no Case is assigned. Let us call a moved category together with its traces a **chain**. In the two examples in (40), then, both the chain (**John, t**) and the chain (**what, t**) have a single Case. Suppose that we reformulate the Case Filter in (39) as in (41).

(41)   Each lexical NP is a member of a chain to which Case is assigned

As Chomsky (1981:331) notes, this reformulation makes its possible to abandon the Case Filter as an independent principle of GB-theory as it can be subsumed under a more general visibility requirement for the θ-criterion applying at S-structure or at LF. The formulation given in (41) leaves open the possibility that more than one Case is assigned to a certain chain, i.e. it leaves open the possibility that Case is assigned to an empty category, but also the possibility that Case is assigned to more than a single member of a particular chain.

The point under discussion is relevant for a more general question concerning the nature of empty categories that was raised in Chomsky (1981:ch.6, 1982). This question is whether there is a single type of empty NP as far as its intrinsic properties are concerned, or whether there are several types of empty categories that can be distinguished in terms of their feature composition. The original idea was that there is indeed a type-distinction between PRO, WH-trace and NP-trace, in that WH-trace is an empty category with Case whereas NP-trace is an empty category without Case, while PRO differs from either in having pronominal features. WH-traces, called variables, are then defined as in (42).

(42) An empty category is a variable iff it bears Case

Because of the bi-conditional, (42) can be read in two directions, i.e. each empty category with Case is a variable and each variable must be Case marked. The approach of distinguishing different types of empty categories in terms of internal properties meets with both empirical and conceptual problems. On the empirical side, examples like those in (43)-(44) (cf.Kayne 1981a:80) suggest that there may be a variable without Case and that a chain may be assigned more than one Case.

(43) a. **Quel garcon** crois-tu t être le plus intelligent?
     b.*Je crois **Jean** être le plus intelligent

(44) a. **Whom** do you believe t has left?
     b. I believe **he/*him** has left

(43) shows that a WH-phrase can be extracted from a position where a lexical NP may not occur. The reason for the ungrammaticality of (43b) is that the lexical NP **Jean** does not receive Case. Hence, the trace in the corresponding position in (43a) does not receive Case either, contrary to the requirement in (42). In (44), the WH-phrase in sentence-initial position exhibits the non-subject form. In the b-example, we see that a pronoun in the same position as the trace of the WH-phrase in the a-example can only take the subject form. Hence, it must be concluded that the chain in (44a) bears two Cases, one of them being the nominative Case assigned to its extraction site of the WH-phrase. Kayne assumes that the matrix verbs **croire** and **believe** assign objective Case to the WH-phrase in the intermediate COMP.

On the conceptual side, a division of empty categories into several different types makes it difficult to explain in a principled manner why the distinct types partition a certain distribution, i.e. the distribution of NP. This conceptual point is the major topic of Chomsky (1981:ch.6, 1982). I shall adopt the approach developed in these references. According to this approach, all empty NP's belong to one and the same type. Differences among them do not follow from differences in intrinsic feature content, but from the functional properties

determined by their antecedents. A simplified version of this functional definition of empty categories is stated in (45)[20].

(45)   i. **e** is a variable iff it is locally A'-bound and
           in an A-position
        ii. **e** is an NP-trace iff it is locally A-bound by
           an antecedent without an independent θ-role
        iii. **e** is PRO iff it is either free or A-bound by an
           antecedent with an independent θ-role

For further refinements and more elaborate discussion, the reader is referred to
the works by Chomsky mentioned above.

If this approach of the functional definition of empty categories is correct,
the Case Filter plays no role in the distribution of empty categories. As far as
lexical NP's is concerned, the Case Filter is subsumed under a general visibility
requirement for the θ-criterion.

2.6. The Status of Variables: Subjacency

In section 2.4. it was argued that the status of Subjacency as a condition that is
restricted in its scope to MOVE α is rather unsatisfactory within the context of
GB-theory. It has always been the case that Subjacency overlapped with other
principles of the theory, at least conceptually. Thus, restricting ourselves to
the most central conditions in Chomsky (1973), the Specified Subject Condition
and the Tensed-S-Constraint imposed a certain locality both on syntactic movements and rules of construal, whereas Subjacency imposed a locality constraint on
syntactic operations only. Koster (1978a) attempts to reduce some of the conceptual redundancy by imposing a general condition on the distribution of empty
categories, his Bounding Condition, and another condition imposing a locality on
possible anaphor-antecedent relations which generalizes over both lexical anaphors and empty categories. Hence, in his system the distribution of empty
categories is constrained by two distinct principles as well. The conceptual
redundancy even increases in the GB-framework, but here a sharp distinction is
made between NP-movement traces and WH-traces. All empty categories are subject
to the ECP which is formulated in (46) below. Furthermore, the distance between

an NP-trace and its antecedent is constrained by the Binding Theory, as traces of
NP-movement are considered to be anaphors, hence subject to principle A of the
Binding Theory. The Binding Theory does not limit the distance between a WH-trace
and its antecedent, however, as traces of WH-movement are assumed to be subject
to principle C of the Binding Theory. Therefore, a locality condition such as
Subjacency is needed to constrain the relation between a WH-phrase and its
extraction site.

(46) The Empty Category Principle (ECP)

> An empty category [$_{NP}$ **e**] must be properly governed,
> where A properly governs B if and only if A governs
> B and a. A = $[+\underline{N}, +\underline{V}]^{o}$ or
>   b. A is coindexed with B

Schematically, the different proposals can be represented as in (47).

(47)

	Chomsky 1973	Koster 1978	GB-theory
MOVE NP	SSC, TSC, SUJ	BC, LP	ECP, BT, SUJ
MOVE WH	SSC, TSC, SUJ	BC, LP	ECP, SUJ
PRO-control	SSC, TSC	BC, LP	"control theory"
anaph.lex.	SSC, TSC	LP	BT

where SSC= Specified Subject Condition
      TSC= Tensed-S-Constraint
      BC = Bounding Condition
      LP = Locality Principle
      BT = Binding Theory
      SUJ= Subjacency

The opacity conditions like SSC and TSC are now subsumed under the Binding
Theory. Roughly speaking, Koster's LP is comparable to principle A of the Binding
Theory. If we consider the various proposals represented in (47), it turns out
that, in general, movements are constrained by the same principles that constrain
anaphor-antecedent relations and furthermore by a principle unique to movements,
Koster's BC, Subjacency and ECP. Comparing Chomsky's (1973) position with GB-
theory, it appears to be the case that WH-movement was assumed to be constrained

by the usual opacity conditions in 1973, but not in the framework of GB-theory. Koster's position equals Chomsky's (1973) position in this respect. However, the difference between Chomsky (1973) and the GB-position is only a matter of appearance, since COMP was defined as an escape hatch for WH-movement with respect to the opacity conditions in Chomsky (1973).

Let us concentrate now on GB-theory. As for MOVE NP, we see that there are three principles that are assumed to constrain either the movement itself (Subjacency) or the result of this movement (ECP, BT). A relevant question, therefore, is whether all three are needed or whether a reduction is possible. The traces left behind by MOVE NP are regarded as anaphors in the sense of the Binding Theory as formulated in (21) above. Therefore, they must be bound in their governing category. This conception of NP-traces, then, has a rigorously delimiting effect with respect to the required structural proximity of the extraction and the landing sites of NP-movements. Consider the examples in (48).

(48) a. **John** seems **t** to be likely **t** to be there in time
     b.***John** seems   that it is likely **t** to be there in time

The assumption here is that **John** is generated in the subject position of the clause **t to be there in time** at D-structure both in (48a) and (48b), but that it occupies the subject position of the main clause due to MOVE α. The ungrammaticality of (48b) can be accounted for in terms of Subjacency (with either S or S' as bounding nodes for Subjacency) as can be seen from the structure in (49).

(49)   **John** seems [$_S$ that [$_S$ it is likely [$_S$ [$_S$ **t** to be there in time]]]]

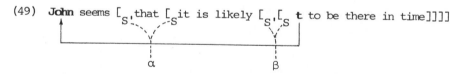

                                α   β

In (48a), on the other hand, the subjacency principle is not violated because **John** is not moved from its base position to its ultimate position in S-structure in a single step, but rather in two separate steps, each of which crosses only a single boundary. Thus, successive application of WH-movement (hence the intermediate trace) evades the restriction of Subjacency in that case. It is important to see, now, that the ungrammaticality of (48b) can be explained by the Binding Theory as well. Starting with the trace in (48b), we ask ourselves what its governing category is. Therefore, we need to determine the governor of the trace and a SUBJECT accessible for it. It is assumed that the trace in the subject position of complement clauses of certain matrix predicates is governed by this

predicate. Below, the way in which this government relation is established will
be further discussed. The accessible SUBJECT for the trace is the subject
position of the clause **it is likely S'** according to the definition of accessible
SUBJECT given in (34), since in this position a possible antecedent for the trace
could be found in principle as in (50).

(50) (I thought that) **John** is likely t to be there in time

Therefore, the clause **it is likely S'** is the governing category for the trace. But
this domain does not contain a suitable antecedent for the anaphor, i.e. for the
trace. Hence (48b) is rejected by the Binding Theory. It might be argued that the
trace does find an antecedent in this domain, viz. the subject **it**. This would be a
correct counterargument, but then (48b) would be rejected by the Θ-criterion,
because **John** would not be assigned a Θ-role (or more specifically, **John** is not a
member of a chain to which a Θ-role is assigned). It turns out, then, that (48b)
is accounted for both by Subjacency and by the Binding Theory. In fact, the
locality imposed by the Binding Theory is more restricted than the locality
imposed by Subjacency. Therefore, it may be concluded that Subjacency is irrelevant as far as NP-movement is concerned[21].

It is impossible at this moment to conclude, however, that Subjacency can be
dispensed with, because MOVE WH is not restricted by the Binding Theory as is MOVE
NP. However, MOVE WH is restricted by the ECP and by Subjacency. The ECP as
formulated in (46) combines two relatively unrelated clauses: an empty category
is either licensed by a lexical governor or by a local antecedent. In this
respect, the ECP overlaps with the Binding Theory in the case of MOVE NP, since
both the Binding Theory and the ECP require a local antecedent. In the case of WH-
movements out of properly governed positions, the two unrelated clauses of the
ECP are redundant as well, as only the first suffices. This implies that for
extractions out of properly governed positions, the ECP could be reduced so as to
contain only the first clause, if the presence of a local antecedent for traces
left behind by WH-movements could be made to follow from an independent principle, such as the Binding Theory in the case of NP-movements. Let us consider some
examples of WH-movements from this perspective. The example in (51) demonstrates
that there are cases of apparent violations of Subjacency.

(51) **Who** do you think that Mary assumed that Bill said
     that John saw **t**?

Such long distances between the WH-phrase and the gap are merely apparent violations of Subjacency. The relation is assumed to be established not in a single operation crossing a larger number of bounding nodes than permitted by Subjacency, but rather by successive cyclic applications of WH-movement, each step only crossing a single bounding node. That this violation is only apparent is evidenced by the fact that if the escape route is not available, (i.e. if it is not possible to split up the unbounded relation in a number of partial steps) such long-distance dependencies are impossible. The relevant cases are WH-islands and complex NP's in the sense of Ross (1967) as in (52)-(53).

(52) *What$_j$ did you wonder who$_i$ John gave t$_i$ t$_j$
     (cf. I thought that John gave Mary a book)
(53) ***Who** did you believe the story that John met **t**

As for (52), it is assumed that, given S as a bounding node for Subjacency, movement of **what** to the sentence-initial complementizer position has to cross two S-nodes in a single operation as the escape route via the COMP of the embedded clause is blocked by the presence of a WH-phrase in this COMP. In (53), the movement of **who** would violate Subjacency by crossing an NP and an S-node in a single step. This is the central part of the empirical domain of Subjacency.

There are examples of WH-movement where Subjacency fails to make the correct predictions. Consider the well-known examples in (54).

(54)   a.***Who** do you think that **t** saw Bill?
       b. **What** do you think that Bill bought **t**?

The difference in grammaticality is not predicted by Subjacency. If S is taken as a bounding node for Subjacency and not S', the two cases in (54) are apparent violations of Subjacency in that there are two S-nodes between the WH-phrase and the gap. However, as in the example in (51), this can be circumvented by assuming that movement is first to the embedded COMP, from which a subsequent movement brings the WH-phrase to its ultimate position. Therefore, as far as Subjacency is concerned, both should be grammatical. What the examples in (54) illustrate is a so-called subject-object asymmetry that we find in many languages in various types of construction. As a simple example, the asymmetry between subjects and objects involving the use of **ne** in Italian could be given. Simplifying the situation, we can say that **ne** must bind an empty nominal projection in an NP containing a quantifier if this NP is in object position, but not if the NP is in preverbal subject position. The following examples, taken from Belletti & Rizzi (1981) illustrate this.

(55) a. Tre settimane passano rapidamente
Three weeks   elapse   rapidly

b.*Tre   ne passano rapidamente
Three of-them elapse rapidly

c. Gianni trascorrera tre settimane a Milano
Gianni will-spend   three weeks   in Milan

d. Gianni ne trascorrera   tre a Milano
Gianni of-them will-spend three in Milan

In fact, a similar kind of asymmetry between subjects of clauses and non-subjects has already been encountered in the case of anaphors. Whereas an anaphor in subject position can be bound to an antecedent outside the clause, non-subject anaphors must always be bound within the domain of their subject (see the discussion above). In Chomsky (1980), this similarity was not captured. The asymmetry in the case of anaphors was accounted for by the opacity condition, whereas the asymmetry in the case of WH-movement observed in (54) was captured by the Nominative Island Condition (NIC).

Earlier in this chapter, some problems with the NIC in the case of anaphors were discussed. The example in (56) shows that the NIC makes the wrong prediction with respect to extraction from subject position as well. Such extractions are not always impossible.

(56) **Who** do you think **t** saw Bill? (cf. 54a)

The asymmetry between (54a) and (56) had been discussed earlier in Chomsky and Lasnik (1977) where the so-called **that-t** filter was postulated to account for the ungrammaticality of (54a). In Chomsky (1981), the ungrammaticality of (54a) is attributed to the ECP, i.e. to the first clause of it, on the assumption that INFL or TENSE cannot be considered to be lexical governors. Hence, the empty category in subject position would violate the requirement of proper government. The second clause of the ECP is motivated by the grammaticality of (56). It is assumed that the trace left behind in the intermediate COMP cannot function as a proper antecedent in the case of (54a). The reason for this is that either this trace is deleted in order to avoid a violation of the filter on doubly-filled COMP's, or that it does not c-command the trace in subject position, due to the branching of COMP.   In (56), on the other hand, the trace in the intermediate COMP need not be deleted and the COMP does not branch. Hence it c-commands the trace in subject position and it licenses this trace in terms of clause b. of the ECP in (46). What this discussion suggests is that as far as the ECP is concerned, the alleged trace in the intermediate COMP in (54b) does not play a role, because the empty category is licensed by the lexical governor **buy**. The presence of a trace in the intermediate COMP is therefore only motivated in terms of Subjacency, at least in these cases.

Before we proceed with the question whether Subjacency can be dispensed with, we concentrate first on the redundancy between the ECP and the Binding Theory. Clearly, this redundancy could be eliminated if the presence of a local antecedent in the case of WH-movements could follow from the Binding Theory as well. In that case, the ECP could be reduced to its first clause. The overlap between the Binding Theory and the ECP is discussed in Aoun (1981), who concludes that the ECP should be dispensed with altogether. I return to his proposal below. The obvious way to approach this situation is to try to subsume the requirement of a local antecedent under the Binding Theory for WH-movements as well.

We noted earlier that under the definition of governing category in (25) it is impossible to define the traces left by WH-movement as anaphors since the antecedent expression for the gap created by these movements will always be outside a possible governing category, if only NP and S are candidates for this function. The idea that WH-traces are not anaphors is supported by the claim in Freidin & Lasnik (1981) that WH-traces are not subject to the usual opacity conditions, i.e. WH-phrases can be extracted from the domain of a specified subject and from the domain of a tensed clause. This was of course the motivation to define COMP as an escape hatch for these opacity conditions in Chomsky (1973), as we noted earlier. Another reason to assume that WH-traces are subject to principle C of the Binding Theory, rather than to principle A is evidenced by their similarity to names (cf. May's 1977 COMP-to-COMP requirement). A relevant example is (57). This would receive an interpretation as in (58). If the x's are replaced by a name like **Bill** as in (59), the parallel behaviour of WH-traces and names is brought to light.

(57) *$[_S, \textbf{Who}_i$ thought $[_S, t_i [_S$ Mary would meet $t_i]]]$

(58)   For which x, x thought that Mary would meet x

(59) ***Bill** thought that Mary would meet **Bill**.

The major argument for the identification of WH-traces with names are the cases of so-called strong crossover (cf. Wasow 1972). In (60a), the pronoun **him** can be coreferential with the WH-phrase, just as **him** in (61a) can be coreferential with the name **Bill**. In the b-examples, however, neither the WH-phrase (nor its trace) can be coreferential with **he,** nor the name **Bill**.

(60) a. **Who**$_i$ t$_i$ said that Mary had kissed him?
     b. **Who**$_i$ did he say that Mary kissed **t**$_i$?

(61) a. Bill said that Mary had kissed him
     b. He said that Mary had kissed Bill

If the claim that WH-traces must be free like names is true, it seems that no locality on the relation between WH-phrase and the gap can be imposed by the Binding Theory.

However, the problems mentioned above can be solved. The first problem, viz. that the WH-phrase is necessarily outside the governing category of the trace it leaves behind given the definition of governing category in (25), has in fact already been solved by relativizing the notion governing category in terms of accessible SUBJECT. Consequently, the set of possible governing categories need not be listed anymore in an a priori manner. The second problem boils down to saying that a WH-trace may not be bound by a category in an A-position. Given the functional definition of empty categories presented in (45), a trace that is bound by a category in an A-position would not even be defined as a variable. Aoun (1981) proposes therefore to generalize the Binding Theory from a theory of A-binding to a theory of A- and A'-binding. Traces left by NP-movements are regarded as A-anaphors, whereas traces left behind by WH-movement, or variables in general, are regarded as A'-anaphors. As these are both anaphors, both are subject to principle A of the (generalized) Binding Theory. A'-anaphors are not only subject to principle A of the Binding Theory, however, but also to principle C.

It seems to me that the latter assumption, i.e. that variables are subject to principle C as well is in fact unnecessary. To see this, consider once more the violation of the COMP-to-COMP requirement given in (57). In this example, the trace is bound by a category in an A-position. Therefore, it is not defined as a variable by the functional approach to empty categories. Furthermore, the structure will be ruled out by the θ-criterion, as will all COMP-to-COMP violations where the landing site is a θ-position. To see this, consider the chain (**who, t, t**) in (57). This chain will bear two θ-roles and is therefore ruled out by the θ-criterion. The same is true for all cases of strong crossover. However, to have these filtered out by the θ-criterion, the formation of chains has to be of a different nature than has been assumed thus far. The formation of chains is described above as follows: a chain is formed by a category and all its traces. This way of defining chains may be called derivational. For the purposes that we are considering here, the formation of chains should be assumed to take place at S-structure where all coindexed elements should be taken to constitute a chain, such that each element in the chain is the local binder of the element following it. This chain algorithm may be called representational (cf. Rizzi 1983). Let us see how this representational characterization of chains works in the case of strong crossover given in (60b).A crossover violation results if **who** and **he** are coindexed. Suppose **who** and **he** are indeed coindexed. Then there are two possible chains that can be formed, both of which lead to ungrammaticality. The first possibility is that a chain is formed consisting only of (**who, he**). Under this possibility, the sentence violates the θ-criterion, because the trace, occupying a θ-position, is not part of a chain that is headed either by a lexical NP bearing Case or by PRO. Therefore, there is a θ-role that is not assigned to a chain that is visible for the θ-criterion. The second possible chain that can be created is (**who, he, t**) which also violates the θ-criterion, because the chain receives two θ-roles, one from the position occupied by the trace and one from the position occupied by **he**. It turns out, then, that the requirement that variables are not bound by a category in an A-position follows from the functional definition of empty categories as well as, in most cases, from the θ-criterion. I conclude, therefore, that there is no need to assume that variables, i.e. A'-anaphors, are subject to principle C of the binding theory.

The next question to ask is how the idea that WH-movement traces are anaphors can be reconciled with the long distances that can be observed to exist between the WH-phrase and the gap. The most obvious solution would be to assume that the local antecedent for the trace in the extraction site is the trace left behind in the intermediate COMP's by successive cyclic movement. In a case like (51), repeated here, a chain would be created consisting of the WH-phrase in sentence initial position as its first member and the trace in the position of the object of **saw** as its final member, with all traces left in the intermediate COMP's by successive application of MOVE WH as the other members, each member being the local antecedent of the next member in that chain.

(51) **Who** do you think that Mary assumed that Bill said

that John saw **t**?

There are two problems with this solution, however. First of all, the discussion above concerning the differential acceptability of (54a) and (56) rested on the assumption that an intermediate trace in a COMP that also contains a lexical complementizer cannot function as a local antecedent, either because this trace is deleted or because it fails to c-command. The intermediate COMP's in (51) are all filled with **that**. Secondly, if WH-traces are to be regarded as anaphors in the sense of the Binding Theory, it is not immediately evident what the governing category for this anaphor should be. Which category functions as the governing category for a particular element depends on two things: what is the governor of this element and what is the minimal accessible SUBJECT. It is fairly easy to determine the governor for the WH-trace. In the example in (51), it is the verb **saw**. Less straightforward, however, is how the question with respect to accessible SUBJECT should be answered. The notion accessible SUBJECT was defined as in (34),and is repeated here.

(34) A is an accessible SUBJECT for B iff A is a position

that may contain a possible identifier for B and B is

in the c-command domain of A, where coindexing A and

B would not violate the i-inside-i constraint.

Before we proceed with our discussion of long distances between WH-phrase and WH-gap, we shall consider a simpler case, as in (62).

(62) $[_{S'}$**Who** $[_S$ did you   see   **t**$]]$

In this example, there are two c-commanding NP's for the trace, **who** and **you**. The governor of the trace is **see**. Suppose that the governing category for this anaphor is S rather than S'. In that case, the sentence should be ungrammatical because there is no possible antecedent for the trace within the governing category. Notice that the NP **you** cannot be an accessible SUBJECT for the trace in object position, because the position occupied by **you** could not host a possible identifier for the trace, for reasons that will be clear by now: if the subject position was coindexed with the object position, a θ-violation would result. If **who** is not coindexed with the object position, the θ-criterion will be violated as well, because the θ-role assigned to the object of **see** would not be visible for the θ-criterion. For similar reasons, INFL in (62) may not be regarded as the accessible SUBJECT either, given transitivity of indexing, since coindexing INFL and the object position would yield a situation in which the subject and object share the same index, resulting in a θ-violation. Aoun (1981) concludes, therefore, that the trace in object position in such a case has no governing category as defined by (29). Then, (63) comes into play (cf. Chomsky 1981:220, Aoun 1981:34).

(63) A root sentence is the governing category for a governed
     element which lacks an accessible SUBJECT

Therefore, in (62) the root clause is the governing category for the trace in object position and in this governing category the A'-anaphor is bound as required by principle A of the generalized Binding Theory. Similar remarks apply in the case of long distances as in (51). Again, we must determine what the governing category for the anaphor is. Surprisingly, this will be the root sentence in this case as well. The embedded Ss and S's do not count as governing categories for the same reasons as in (62): their subjects and AGRs do not count as possible accessible SUBJECTs, since in all cases a violation of the θ - criterion would result, because the trace would be A-bound. Therefore, the trace lacks an accessible SUBJECT and consequently, (63) comes into play. Therefore, for WH-traces in non-subject positions, it turns out that the root sentence will always be the governing category, at least this is what Aoun concludes.

The situation concerning WH-movement from subject position is slightly more complicated. Consider again the contrast between (54a) and (56), repeated here.

(54a)*Who do you think that t saw Bill ?
(56) Who do you think   t saw Bill ?

Recall that this contrast was used to motivate clause b in the formulation of the ECP. According to Aoun (1981), the contrast can be accounted for by the Binding Theory as well. He assumes that the governing category for the trace in subject position is the embedded S', because in this domain the trace finds both its governor (INFL) and an accessible SUBJECT (AGR). Therefore, the trace must find an antecedent in this domain. This is the case in (56), viz. a trace in COMP, but not in (54a), because either there is no trace or if there is a trace in COMP, it fails to c-command the anaphor, due to the internal branching of COMP. Therefore, Aoun (1981) concludes that, given the generalized Binding Theory, the ECP can be dispensed with altogether. I will not take over this latter conclusion. In the discussions below, it will be shown that the ECP still has a relevant empirical domain. I also do not accept Aoun's conclusion that in the examples in (54a) and (56) the embedded S' should be regarded as the governing category of the anaphor in subject position. The difference in acceptability follows from the ECP, as the subject position of a **that**-clause is not properly governed on the assumption that INFL is not a member of the set of lexical governors. It will tentatively be assumed that the subject position in (56) is properly governed by the matrix verb **think** as a result of S'-deletion, an operation that is possible in the complement of a restricted class of predicates, provided that the COMP is empty[22]. Such a government relation is possible only with those matrix predicates that also take an infinitival complement with a lexical subject, like **think** and **believe,** the so-called Exceptional Case Marking Verbs (ECM verbs). This restriction accounts for the fact that no difference in acceptability is observable in the case of adjectival complement clauses as the following examples, taken from Kayne (1980 : 77 ff.), illustrate.

(64) a.*The only person **who** it's not essential (that) **t** talk to her, is Bill

    b.*Your son, **who** it is in my opinion not possible

       (that) **t** could fall in love with any girl, ...

    c.***Who** is it likely (that) **t** will forget the beer

Another piece of evidence that the subject in such constructions is governed by the matrix verb derives from cases like (44a), in which the WH-phrase that is extracted from the subject position of a tensed clause exhibits objective Case.

    Hence, I conclude that (54a) is ruled out by clause a. of the ECP. Let me turn now to the reason for not adopting Aoun's conclusion that the embedded S' is the governing category for an A'-anaphor in the subject position of a tensed clause. In order to demonstrate this, we have to turn to WH-islands. It should be remembered that WH-islands belong to the central empirical domain of the principle of Subjacency. I will now argue that the WH-island constraint follows from the generalized Theory of Binding. Aoun (1981) does not discuss these cases. It is difficult to see how the constraint on extraction from islands could be reconciled with his conclusion that it is always the root clause that functions as the governing category for WH-traces in non-subject position. Consider an example like (65).

(65) ***What** did you wonder   whether Bill bought **t**?

According to Aoun, **bought** is the governor of the trace and the root clause is its governing category for the same reasons as in the cases discussed above. Therefore, as the trace is bound in this domain, Aoun has to appeal to another principle (perhaps Subjacency) to exclude (65). However, the ungrammaticality of (65) can be derived from the generalized Binding Theory in the following way. The way to proceed would be to arrive at a situation that the embedded S' is the governing category in this case, but not in cases like (51). Therefore, the embedded S' should contain an accessible SUBJECT for the anaphor. This is exactly the case under the definition of accessible SUBJECT given in (34). The embedded COMP qualifies as an accessible SUBJECT, because a possible antecedent expression for the WH-phrase could occur in this position, as in (66). In this respect, the COMP embedded under a verb like **wonder** will always be the accessible SUBJECT for a WH-trace in the domain of this COMP, unlike a COMP embedded under verbs like **think,** as we can see in (67).

(66) I wonder **what** Bill bought **t**
(67)*I think **what** Bill bought **t**

So, even in a case like (65) where the COMP does not contain a possible antecedent expression, COMP functions as an accessible SUBJECT, making the embedded clause opaque for binding from outside. In this respect, the COMP under verbs selecting an indirect question is comparable to the subject of a clause: both the subject of a clause and this specific COMP are always present, so that consequently there is no variation in choice of governing category for anaphors in their domain. On the other hand, such a COMP is comparable to AGR in that both can be accessible SUBJECTs without being possible binders.

If the reasoning presented just now is sound, then the conclusion that in the examples (54a) and (56) the embedded clause is the governing category is false. Our contention that the ungrammaticality of (54a) is not due to the Binding Theory would then be correct. This implies, however, that some other principle is called for to account for the ungrammaticality of examples like (54a). I claim that this other principle is the ECP. An important result of the discussion above is that the Subjacency Condition is superfluous as far as the WH-island constraint is concerned, just as it is superfluous for those cases that were always said to be apparent violations of it. It should be noted that on the assumption that MOVE α is only a metaphor, i.e. that D-structure is present as a property of S-structure, the Subjacency condition would even make less sense than it does on a realistic interpretation of MOVE α. If chains are generated not by movement but

rather by an algorithm applying to S-structure, as we suggested above, following
Rizzi (1983), it is obvious that in cases of multiple application of WH-movement
from COMP-to-COMP the traces left behind in the intermediate COMP-positions are
totally irrelevant in those cases where the lexical complementizer is retained.
These traces are either deleted in order to avoid a violation of the doubly-
filled-COMP filter, or they do not c-command the next trace. Straightforward
evidence that the intermediate traces must be absent at some levels of representation comes from examples such as (68). In order to guarantee proper government
of the trace in the subject position of the embedded clause, the S' barrier must
be removed, either by S'-deletion or by some other mechanism with the same
effect. In any event, this effect cannot be achieved if the COMP contains any
material, i.e. the COMP must be empty.

(68) Who did **John** seem $[_{S'} \emptyset [_S$ **e** to like **t**$]]$

Therefore, either the movement of **who** from the object position of **like** must have
taken place in a single step, crossing two S-nodes in violation of Subjacency, or
it has taken place in two steps, with the intermediate trace being eliminated
before the ECP applies. If something like the Case Filter is assumed to apply at
S-structure, instances of exceptional case marking (cf. below) that require that
the S' barrier is removed just as in the example in (68), would even require that
the intermediate trace is eliminated before S-structure.

(69) **Who** did you believe $[_{S'} \emptyset [_S$ Bill to like **t**$]]$

Again, either the trace only plays a role within the MOVE α component, as forced
by Subjacency, or the movement of **Who** is carried out in a single step, in
violation of Subjacency[23].

   Before we turn to the CNPC facts, which are also assumed to fall under Subjacency, we shall quickly review Rizzi's (1982:chap. 2) proposal on the nature of
Subjacency. Rizzi shows that the WH-island constraint can be violated in some
situations in Italian. Rizzi proposes that the set of bounding nodes for Subjacency is subject to parametric variation. On the assumption that in English S is a
bounding node for Subjacency, whereas in Italian S' is the relevant one, the WH-
island violations in Italian are not genuine, as the following schematic representation makes clear.

(70) English

$$[_{S'} \text{ WH-phrase } [_S \ .....[_{S'} \text{ WH-phrase } [_S .... \text{ t } ...]]]]$$

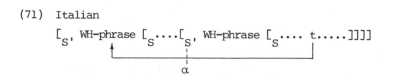

(71) Italian

$$[_{S'} \text{ WH-phrase } [_S ....[_{S'} \text{ WH-phrase } [_S .... \text{ t }.....]]]]$$

The representation in (70) would thus be relevant for languages in which the WH-island constraint is obeyed, whereas (71) would be relevant for those languages, like Italian, in which WH-island violations do occur. There are various problems with Rizzi's proposal, however. First of all, the proposal does not generalize to other languages. Engdahl (1980) argues that the violations of the WH-island constraint in the Scandinavian languages, specifically Swedish, cannot be accounted for along the lines proposed by Rizzi. Secondly, the hypothesis makes a false prediction. Rizzi points out that his proposal predicts that extraction out of subject NP's in Italian should not give the same problems as in English. Again, this can be illustrated in the following way.

(72) Languages with S cyclic for Subjacency

$$[_{S'} \text{ WH-phrase } [_S [_{NP} ..t..]....]]$$

(73) Languages with S' cyclic for Subjacency

$$[_{S'} \text{ WH-phrase } [_S [_{NP} ..t..]....]]$$

This prediction seems to be borne out if one looks at the following examples.

(74) *Who did a picture of terrify him?

(75) Di che cosa e   appersa una foto?
      of which thing is appeared a photograph

However, the proposal predicts more generally that languages that do allow WH-island violations also allow extractions out of subject NP's, whereas languages that allow extractions out of subject NP's also allow WH-island violations. Cinque (1980), however, shows that there are many cases in Italian where extractions from NP to COMP give bad results, whereas extractions from the subject NP in Dutch are freely allowed, although Dutch is at least as strict as English with respect to the WH-island constraint. Therefore, Rizzi's reinterpretation of Subjacency as a parametrizable condition cannot be considered satisfactory. The languages, then, that violate Subjacency also violate the account of the WH-island constraint in terms of the generalized Binding Theory. How these violations must be accounted for is left for future research. From the discussion in the literature, which I shall not review here in detail, no clear alternative emerges (cf. Rizzi 1982, Engdahl 1980, Reinhart 1979, Koster 1982). The data put forth in support of the various analyses are disparate as well. It appears to be the case that the kind of violations found in Italian differ from the kind of violations found in the Scandinavian languages, which in turn vary from the kind of violations found in Hebrew. Koster's (1982) analysis assumes that the violations result from marked aspects of the languages involved. Specifically, he adopts Reinhart's (1979) two-COMP analysis as a marked option and assumes furthermore that extraction out of S' is itself a marked phenomenon. Whether these suggestions are correct is hard to judge from the slender evidence.

It should be noted that the account of the WH-island constraint given above carries over quite easily to the double-R-phenomenon studied by Van Riemsdijk (1978b). The relevant data are given in (76).

(76) a. ***Wie** heb je met Piet over t gesproken?
   b. **Waar** heb je met Piet over t gesproken?
   c. **Waar**$_i$ heb je **er**$_j$ met Piet over t$_{j/*i}$ gesproken?

Extraction of a normal NP from a PP as in (76a) is impossible. Van Riemsdijk accounts for this impossibility in terms of Subjacency under the following assumptions:

A. PP is a bounding node for Subjacency
B. In Dutch, S (bare S) is a bounding node for Subjacency.

It should be noted that, if these assumptions were correct, it would follow that preposition stranding, which is impossible in Dutch, is allowed in Italian, which is, however, contrary to fact. Preposition stranding is possible in Dutch,

however, if the element to be extracted from PP carries the feature [+R] ,
basically a morphophonological feature shared by a handful of pronominal elements
(see Van Riemsdijk 1978a for an account of these R-forms). In order to explain
this contrast between extraction of an R-form and a regular NP, it is assumed that
extraction of R-forms escapes the effects of Subjacency, because in (76b) **waar** is
not moved to its ultimate sentence initial position in a single step, but rather
in two successive steps, each of which passes a single bounding node. The first
step moves the R-form from inside the PP to a base-generated clitic position that
accepts only categories marked with the   [+R] feature. From this position, it is
moved into the sentence-initial COMP. This is schematically represented in (77).

(77) $[_{s'}$ waar $[_{s}$ ...$[_{+R}$ t] ..$[_{PP}$ over t   ] ..]]

The analysis derives support from (76c): the sentence ought to be ambiguous
between an interpretation in which **waar** is locative and **er** binds the complement
of **over,** and an interpretation where **er** is locative and **waar** questions the
complement of **over,** as in the b-example. However, the second interpretation is not
available. This is explained by Subjacency, because in order to arrive at this
interpretation, **waar** has to be moved into the sentence-initial COMP in a single
step, just as **wie** in (76a), because the escape route is occupied by **er.** This
analysis by Van Riemsdijk can be reinterpreted in a straightforward manner within
a framework that dispenses with Subjacency in favour of the generalized Binding
Theory. Suppose that **er** in (76c) is contained within the V-projection or in S
(below, I shall argue that these are the same). We then need to know what the
governing category for the anaphoric trace inside the PP is. Obviously, this is
the V-projection containing **er** ,since it is the minimal projection containing the
anaphor (the trace), the governor of the anaphor (the preposition) and a SUBJECT
accessible for the anaphor. **Er** qualifies as an accessible SUBJECT, because it is
in a position that can have a content that identifies the trace. In this case, it
is **er** itself. Hence, the trace must receive an antecedent in this V-projection,
which it would not have if **waar** is to be considered its antecedent. Hence, there
is only a grammatical outcome if the trace is coindexed with **er,** as required. This
discussion of the double-R-phenomenon shows that our interpretation of the notion
accessible SUBJECT is not ad hoc.

Now it is time to turn to extractions out of NP's, specifically out of complex
NP's in the sense of Ross (1967). Extractions out of NP's are in general not very

acceptable. In Chomsky (1973), the Subject Condition was proposed to prohibit extractions out of subject NP's (cf. (74)), but extractions out of NP's other than the subject do not always yield good results either. This led Horn (1974) and Bach & Horn (1976) to replace Subjacency by an even stronger condition, the NP Constraint. This captures not only the Subject Condition, but accounts for the following cases as well.

(78) *__Who__ did you destroy [$_{NP}$ a picture of t]

(79) a   Who did you see a picture of?
     b.?Who did you see the picture of?
     c.*Who did you see John's picture of?

In order to account for the grammaticality of (79a), Bach & Horn assume that the verb **see** is subcategorized to take either an NP complement or an NP followed by a PP, whereas a verb like **destroy** can only take an NP complement. Therefore, in (79a), **who** is not extracted from inside an NP (this would be forbidden by the NP-Constraint), but rather from an independent PP.

Chomsky (1977) subsumes the NP-Constraint under Subjacency by changing the set of bounding nodes for Subjacency from S' and NP to S and NP. This change implies that extractions out of NP's are always impossible in a language that takes S as a bounding node for Subjacency, unless some other device circumvents the effects of Subjacency. We saw above that this prediction cannot be upheld in this unqualified form. In order to account for those cases where it seems that WH-movement has extracted an element from inside an NP, as in (79a), it is assumed that a process of reanalysis applies that rearranges the PP out of the NP. I think, however, that this account leaves much to be desired. Firstly, it is unclear why this reanalysis (let us call it extraposition of PP from NP) should be possible only in some cases and not in others (e.g. in (78)). Secondly, it is unclear why a definite determiner should block the application of PP-extraposition, or at least make it less easy to apply it, whereas a genitive determiner makes it totally impossible. These problems are so much worse in an approach like Bach & Horn's, where it is totally unclear how the specifier of the NP could be relevant to a possible extraction out of an independently generated PP. In general, such an effect cannot be observed in, those cases where the independent status of the PP is unquestionable, cf. (80).

(80) a. What did you accuse a representative of the government of?

b. What did you accuse the representative of the government of?

c. What did you accuse Reagan's secretary of?

Similarly, the following cases illustrate that the specifier of NP does not have the same effect on real extraposition from NP:

(81) Did you see some/those/Bill's pictures yesterday
      of that huge tornado?

Comparing the examples in (79) with examples like those in (82), one can hardly avoid being struck by a certain parallelism. This suggests that the Binding Theory, which is responsible for the contrast in (82), would be relevant in the case of (79) as well.

(82) a. **We** heard some stories about **each other**
     b.***We** heard their stories about **each other**

Their in (82b) is an accessible SUBJECT for the anaphor **each other** and therefore, the anaphor may not be bound outside the NP. In contrast, **some** in (82a) is not an accessible SUBJECT, hence the NP is not the governing category for the anaphor and binding **each other** by **we** is permitted. Aoun (1981) points out that WH-extraction from NP seems to be subject to opacity conditions as well, at least in some languages, including French. Consider the following examples.

(83) a. L'artiste **dont** tu as vu [$_{NP}$ le portrait d'Aristote **t**]
     b. *L'artiste **dont** tu as vu [$_{NP}$ le portrait **t** de Rembrandt]

Extraction of the subject, i.e. the PP that expresses the logical subject, as in (83a) is permitted, whereas extraction of the PP expressing the object is impossible if the subject is present. This is Aoun's motivation to derive these results from the Binding Theory. He achieves this by assuming that the determiner **le** is coindexed with the logical subject and acts like an operator, thus making the NP opaque for WH-extractions of something other than the subject.

There is one important aspect of extractions out of NP's, at least in English, which Aoun fails to discuss, viz. the fact that in the case of complex NP's in the sense of Ross, the possibilities of extraction do not seem to depend on the determiner. Compare (79) with (84).

(84)*__Who__ did you hear John's/the/a story that Peter would have met __t__

If one wants to account for the differences in acceptability of the examples in
(79) in terms of the Binding Theory by arguing that the NP is the governing
category for the trace left behind by extraction in some cases but not in others,
it would be hard to see how this result could be achieved given our conception of
accessible SUBJECT; the determiner of NP can never host an identifier of a WH-
trace in the complement of a noun. It should be noted in this connection that it
has frequently been remarked that the difference in acceptability of the examples
in (79) is due to some obscure constraint, called the Specificity Constraint (cf.
Chomsky 1981:235). Clearly, unlike Subjacency, the Specificity Constraint is not
a structural principle. Now, one might reason that whereas the differences in the
case of (79) are accounted for in terms of this non-structural principle, the
absence of similar contrasts in the case of (84) strongly indicates that a
structural principle like Subjacency should be held responsible for the ungrammaticality. It turns out, however, that extractions out of complex NP's in languages other than Dutch and English are governed by some sort of Specificity
Constraint as well. The following examples, taken from Taraldsen (1978b
:627,fn.6) illustrate the effect of the determiner on the extractability from
complex NP's in Norwegian.

(85) a. __Hvilket krydder__ visste du om en butikk som solgte billigst __t__
        Which spices did you know a shop   that sold cheapest

     b.*__Hvilket krydder__ visste du om den butikken som solgte billegst __t__
        Which spices did you know   the   shop   that   sold cheapest

Similar examples from Swedish are given in Engdahl (1980:95 ff.).

(86) __Johann__ kanner jag ingen/?en flicka/*flickan som tycker om __t__
     Johann know   I no one/ a girl /the girl that likes t

Taraldsen (1981b) proposes that the problem for Subjacency could be avoided by
assuming that extraposition of the relative clause feeds the extraction operation, in which case the movement would cross only a single boundary node. This
suggestion is taken over in Kayne (1981a:112 fn.31). It seems, however, that
Taraldsen's solution is misdirected. Engdahl (1980) shows that extraction is
permitted also in cases where extraposition of the relative clause cannot have

applied. In Dutch, extraction out of an extraposed relative clause is just as bad as extraction out of a non-extraposed relative clause as the following examples indicate.

(87) a. ik heb het verhaal dat Piet een muis kocht gehoord
        I have the story that Peter a mouse bought heard
     b.*Wat heb je het verhaal dat Piet t kocht gehoord?
        What have you the story that Peter t bought heard
(88) a. Ik heb het verhaal gehoord dat Piet een muis kocht
        I have the story heard that Peter a mouse bought
     b.*Wat heb je het verhaal gehoord dat Piet t kocht?
        What have you the story heard that Peter t bought

In order to accommodate the CNPC violations in Swedish and Norwegian, Engdahl adopts Reinhart's two-COMP analysis (Reinhart 1979). From this hypothesis, the possibility of WH-island violations follows as well. It was remarked above that this analysis also fails to generalize, since in Italian WH-island violations are found, while the CNPC is strictly obeyed.

As in the case of WH-island violations, then, it seems that the violations of the CNPC are not easily reconcilable with Subjacency. The discussion above reveals that extractions out of NP are generally rather marginal, and that they become worse if the NP has a more definite interpretation, which is not easily explainable in terms of a structural principle. A solution to the problem of NP extractions that does not invoke Subjacency is offered in Kayne (1981a:106 ff.). The principle he proposes is the extended ECP. Kayne's proposal meets with the same problems as Subjacency in the case of CNPC-violations and is incapable of explaining the effects of Subjacency in the case of WH-islands. I shall not go into Kayne's extended ECP proposal, but note that it could be adopted to account for the cases in which extraction out of NP's is impossible.

It turns out, then, that no firm conclusions can be reached in the case of extractions out of NP's. Conditions on such extractions resemble quite closely the conditions on extraposition from NP as discussed by Guéron (1980). I conclude therefore that in general NP's are not suitable bridges in the sense of Erteschik (1973), who intends this notion as a pragmatic rather than as a structural one. Further research is needed to determine whether the non-bridge character of NP can be captured in structural terms, or whether it should be considered a pragmatic factor[24].

Summarizing then, we have seen that the principle of Subjacency does not play a role as far as NP-movements are concerned, since the required locality can be derived from the Binding Theory. The same holds for WH-movements if the traces left behind are regarded as anaphors in the sense of the Binding Theory. The fact that the usual opacity conditions for A-binding are irrelevant for WH-traces does not have to be stipulated, but follows independently from the functional defini- tion of empty categories, and in almost all cases from the θ-criterion as well. The fact that the distance between gap and antecedent can be fairly long in the case of WH-movements follows from the relativized notion of governing category, which is formulated in terms of accessible SUBJECT. The θ-criterion, from which the crossover phenomena follow, prevents most clauses from functioning as a governing category, since there are no candidates for accessible SUBJECT. There- fore, the root sentence is normally the governing category for WH-traces, with the exception of WH-islands where the COMP is interpreted as an accessible SUBJECT for the anaphor. In order to achieve this result, we slightly changed the notion of accessible SUBJECT, which is motivated independently by the double- R-phenomenon in Dutch. Therefore, we concluded that the Subjacency Principle can be dispensed with, a desirable result given its odd conceptual status in a framework that focusses on wellformedness conditions on representations rather than on derivational constraints.

A number of problems remain, specifically those cases that were problematic for Subjacency, i.e. the violations of the WH-island constraint. Another problem that is not dealt with satisfactorily here is extraction out of NP. We have examined a number of proposals, without reaching a firm conclusion. We might adopt Kayne's extended ECP account or we might explore the possibility that some non-structural explanation should be given for the relevant cases.

2.7. Complement selection and ordering

After this overview of the main subtheories of GB-theory, it is now time to return to the questions raised in the section on the Base Component. Let me start by repeating the main issues here.

a. The stipulation of specific orderings of complements by means of PS-rules is non-explanatory. It is even descriptively inadequate given the existence of a freely operating rule MOVE α.

b. Whereas category-specific PS-rules may in principle account for the non-occurrence of specific phrase types in their environment, i.e. by not mentioning them in the expansions for the various categories, the possible and impossible choices are not explained in this way.

c. PS-rules invariably allow for expansions that are never realized. It is not always possible to collapse various options so as to avoid this overgeneration, nor would such an undertaking have any explanatory power. The expansions listed for various categories are entirely dictated by the possibilities which happen to occur.

d. The stipulations of the PS-rules introduce a massive redundancy in the grammar as a whole in that they repeat the information already contained in the subcategorization features of the lexical items in the lexicon.

From these considerations, the conclusion should be drawn that PS-rules should be dispensed with. In large measure, the principles of X'-theory are deducible from other principles of grammar, specifically from the Projection Principle and the θ-criterion. The requirement that all phrases are endocentric follows from the fact that a lexical head is required in order to supply the θ-structure in its phrasal domain. If all phrases have subjects, an assumption that will be extensively dealt with in this section and in the following chapter, and if subjects of phrases are defined as (SPEC, Xmax), it follows from the θ-criterion that only maximal projections can occur as complements and specifiers. It will be seen below that the notion of maximal projection itself is rather problematic, specifically because it is unclear whether all complements and specifiers are indeed of the same projection level.

There is one serious problem if PS-rules are abandoned. In the preceding discussion we have followed the standard assumption within the framework of generative grammar that there is an asymmetry between subjects and non-subjects in that only the subject can be a θ'-position, i.e. a position to which no θ-role is assigned. Therefore, the presence of a subject cannot be derived from the Projection Principle and the θ-criterion. Nevertheless, it has always been assumed that the subject of a clause is obligatory, unlike all other elements, such as complements, subject of NP etc. (cf. Jackendoff 1977:43). From the difference in obligatoriness between subjects of clauses and subjects of NP's, Emonds (1976) concluded that VP was to be regarded as the maximal projection of V, while the obligatory nature of the subject of S was accounted for in terms of the rather unique rule S->NP AUX VP. This solution is also adopted in Chomsky (1981). It will be evident, of course, that this solution is not available within a framework that dispenses with PS-rules. Therefore, the obligatory nature of the subject of S must be stipulated in some fashion, at least as far as θ'-subjects

are concerned. Alternatively, one might question the universal character of the
subject position. Anticipating the discussion of the structure of the clause in
Dutch below, I would like to suggest here that the obligatory presence of the
subject position in S can be derived in Dutch from the obligatory governance of
this position by INFL. Arguably, the subject position is not obligatory in those
V-projections in Dutch that lack INFL. As these matters require that at least
some firm conclusions are drawn with respect to the issue of what is to be
regarded as the maximal projection of V, the question will be left open here[25].

Let us now focus on the question as to which principles determine the order of
complements with respect to the head and with respect to each other. In section
2.2. it was concluded that Dutch differs from English in that in English all
complements follow their head, whereas in Dutch the [+V] categories follow their
complements while [-V] categories precede them. It might be argued that this
situation does not require any deep explanatory principle: the principles of UG
just have to allow e.g. the object NP either to precede or to follow the head. The
evidence as to which position the object happens to take in a certain language is
readily available, so that deep explanations are not called for. This line of
reasoning, which is found in Lightfoot (1983), would seem to be correct in
principle. The following discussion demonstrates, however, that the principle
determining the order of the object, which is indeed subject to parametric
variation where actually occurring sequences of verb and object are enough to fix
the parameter, has a number of consequences that go far beyond the determination
of the order of the verb and its object. The relevance of the principles to be
discussed, therefore, should not be measured in terms of the fact that it
accounts for the order of the verb and its object, but rather in terms of the
other consequences.

Stowell (1981) proposes to capture the fact that in English all complements
follow their head by the stipulation that complements follow their head. Although
a stipulation, it is far more elegant then the set of stipulations it replaces.
Along the same lines, we might stipulate for Dutch that complements of [-V]
categories follow their head, but complements of [+V] categories precede their
head. The question that comes up at this point is at what level such a statement
is supposed to apply. Evidently, if it is relevant for D- structure, the problem
that the phrases can be moved arbitrarily by the transformational component
remains. If it applies at S-structure, we face the problem that the statement is
not true as far as [+V] categories are concerned, since sentential complements
must and prepositional complements may follow the verbal head.

One way to overcome these problems is to assume that a rule of sentential extraposition and a rule of PP-over-[+V] apply in the left-hand component of the grammar, i.e. in the component that derives surface structures from S-structures. These rules may then be considered stylistic. Suggestions to that effect have been made in the literature, but such a move strikes me as fairly unsatisfactory given the small amount of attention paid to this component on the one hand and the centrality of the phenomenon on the other. It would seem to be a priori more desirable if a more principled explanation could be put forward for the distribution of phrases (cf. also Guéron 1980 who shows quite convincingly that extraposition must be a rule of syntax rather than a stylistic movement rule).

Another way, then, to overcome the problem mentioned above, would be to formulate other requirements besides the requirement of position with respect to the head. One such extra requirement is proposed in Stowell (1981), viz. the requirement that NP's must occur in Case-marked positions, while clauses are not allowed in such positions (his Case Resistance Principle). Stowell argues that this has the immediate effect of placing sentential complements in a peripheral position, as they have to move from the position immediately adjacent to the verb. This proposal will be considered in more detail below.

A more principled question would be why there is an asymmetry between Dutch and English as the one observed above. Preferably, an answer to this question has consequences beyond a mere account of the different orientation of complements towards their heads in the two languages. The proposal that I would like to make is that this difference is a consequence of the directionality of government, i.e. government is asymmetric in that it holds only in a single direction for each category. This direction can be different from language to language and from category to category, although a theory of markedness might place a higher value on some distributions than on others, as appears to be the case if one considers the tendencies of ordering across categories in the different languages of the world (cf. Greenberg 1963 and all the later work done in explaining the word order correlations observed there as e.g. Vennemann 1974,1976, Keenan 1979, Lehmann 1978 and references cited there). This implies that the occurrence of a VO combination suffices to establish that the direction of government is to the right for the verb. This direction is found in English, whereas the verb in Dutch governs to the left. It will be shown in the rest of this study that this positional difference of the verb brings with it a fair number of subtle and substantial differences that can be accounted for in terms of the central concepts of the GB-theory, i.e. the notion of government and the ECP. I shall start, therefore, with a more elaborate discussion of the notion of government that was already introduced in section 2.4. above (cf. (24)).

2.7.1. Government

The notion of government within GB-theory corresponds to the traditional notion
that verbs and prepositions govern their complements. This traditional notion
constitutes the core or archetypal instance of the theoretically more elaborate
notion that accommodates other relations between constituents as well. The
standard definition that is generally adopted is the one developed in Aoun &
Sportiche (1981). It is formulated in (89) (=(24) above).

  (89) x governs y iff for all F, F a maximal projection,
       F dominates x iff F dominates y

According to this definition x governs y if they share all maximal projections.
This particular definition depends in large measure, as we shall see below, on
the status of S and the projection of V. In Jackendoff (1977) it is assumed that S
is the maximal projection of V, i.e. that the subject of a clause is a specifier.
This position was never undebated (cf. Hornstein 1977, Brame 1979 among others).
The main problem for Jackendoff was the fact, which we mentioned above, that the
subject of S seems to be obligatory, whereas the subject of NP is optional.
Another problem for Jackendoff concerns the way in which S should be fitted in if
S=Vmax (cf. Jackendoff 1977:47).

  More recently, other candidates have been introduced as the head of S and S',
specifically INFL. Taking INFL as the head of the sentential projection and VP as
the maximal projection of V, the structure of a full sentence might be represented as in (90).

  (90)

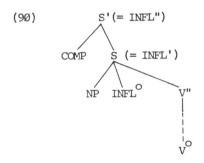

One of the main arguments for VP as Vmax rather than S and for the definition of

government in (89) at the same time, is presented in Aoun & Sportiche. The
question addressed there is the following. Is NP in (91) governed by X^o or not?

(91)   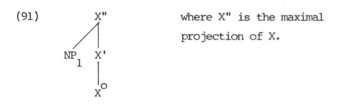   where X" is the maximal
                                               projection of X.

Aoun & Sportiche give a positive answer to this question which is based on the
difference in acceptability between (92a) and (92b).

(92) a. *I like [$_{NP}$ PRO [picture of Bill]]
     b. I like [$_{NP}$ PRO [reading a book]]

Their argumentation for this positive answer runs as follows.

1. PRO must be ungoverned (theorem of the Binding Theory)
2. PRO in (92a) is rejected,hence it is governed
3. PRO in (92b) is accepted, hence it is ungoverned
4. the innermost brackets in (92a) = N'
5. the innermost brackets in (92b) = VP

On the assumption that VP=Vmax, line 3 of this argument is correct, given (89).
Line 2 follows from lines 1 and 4 on the assumption that the structure of (92a) is
as indicated, i.e. with PRO. Therefore, Aoun & Sportiche conclude that N' does
not prevent PRO from being governed by the lexical head of the NP, i.e. they
conclude that NP_2 in (91) is indeed governed by X^o. However, the flaw in the
argument clearly stands out: the argument is based on the assumption that the
presence of PRO is the only possible reason for the ungrammaticality of (92a). A
further, rather obvious reason, might be that some nouns require the presence of
a determiner which other nouns do not allow, cf. (93).

(93) a. I like that picture of Bill
     b.*I like that reading a book

Therefore, the conclusion that NP_2 in (91) is governed by X^o cannot be based on
this argument, which implies that the assumption that VP rather than S is the
maximal projection of V is undermined. Notice that if NP_2 in (91) is not governed

from below, no problem arises in the case of (94), where it is immaterial whether or not S is regarded as Vmax or not.

(94) They tried $[_{S'}$ $[_S$ PRO to go]]

The assumption that governor and governee share all maximal projections runs into problems in the central case for which the notion of government was introduced in the first place, i.e. to establish a relationship between a verb and the subject of a sister projection. Specifically, in the case of tenseless complements to verbs like **believe**, it is assumed that the lexical subject of the complement clause receives Case from the matrix verb. As Case is assigned under government, the traditional notion has to be extended so as to allow government of the embedded subject across a clause boundary. Aoun & Sportiche can avoid this problem by assuming that for the matrix verb to govern the subject of an embedded clause, it is required that the S'-barrier is deleted. On the assumption that S', but not S is a maximal projection, the result of S'-deletion would be that no maximal projection intervenes between the matrix verb and the embedded subject.

(95) They believed $[_{S'}$ $[_S$ Bill to be a liar]]

$$\Downarrow$$

$$\emptyset$$

However, this approach does not work in the case of so-called small clauses. The analysis of small clauses will be discussed in more detail in the next chapters. Anticipating this discussion, however, we assume that the complement structure of **consider** in (96) is as indicated in (97), i.e. with **John** as the subject within the maximal projection of the adjective **foolish**.

(96) I consider John foolish
(97) I consider $[_{A''}$ $[_{NP}$ John]$[_{A'}$ $[_{A^o}$ foolish]]]

If the small-clause analysis is correct, **John** is contained within a maximal projection, but it must receive Case from and hence be governed by the verb **consider**. Therefore, in these cases, a maximal projection intervenes between the governor and the governee. It must be concluded therefore, that Aoun & Sportiche make the wrong predictions in both directions, i.e. according to their definition, NP_1 in (98) is governed by X^o, while NP_2 is not. Just the opposite is the case, however.

(98)

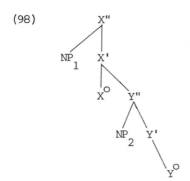

The idea, then, that the roof for government is set by maximal projections, is
misdirected, at least for the general government relation. Does this imply that
we have to return to Reinhart's definition of c-command to define government,
such that the roof for government is set by the first branching node dominating
the governor? Aoun & Sportiche convincingly point out that this position has
various unwanted consequences, e.g. that the subject would be governed by the
verb just in case the verb is intransitive and not accompanied by any modifiers,
but never when the verb is transitive etc. This conclusion, however, is not at all
imperative. Just as one can refer to Xmax as setting the upper boundary for
government, one may equally well refer to X', i.e. the first-order projection
(see Selkirk 1981 who uses this notion as well). Therefore, I propose to replace
(89) by the definition in (99), which is in all relevant respects identical to the
notion of government considered by Chomsky in his Pisa lectures[26].

(99)   a node x governs y iff y is contained in the first- order
        projection of x and there is no z such that y is contained
        within the first-order projection of z and x is not

Actually, (99) is the general definition of government. Specific relations may
impose further conditions on the relation between the governor and the governee
(Safir 1982 calls these adaptor conditions). More specifically, I will distinguish between two notions of government, viz. structural government and θ-
government. θ-government obtains if a category governs another category in the
sense of (99) and θ-marks this category as well. Structural government, on the
other hand, is a blind structural relation which is defined in (99). In a
configuration like (98) NP_2 is merely structurally governed by X^0, i.e. X^0 does

not θ-mark NP_2. Not all categories have the property of being a structural
governor. Generally, this property is restricted to members of the category V,
while in some languages prepositions may be structural governors as well (cf.
Kayne 1981c who argues that prepositions are structural governors in English, but
not in French). It may also be the case that only specified members of a certain
category have the structural governor property, e.g. **met** 'with' in Dutch, **avec** in
French[27].

My claim is that structural government is parasitic on θ-government, in that
it always holds in the direction of θ-government, typically government of the
object. Below I will adduce support for this claim. First, however, we return to
the question of the nature of Vmax, after having established that there is no
argument in favour of (90) that derives from the theory of government, now
redefined as in (99).

I will proceed by exploring the consequences of replacing (90) in the grammar
of Dutch by the configuration in (100).

(100)

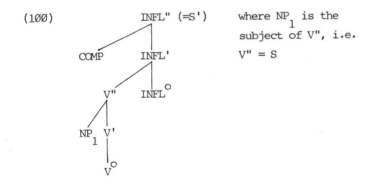

where NP_1 is the
subject of V", i.e.
V" = S

Given the definition of government in (99), the NP specifier of V' (i.e. the
subject) is not governed by the verb, but it would be governed by INFL if INFL is a
structural governor.

It should be noted first that the proposal in (100) does not easily extend to
English or SVO languages in general[28], if the process of merging $INFL^o$ with V^o is
assumed to be a local operation that requires adjacency of these categories, as
the discussion of AUX in Chomsky (1957) suggests. It might be the case, therefore, that the status of INFL in various languages is subject to variation. One
could wonder whether there is any evidence that Dutch and English vary in this
respect. Without going into this matter in any detail, I would like to suggest
some differences that might be related to a difference in the status of INFL in

these languages. First, whereas there is reasonable evidence to assume the
existence of a separate category AUX in English (cf. Chomsky 1957, Lightfoot
1979a), there is no convincing reason to treat the alleged auxiliaries in Dutch
as different from main verbs (cf. Evers 1975 and the discussion in section 4.4.).
Secondly, whereas the phenomena described as VP-preposing and VP-deletion are
found in English, these are typically absent in Dutch. This difference might be
related to the alleged difference concerning the status of INFL, and more
relevant in this respect,the concomittant difference in the status of Vmax, which
would be VP in English, but S in Dutch. A third difference that might be related
to the alleged difference concerning the status of Vmax is the possibility of
having a Ø-subject in some construction types in Dutch, but not in English.
Below, an account of this possibility in Dutch will be offered that crucially
depends on the correctness of (100). These differences between Dutch and English
may be further investigated in order to establish whether the suggestion made
here, viz. that the status of INFL and Vmax differs in these languages, is
correct[29].

We shall continue, now, by exploring the consequences of the proposal in
(100) and the definition of government in (99), in conjunction with the hypothesis that government is unidirectional.

2.7.2. Unidirectional government and the status of S

2.7.2.1. The distribution of sentential complements

It was observed above that, although complements of verbs generally precede the
head, sentential complements obligatorily occur in postverbal position. Traditional generative studies accounted for this fact by assuming that sentential
complements in general are generated by means of the expansion of NP, i.e. in
preverbal position for object clauses, and that they are subsequently moved out
of this position by a rule of extraposition, the obligatory effect of which was
derived from the Internal-S-Constraint (Kuno 1973). The generation of sentential
complements by means of the expansion of NP was necessary in order to account for
the fact that a clause in postverbal position could either have the function of
subject or object, these functions themselves being defined as (NP,S) and (NP,VP)
respectively. However, this conception quickly ran into problems because it is

unclear in this view how an account could be given for the fact that some verbs
only allow NP complements whereas others take a clausal complement, i.e. not all
verbs taking NP's also take clauses and -vice versa- not all verbs taking
sentential complements take NP's (cf. Grimshaw 1979). Another problem was created
by the introduction of Subjacency: the assumption that all clauses are dominated
by NP implies that all clauses are islands for extraction, since in each case of
extraction the extracted constituent has to cross at least two bounding nodes.
The obvious way to get around this problem is to assume that extraposition feeds
the rules of extraction, but that solution conflicts with the idea that extraposed phrases get frozen (cf. Ross 1967). In section 2.6. above, we saw that
Taraldsen's proposal to this effect does not yield the required result in the
case of extraposed relative clauses (cf. (87)-(88)).

For these reasons, the position that sentential complements are generated as
expansions of NP was abandoned[30]. It is now commonly assumed that sentential
complements are introduced in the expansion of V' (cf. Jackendoff 1977).Neverthe-
less, the idea that clausal complements were generated in preverbal position was
generally maintained.The only linguist of whom I know that he explicitly argues
that sentential complements in Dutch must be generated in postverbal position is
De Haan (1979). His argument for this assumption is based on the idea that matrix
verbs are subcategorized for the complementizer of their sentential complement
(De Haan 1979: 40 ff.). This argument seems to me to be fallacious. According to
De Haan, an element may be subcategorized for a category in the domain of its
sister only when this category is string adjacent to the subcategorized element,
in this case a verb that subcategorizes the complementizer of its sister clause.
As complementizers occur clause-initially, this would require that the clause
itself is in postverbal position in order to satisfy the string-adjacency requirement. However, other phrase introducers, like prepositions of prepositional
objects and complementizer-like elements introducing predicative complements ,
are not string adjacent to the subcategorizing verb. Moreover, I doubt whether
the traditional assumption that the complementizer is subcategorized by the
matrix verb is correct. It appears to be the case that various aspects of the
make-up of matrix clauses determine the choice of an embedded interrogative or an
embedded declarative clause, cf. the examples in (101).

(101) a. I know that/*whether John will come

b. I do not know that/whether John is coming

c. If someone had told me,I would have known that/
   whether John is coming

Therefore, both the string adjacency requirement and the assumption that matrix verbs subcategorize the complementizer of their complement clauses seem to be incorrect.

A more principled objection against De Haan's position and against any effort to account for the surface distribution of clausal complements in terms of PS-rules has been discussed above, i.e. the obligatory postverbal position would not be explained in this fashion. A more promising effort is made by Stowell (1981), as we mentioned above. Stowell proposes that clausal complements may not occur in Case-marked positions. This proposal effectively eliminates S' in the positions indicated by X in the following structures, since these are all Case-marked positions.

(102)

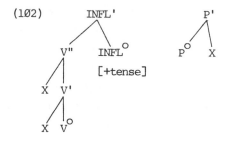

If Case marking applies at the S-structure level, the following examples illustrate the correctness of the proposal made by Stowell.

(103) a.*dat [$_{S'}$ dat Peter ook komt] mij ergerde
            that   that Peter also comes me annoyed
            "that it annoyed me that Peter also comes"

     b.*dat Jan [$_{S'}$ dat hij ziek geweest was] vertelde
            that John that he ill been   was   told
            "that John told that he had been ill"

     c.*dat Jan over [$_{S'}$ dat Piet ook mee ging] klaagde
            that John about that Peter also along went complained
            "that John complained about the fact that Peter
            went along as well"

The examples in (103) are all completely acceptable if the S's are replaced by NPs. They are equally acceptable if the S's are moved into postverbal position.

In cases a. and c., a pronominal element occupies the position taken by the clause in the examples in (103). In subject position, this pronominal form is **het** 'it'; in the complement position of the preposition, the form is **er** 'there' which precedes, rather than follows the preposition[31].

(104) a. dat het mij ergerde [$_{S'}$ dat Piet ook komt]
        that it me annoyed   that Peter also comes

    b. dat Jan vertelde [$_{S'}$ dat hij ziek geweest was]
        that John told   that he ill been was

    c. dat Jan er over klaagde [$_{S'}$ dat Piet ook mee ging]
        that John there about complained that Peter also along went

There are, however, reasons to doubt the adequacy of Stowell's proposal. In the examples in (105), NP and S' overlap in distribution. As NP's must receive Case, I assume that the position is a Case-marked position.

(105) a. Voor $\left\{ \begin{array}{l} [_{NP} \text{ de maaltijd}] \\ [_{S'} \text{ dat de maaltijd begint}] \end{array} \right\}$ drinken we eerst iets

        Before the meal/that the meal starts drink we first something

    b. Door $\left\{ \begin{array}{l} [_{NP} \text{ de hitte}] \\ [_{S'} \text{dat het zo heet was}] \end{array} \right\}$ konden we niets doen

        Through the heat/that it so hot was could we nothing do

Let us replace Stowell's proposal of prohibiting sentential complements in Case marked positions by the following requirement. This requirement will be derived from a more general principle below.

(106)   S' may not be governed by V

Let us first investigate the effect of (106). In the case of object clauses, it is evident that the requirement that they do not occur in preverbal position follows from the assumption that in Dutch the verb governs to the left. As for prepositional object clauses, this is less immediately clear, since the clause is contained within PP. It is necessary, however, to distinguish between those PP's that may

contain a sentential complement, like those in (105), and those that do not allow
that (i.e. in the case of prepositional objects). Notice that in the latter case
the preposition may be taken to assign Case to its complement, but that it is the
verb that determines the θ-role of the complement. While it is reasonable to
assume that Case is assigned under structural government (indeed, this is the
main reason to introduce the notion of (structural) government in the first
place), this is not true for θ-government. We might say that a phrase is opaque
for θ-assignment from outside, if the θ-structure in the domain of that phrase
is uniquely determined by the head of that phrase. This would adequately discriminate between the two kinds of PP's as desired. Notice that we may even go
further than this. Given the abandonment of PS-rules, there is really no need to
assume that all phrases are of the same projection level, i.e. there is no need to
hold on to the assumption that all phrases are of level three as X'-theory in
Jackendoff's version requires. Above, we argued that the internal structure of
phrases can be derived from the Projection Principle and the θ-criterion. On
the assumption that prepositional object PP's do not have subjects, there is no
reason to assume that they have an internal structure with three levels, i.e. we
may assume that they are really exocentric rather than endocentric, as standard
X'-theory assumes. The reason for calling them exocentric is that the presence of
a complement is always required, not by the preposition, but rather by the
governing verb, whereas prepositional objects and other PP's that we may call
argument PP's do not exhibit the specifier structure that Van Riemsdijk (1978a)
uses to argue for the inclusion of prepositions in the set of major lexical
categories. A similar proposal can be found in Moortgat (1980). In this sense,
then, prepositions of prepositional objects are not proper heads. Their only
function is to provide Case for their complement. If this hypothesis is correct,
the ungrammaticality of (103c) follows from principle (106)[32].

As for subject clauses, the prohibition for them to actually occupy the
subject position as in (103a) can be derived from (106) only if the subject
position is governed by the verb. Above, we made an effort to argue that the
subject position is normally not governed by the verb. How, then, can the desired
result be obtained?

Before proceeding to answer this question, let us first go into the nature of
(106). Stowell's idea has a strong intuitive appeal. It basically says that
categories that are able to assign Case may not receive it and, vice versa, that
categories that must receive Case cannot assign it. Adjectives and nouns cluster
together as categories that are unable to assign Case, as mentioned above, but
they must be Case marked, whereas prepositions and verbs, the categories that

assign Case, may not receive Case themselves. A similar idea is put forward in Kayne (1982a). Verbs and nouns are notions that belong to a different paradigm than the paradigm to which notions like predicate and argument belong. The most natural way to relate these differential notions is to associate verb with predicate and noun with argument. The most natural case, therefore, seems to be that verbs take nouns or projections of nouns as arguments. Similarly, whereas adjectives and prepositional phrases are natural modifiers of nouns, nominal projections do not so easily combine with nouns. Kayne proposes two principles:

(i)   no projection of V can be an argument
(ii) a non-maximal projection of N must not govern a maximal
      projection of N

Kayne adduces considerable support for these hypotheses. If we generalize these two hypotheses as far as possible, we arrive at the following statement[33].

(107)   The Unlike Category Condition

        At S-structure, no element of $[\alpha N, \beta V]$ may
        govern a projection of $[\alpha N, \beta V]$

This Unlike Category Condition (UCC) has a number of nice consequences, as well as a number of counterexamples. First of all, it follows from the UCC that nouns cannot take NP complements, though they may take NP specifiers in the case of appositives.

(108) a. *de verovering de stad
         the capture   the city
      b. mijn broer, de voorzitter van deze commissie
          my brother, the chairman of this committee

The difference in acceptability of the examples in (108) follows from the UCC, if the internal structure of these NP's is as in (109) and if our definition of government in (99) is correct.

(109)

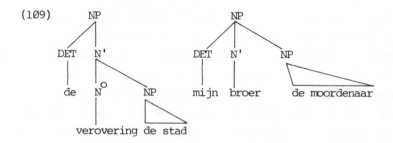

Because the appositive NP is not contained in the first-order projection of the noun, it is not governed by it[34]. A problem for the UCC in the domain of NP are partitives as those in (110).

(110) a. een emmer bramen
           a bucket blackberries

      b. een bos bloemen
         a bunch flowers

It should be noted that these nominal complements in partitives in English must be preceded by the preposition **of** (cf. Selkirk 1977)[35]. A full discussion of partitives in Dutch would take us too far afield (cf. Wiers 1978, Bennis 1978).

Turning to adjectives, we see that the UCC predicts that adjectives may not take AP complements. A case where an AP complement to an adjective would be expected is the case of raising adjectives. Consider the following examples.

(111) a. John is certain $[_{S'}$ $[_S$ e to win]]
       b.*John is certain $[_{AP}$ e dead]

The structure in (111b) presupposes the so-called small-clause analysis, according to which all maximal projections have subjects. While the adjective **certain** may take a sentential complement from which it induces subject raising as in (111a), it cannot take an AP complement as in (111b). This fact in itself may be taken as a lexical idiosyncrasy of the adjective **certain,** but the relevant observation is that no raising adjective can take an AP complement. This cannot be attributed to Case theory, as the trace left behind in (111a) does not receive Case either. Hence the fact that no raising adjective in English can take AP complements may be regarded as a consequence of the UCC. Below we shall see that it follows from the UCC as well that there are no raising adjectives in Dutch at all.

The clearest problems for the UCC arise in the case of prepositions. Whereas prepositions usually take NP complements -a reason for structuralist and traditional analyses to define prepositions syntactically as elements that combine with nouns- some prepositions may also take complements of other categorial types, inter alia PP's (cf. Jackendoff 1973, Van Riemsdijk 1978a). Examples of this are given in (112).

(112) a. voor bij de maaltijd
        for with the meal

      b. voor na de lunch
        for after the lunch

      c. van voor de oorlog
        from before the war

Other violations of the UCC are the absolute constructions with **met** 'with' and **zonder** 'without' in (113), if the small-clause complements are analyzed as PP's (cf. Beukema & Hoekstra 1983a,1983b).

(113) a. met [$_{PP}$ Cruyff in het doel]
        with Cruyff in the goal

      b. zonder [$_{PP}$ een das om zijn nek]
        without a tie around his neck

At present, I have no insights to offer how these potential counterexamples can be explained. Pending further research, however, I would like to maintain the UCC in its full generality[36].

Let us now turn to the structure in (114). This structure should be excluded for Dutch, since an S' must occur in postverbal position at S-structure.

(114) [$_{V'}$ ....S' V$^{\circ}$]

It would be desirable if (114) could be excluded by the UCC. This result can be achieved if we accept the following assumptions:

(i) the verb governs to its left

(ii) S' is a projection having the features [-N,+V] in common with V^{o}

Assumption (i) has already been introduced: it is one of the central claims that I want to defend concerning the notion of government, i.e. that government is a unidirectional notion and that the orientation of government in Dutch is to the left for the category V. The assumption in (ii) would be correct given the structure of S' in (100), if INFL is non-distinct from [-N,+V]. This does not seem to be an unreasonable assumption. One other consequence of this claim would be that the merger process of INFL and V^{o} can be regarded as an instance of the rule of V-raising, a rule that is needed in the grammar of Dutch (and German) independently. The rule of V-raising itself will be discussed in the next section (2.7.2.2.). In the remainder of this section, I shall provide evidence to support the caim that the merger of INFL and V^{o} is indeed an instance of V-raising, thereby lending support to the claim that INFL is non-distinct from V in its feature content. Therefore, if the argument that follows is correct, the conclusion may be drawn that the configuration in (114) is correctly ruled out as a consequence of the UCC.

It was pointed out above that sentential complements in postverbal position have a corresponding pronominal element in preverbal position, **er** in the case of "extraposed" prepositional object clauses and **het** in the case of "extraposed" sentential subjects, but that there was no such pronominal form in the case of "extraposed" sentential objects. This description is not entirely accurate, however. While it is true that **er** is obligatory with prepositional object clauses, **het** is sometimes found with sentential objects, especially with factive predicates (cf. Van den Hoek 1970), whereas **het** can be left out in many cases with sentential subjects. The difference in obligatoriness of a pronominal form between prepositional objects and objects of V may be explained in terms of the ECP, along the lines of Kayne (1981c). According to Kayne (o.c. 266 ff.), V and P in French govern in different ways, whereas they govern in identical fashion in English. Kayne is able to derive a number of differences between English and French on the basis of this hypothesis, one of them being that preposition stranding can be found in English, but not in French. Kayne's explanation is that French prepositions do not license an empty category, unlike verbs. Generalizing Kayne's hypothesis concerning French prepositions to Dutch, this may not only explain why preposition stranding is generally impossible in Dutch (cf. Van Riemsdijk 1978a), but also why a pronominal form is required to accompany the

preposition of a prepositional object with an "extraposed" sentence. The fact
that **het** may occur in the case of object clauses in postverbal position should
cause no surprise. The relevant point is that it may always be absent, a fact that
is explained by the ECP.

Turning now to the case of sentential subjects, we note that these too have to
appear in postverbal position. In the position of the syntactic subject position,
we may find either **het,** or **er** or Ø. As for the choice between **het** and **er,** the
reader is referred to Hoekstra (1983). Here I shall concentrate on the Ø-option,
which is surprising from a theoretical point of view. Examples of a Ø in the
position of the syntactic subject can be found in (115).

(115) a. omdat **e** duidelijk was [$_{S'}$ dat Piet ook mee ging]
        because clear was   that Peter also along went

b. Onder die omstandigheden was **e** gewenst [$_{S'}$ dat Piet ook mee ging]
        Under those circumstances was desirable that Peter also along went

There are all sorts of peculiar restrictions on the use of the Ø-option that I
shall not go into here. What is relevant is that a Ø-subject is unexpected in a
non-PRO-drop language. In general, the following three phenomena cooccur in a
PRO-drop language such as Italian:
a. absence of a subject pronoun: Arriva "He arrives"
b. free inversion of the subject: Gianni arriva /Arriva Gianni
                 "John arrives"
c. long subject extraction: **Chi** pensi che **t** verra
                 "Who do you think that comes"
In English, a non-PRO-drop language, each of these phenomena is absent. In order
to explain this cluster of differences between languages, it is assumed that
their absence or presence follows from a single parameter of UG. The initial way
of formalizing this parameter was the assumption that the subject position is
properly governed in PRO-drop languages, but not in non-PRO-drop languages. The
differences would then follow from the ECP. This idea was primarily inspired by
the phenomenon of long subject extractions, a phenomenon that was previously
captured by the **that**-trace filter in Chomsky & Lasnik (1977) and later by the
Nominative Island Constraint in Chomsky (1980). The NIC was subsequently reduced
to the ECP on the assumption that the subject position is not properly governed,
since INFL or AGR was not considered to count as a proper governor. The apparent
violations of the **that**-trace filter in PRO-drop languages could then be explained

on the assumption that in those languages, AGR could count as a proper governor, in view of its person and number features which make AGR more specific. The idea was not to consider AGR as lexical in the PRO-drop languages, but rather to consider it as a pronominal category, since it has person and number features. This pronominal category, PRO, could then count as a proper governor in the sense of being a local antecedent, coindexed with the subject (cf. (46) above and the discussion following it). This execution of the PRO-drop parameter has a very strong intuitive appeal in that it relates the phenomenon to the observable specifity of verbal agreement (cf. Taraldsen 1978a for discussion).

In spite of its intuitive appeal, however, the initial execution sketched above was abandoned. The motivation for this is found in Kayne's (1981d) paper on subject extractions where he argues that the ECP applies to empty categories that result from so-called quantifier raising (May 1977) and WH-movement in the LF component of the grammar. The following examples illustrate that these movements are indeed subject to the ECP.

(116) a. je n'ai exigé qu'ils arretent personne
      b. je n'ai exigé que personne soit arreté
      c. j'ai exigé que personne ne soit arreté

The ungrammaticality of (116b) is explained by assuming that **ne** is the scope indicator of **personne** and that **personne** has to be moved in the LF component to its scope indicator by May's rule of quantifier raising. This movement would leave an empty category behind in subject position. If empty categories created by movements in LF are subject to the ECP, the ungrammaticality of (116b) would be explained. Similar remarks can be made with respect to multiple interrogations.

The prediction following from this hypothesis in conjunction with the execution of the PRO-drop parameter formulated above is clear: extractions from the subject position by LF movements should be possible in Italian. Rizzi (1982:ch.4) demonstrates, however, that this prediction does not seem to be borne out. The following examples are relevant.

(117) a. non voglio che tu parli con nessuno
         not I-want that you talk with nobody

      b. non voglio che nessuno venga
         not I-want that nobody goes

Nessuno in (117a) can have wide scope, i.e. (117a) can be interpreted as "for no x, I want you to talk to x". Alternatively, (117b) cannot be interpreted with **nessuno** taking wide scope, i.e. it can only have the reading "I want for no x that x comes", and not "there is no x such that I want that x comes". The impossibility of a wide scope reading would follow from the ECP if the wide scope reading is accounted for by quantifier raising in LF, leaving an empty category behind that violates the ECP. If that is to be concluded, the possibility of long subject extraction in the syntax cannot be attributed to AGR being a proper governor for the subject trace. Therefore, Rizzi argues that the possibility of long subject extraction should be reduced to the second property of PRO-drop languages, viz. the possibility of free inversion. According to this suggestion, the WH-phrase in sentence-initial position that is the understood subject of an embedded clause is not extracted from preverbal, but rather from postverbal position, i.e. from the inverted structure[37]. Assuming that this position is properly governed by the verb (cf. Belletti & Rizzi 1981), this extraction is allowed as far as the ECP is concerned.

This reduces the cluster of PRO-drop properties to the first two, i.e. free inversion and the absence of pronominal subjects. These two properties are accounted for in more or less the opposite way in which they were accounted for under the initial execution of the PRO-drop parameter. Whereas it was initially assumed that the subject position was properly governed in PRO-drop languages by AGR, it is now generally held that the difference between PRO-drop and non-PRO-drop languages is that the subject position is always governed in the non-PRO-drop languages, whereas it may be ungoverned in PRO-drop languages. Since the subject position of tensed clauses may be ungoverned in PRO-drop languages, the subject may be PRO (cf. Rizzi o.c., Chomsky 1981). This difference is assumed to follow from the following option, which may be regarded as the PRO-drop parameter: there is a rule, call it R, that moves AGR to V; in PRO-drop languages, rule R optionally applies in syntax, whereas it obligatorily applies in the left-hand component of the grammar in non-PRO-drop languages. Therefore, at S-structure the subject position is always governed by AGR in non-PRO-drop languages, whereas it may be ungoverned in PRO-drop languages, viz. in those cases where R has applied in the syntax.

Let us now return to the Ø-option in Dutch. This Ø-option is found in at least four different constructions, only three of which will be discussed here. The fourth case basically falls under the second one mentioned here and will be discussed in greater detail in section 3.3.3. The relevant instances are:

a. with "extraposed" subject clauses (cf. (115)).

b. with impersonal passives (cf. (118) below).

c. with long subject extractions (cf. (119) below).

(118) a. Gisteravond werd **e** over dat onderwerp gesproken.

      Yesterday-evening was about that subject talked

b. Daarna werd **e** niet meer verder gediscussieerd.

    Thereafter was not more further discussed

(119) a. Wat denk je dat **e** tijdens die vergadering gebeurde?

      What think you that during that meeting happened

b. Wie geloof je dat **e** dat gedaan heeft?

    Who believe you that that done has

The possibility of dropping a subject pronoun with definite interpretation is typically absent. If a θ-role is assigned to the subject position, the subject position can only remain empty at S-structure if coindexed with a category in an A'-position as in the examples in (119). As for the examples in (115), I shall assume that the sentential complement is in an A'-position as well[38]. The other instance of an empty subject position is the case where no θ-role is assigned to the subject position, as in the examples in (118). How can the Dutch Ø-option be explained?

Cases of long subject extraction in Dutch have tentatively been explained along the following lines. On the assumption that the ECP contains two possible proper governors, i.e. lexical governors and local antecedents, the empty category in subject position may be said to be properly governed by a trace in COMP as a local antecedent, in spite of the presence of a lexical complementizer. There are various ways in which this result can be obtained. One way would be to assume that in English the trace in COMP that also contains a lexical complementizer has to be deleted in order to avoid a violation of the doubly-filled COMP filter (cf. Chomsky & Lasnik 1977), while the trace may be retained in Dutch because either the filter is absent in Dutch or is at least not as strong as in English. In this connection, the examples in (120) are relevant.

(120) a. ik vroeg me af [$_{S'}$ [$_{COMP}$ wie of dat] Jan gezien had]

     I wondered   who whether that John seen had

b. ik wist niet [$_{S'}$ [$_{COMP}$ wat of] ik moest doen]
   I did not know   what whether I had to do

Retention of **of** is optional in Dutch for most speakers, while for some speakers **of** may even be followed by **dat**. Another way to establish that the subject trace is properly governed is by assuming that there is a rule in Dutch similar to the **que→qui** rule in French, illustrated in (121), which does not have any phonological effect on **dat** (see Pesetsky 1982 for discussion of complementizer-trace phenomena).

(121) a.*L'homme que tu crois **que** e viendra nous rendre visite, ...
       The man that you believe that will-come pay us a visit, ...

      b. L'homme que tu crois **qui** e viendra nous rendre visite,...

It will be clear that these efforts to explain the possibility of long subject extraction have not been designed with a view to generalize over the three different cases of empty subjects mentioned above. Moreover, an appeal to a local antecedent to rescue an empty category from the ECP is not open to us, as the ECP has been reduced so as to allow only for empty categories that have a lexical category as a proper governor.

It would be more desirable, therefore, if it could be argued that the possibility of a Ø-subject is not due to a local antecedent, but rather to the presence of a lexical governor. How can this be accomplished within the framework of assumptions of GB-theory?

What I want to propose is that it the process of merging V^o and $INFL^o$ as an instantiation of V-raising that achieves this result. Recall that it is our aim to argue that this merger is indeed an instantiation of V-raising, so as to support our claim that INFL is non-distinct from V in its feature content. This result is necessary in order to derive the obligatory postverbal position of clausal complements from the UCC. It is generally assumed that a clause becomes more or less transparent as a consequence of V-raising, which Evers (1975) formalizes in terms of a pruning convention applying to any projection the head of which is removed. Later we shall go into this matter in more detail. Here I would like to suggest that collapsing V^o with $INFL^o$ is responsible for the relatively low degree of configurationality that has been claimed for Dutch and German in recent linguistic literature.

At any rate, if the merger process is regarded as an instance of V-raising, this has the result that the subject position in a configuration like (100) is now properly governed by a lexical item of the category V, a structural governor. Therefore, the subject position may be empty as far as the ECP is concerned.

A relevant question at this point is why there is no possibility of dropping a definite pronoun in Dutch, which is allowed in real PRO-drop languages. It would seem that this is not a matter of the ECP, but rather of the θ-criterion, which requires that each θ-role is assigned to a chain that contains a referential expression. In Dutch, this referential expression would be absent if the pronoun is dropped. In the relevant cases in real PRO-drop languages, however, there is no problem with the θ-criterion, because the coindexing of AGR and the subject position constitutes a chain that does contain a referential expression, viz. AGR which possesses person and number features in these languages. Thus, the empty category resulting from dropping a definite pronoun is licensed not by V^o in these languages, as it is in Dutch and German, but rather by AGR, as claimed under the initial formalization of the PRO-drop parameter found in Taraldsen (1978a). In this way, then, the intuitions behind the original ideas about PRO-drop are retained.

It is interesting to note that the situation with respect to Ø-subjects in Dutch is also found in Italian gerunds and specific types of infinitival constructions. In these constructions, in which AGR is absent, nominative pronouns with a definite interpretation are equally obligatory as in Dutch. A null subject in these constructions is possible "when the subject is interpreted as a "dummy element", with an extraposed sentential complement or with a postverbal subject" (Rizzi 1982:128). This suggests very strongly that it is indeed AGR that determines the possibility of a null subject with the interpretation of a definite pronoun.

If this argument is convincing, the obligatory postverbal position of sentential complements can be derived from the UCC. It turns out, then, that the position of sentential complements in Dutch can be accounted for without any appeal to ordering stipulations in PS-rules or construction-specific transformational operations like extraposition.

There is one type of clausal complement in Dutch that requires further comments, however. This will be treated in the next section where further differences between Dutch and English are discussed.

2.7.2.2. Exceptional Case marking and V-raising structures

Constructions of the type in (122) are often claimed to be exceptional, which is reflected in the term Exceptional Case Marking (ECM) that is frequently used in the description of structures of this type.

(122) I believe John to be a fool

The peculiarity of this construction is that a lexical NP can appear in subject position of a tenseless clause. This means that it cannot receive Case from within the clause, since there is no TENSE to provide nominative Case for this NP. Therefore, it must be concluded that the lexical NP is licensed by the matrix verb. One way in which this could be handled is to assume that the NP **John** is raised from the complement clause into matrix object position by a rule of "Raising to Object" (cf. Postal 1974). However, such a rule is impossible within the framework of GB-theory for reasons discussed above (cf. p. 38). It is assumed, therefore, that the position of the embedded subject comes within reach of the matrix verb, i.e. that the matrix verb may govern this position. This possibility is surprising under the definition of government by Aoun & Sportiche (1981), formulated in (24) above, if the structure is as in (123).

(123) I believe $[_{S'} [_S$ John to be a fool]]

The governee, **John,** would be contained within a maximal projection, S', which does not contain the governor. A way out for Aoun & Sportiche is to assume that some verbs trigger the deletion of S' in their complement, leaving a bare S which is not a maximal projection in their view.

The exceptional nature of this construction would then follow from the exceptionality of the rule of S'-deletion. Such an explanation goes against the spirit of the GB-framework, as it states differences among languages in terms of absence vs. presence of a specific rule. Moreover, it is not correct to claim that S'-deletion is restricted to languages like English: S'-deletion must be present in the grammars of Dutch and French as well. To see this, note that the ECP requires that empty categories be properly governed. Therefore, S'-deletion should be available in the grammar of any language that allows for subject raising, including the grammar of Dutch and French.

(124) John seems $[_{S'} [_S$ **e** to be ill]]
(125) Jan schijnt $[_{S'} [_S$ **e** ziek te zijn]]
(126) Jean semble $[_{S'} [_S$ **e** être malade]]

The empty category in the subject position of the embedded clause, resulting from moving the NP **John/Jan/Jean** to matrix subject position, must be properly governed by the verb **seem/schijnen/sembler**. Since S', a maximal projection, is an absolute barrier for government, it must be deleted in (124)-(126), in order for proper government to obtain.

The exceptional Case-marking contexts, then, appear to be a proper subset of the contexts where proper government across a clause boundary holds. That this is so can also be seen in French in the following examples, taken from Rouveret & Vergnaud (1980:127).

(127) a.*Jean suppose $[_{S'} [_S$ Marie avoir résolu le problème]]
      b. **Marie** est supposée $[_{S'} [_S$ **e** avoir résolu le problème]]

The empty category in the b-example is accepted, whereas the lexical NP in the corresponding active in the a-example is rejected. Hence it must be concluded that the relevant position is properly governed, but that no Case is assigned to it. Given this conclusion, one might be inclined to think that the property of assigning Case across a certain boundary (across S in this case) is a lexical property of verbs, which is absent in those languages that differ from English in not having exceptional Case-marking constructions. Such a position, however, is, apart from being uninteresting, also obviously wrong, as we shall see below. I will adopt the view that the assignment of structural Case is a purely configurational matter, i.e. that it is determined by the structural relation between a Case assigner and an NP, the only restriction being that a structural-Case assigner like a verb will only assign Case if it also assigns a θ-role to its subject. This restriction will be extensively dealt with in the next chapter. According to this view, then, Case assignment is a blind process.

In order to illustrate that assignment of Case across a maximal projection boundary appears to be possible in Dutch, the analysis of ergativity and small clauses that is the subject of the next chapters has to be anticipated. The term ergativity is used in recent generative grammar to refer to structures in which the verb does not assign a θ-role to the subject, although it may select a complement. The hypothesis that such structures exist is originally due to Perlmutter (1978). The relevant class of verbs is studied in impressive detail

for Italian in Burzio (1981). The concept of ergativity may be exemplified by the
following cases.

(128) a. the enemy sank the boat
      b. the boat sank

According to the ergative analysis, **the boat** in (128b) is generated in object
position, just as in (128a), but it is subsequently moved to the subject position
by MOVE α. This movement is forced by the Case filter, on the assumption, that
structural Case fails to be assigned by a verb that does not θ-mark its subject.
This would be the case in (128b), but not in (128a). It is not entirely clear
whether this ergative analysis is applicable to English, however (cf. Keyser &
Roeper 1982, who claim that ergativity in English is an entirely lexical matter).
   Schematically, the ergative analysis can be represented as in (129).

(129)

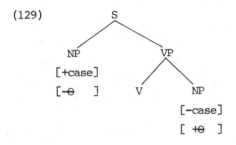

The (NP,VP) is governed by V, but it does not receive Case from this verb, since
(NP,S) does not receive a θ-role. The diagram in (129) is in fact relevant for
the analysis of passive as well, as we shall see below. It should be noted that
apart from passives on θ-governed NP's (i.e. on direct objects), there are also
passives in which the subject position is filled by an NP that is merely
structurally governed by the verb. A **believe**-passive as in (130) is a case in
point, but a passive as in (131) involves passivization of a non-θ-governed NP
as well.

(130) **John** was believed [_S', [_S **e** to have done it]]
(131) **John** was considered [_sc **e** foolish]

The label sc in (131) stands for small clause. Following Stowell (1981), I shall
assume that the categorial label for which sc stands in (131) is determined by the

category of the predicate, i.e. sc = AP in (131), as **foolish** is an adjective. This means that not only NP and S have subjects, but that in fact all phrase types can have subjects. Under this hypothesis, the structure of (131) would be as in (132).

(132)

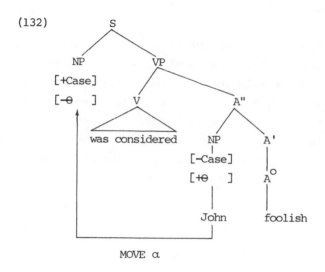

MOVE α

If the small-clause analysis is accepted, it has to be concluded that government across a maximal projection boundary is possible: in (131) in order to obtain proper government of the empty category left behind by MOVE α, and in its active counterpart in order to assign Case to the subject of the AP. In other words, Stowell's execution of the small-clause concept is irreconcilable with Aoun & Sportiche's definition of government.

Earlier we saw that the ECM structure in (130) did not provide a problem for the Aoun & Sportiche definition of government if one assumes that S'-deletion applies and that S does not count as a maximal projection. It was noted that the exceptionality of the type of structure in (130) cannot be due to the exceptional status of S'-deletion, as this process is needed in the grammar of other languages as well. Therefore, the exceptionality might be due to the assignment of Case across certain boundaries. The following examples are relevant to illustrate that assignment of Case across a maximal projection boundary appears to occur in Dutch as well.

(133) a. dat ik vind dat Jan vervelend is
         that I think that John is boring

    b. dat ik Jan vervelend vind
       that I John boring   find

The verb **vinden** 'find, think' in (133a) assigns two θ-roles, an internal role to
the complement clause and an external role to its subject. The minimal assumption
would be that the θ-grid of **vinden** is not changed for a structure like (133b),
i.e. that **vinden** in (133b) again assigns two θ-roles, the external role to the
subject and the internal θ-role that is assigned to the clausal complement in
(133a), but to the small clause AP in (133b). If this line of reasoning is correct
(I shall return to this matter in great detail in the final chapter), the
structure of (133b) would be as in (134)

(134)

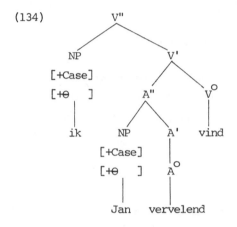

The subject of the A", **Jan,** receives its Case from the verb **vinden** as becomes
clear when we passivize the matrix verb, i.e. when we eliminate the assignment of
a θ-role to the subject. As stated above, this results in suspension of the
assignment of Case to a governed NP. The result is that the NP **Jan** has to move to
the matrix subject position as can be seen in (135).

    (135) dat Jan (door mij)   vervelend wordt gevonden
          that John (by me)   boring   is   found

It must therefore be concluded that if the small-clause analysis is correct,
government across a maximal projection boundary is permitted in Dutch as well as
in English, as is assignment of Case under government. A further question is
whether Case can also be assigned across a sentence boundary. The examples in

(127) suggest that in French, government across a sentence boundary is permitted but Case assignment is not. The examples in (136) again illustrate that, in general, Case marking across a sentence boundary is not permitted in French (see, however, Kayne 1981c:353, fn.9). Case assignment across a small-clause boundary is not impossible, even with the same verbs as those in (136), as is shown in (137).

> (136) a. *Jean crois Bill avoir menti
>   b. *Je croyais Jean etre arrivé

> (137) a. Je crois Jean intelligent
>   b. Je croyais Jean à Paris

In Beukema & Hoekstra (1983a) it is demonstrated that assignment of Case across a small-clause boundary in less restricted in Dutch, as is evident from the absolute **met**-construction. It is argued there that the structure of the absolute **met**-construction in (138) is as in (139), where it is required that the subject of the small clause receives its Case from the preposition **met** 'with'.

> (138) a. Met je mond open zie je er dom uit
>   With your mouth open,you look dumb
>
>   b. Met voetbal op de televisie is er niemand op straat
>   With football on the television, is there nobody on the street

(139)

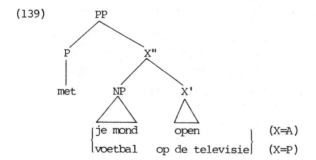

Whereas the complement of **met** in this absolute construction can be a small clause, **met** may not take a normal clause as complement. It is argued in Beukema & Hoekstra (1983a) that the reason for this is that the preposition may not assign

Case across a sentence boundary. Note that it must be assumed that the subject of the small clause in (138) receives Case from the preposition. This is evidenced by the fact that the NP receives dative Case in the German **mit**-construction, a Case that is governed by the preposition **mit**[39].

(140) Mit dem Fenster offen schläft man meist besser
      With the window open, one usually sleeps better
          [+dative]

Let us now turn to examples like (141) that suggest that Case assignment across a sentence boundary is possible in Dutch.

(141) dat ik [Jan mooi zingen] vind
      that I   John beautifully sing find

Again, **Jan** receives Case from the verb **vinden,** although this cannot straightforwardly be demonstrated by passivization, as in example (135), because passivization is impossible in this kind of structure. First, however, it must be determined what the structure of (141) is: if the phrase **Jan mooi zingen** is a clause, the structure should be rejected by the UCC, since the matrix verb would govern a clause. Fortunately, (141) is ungrammatical as it stands. The order of matrix and embedded verb is obligatorily changed as a result of applying V-raising[40]. Hence, instead of (141), which may be taken to represent D-structure, the surface form of the sentence is as in (142).

(142) dat ik Jan mooi vind zingen

Let us now address the question what the label of the bracketed part in (141) should be. Suppose that it is a projection of INFL, i.e. S'. Then, given the reasons that we gave earlier for the obligatory nature of extraposition of sentential complements, (i.e. they are projections of INFL, INFL is non-distinct from V in its feature content, therefore the UCC forbids that they occur in the goverment domain of V, V governs to the left), the bracketed part should occur in postverbal position as a whole. Furthermore, given that the COMP node is the specifier of the INFL-projection, there is no apparent reason for the absence of a lexical complementizer in these preverbal complements. All these preverbal clauses lack a complementizer as well as the possibility of being introduced by a WH-phrase. Finally, if the INFL hypothesis is maintained, **Jan** would be governed

by INFL rather than by **vinden,** which we argue is the governor of **Jan.** The
conclusion must therefore be that, given our definition of government, **Jan** is not
governed by INFL and this conclusion implies that the bracketed part in (141) is
not a projection of INFL.

   If it is assumed that (100) correctly represents the structure of full
sentential structure, an alternative possibility for the labelling of the bracketed part in (141) is possible, viz. S=V". This would lead us to assume that the
correct representation of (141) is as in (143). In this structure, **Jan** is indeed
governed by the matrix verb **vinden,** as required, whereas the absence of a
complementizer and the possibility of WH-movement is automatically explained.

(143)

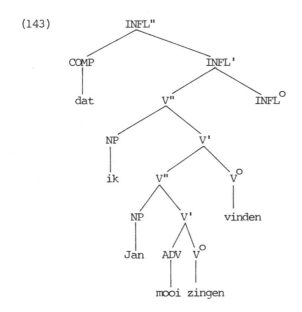

Notice that the absence of INFL in the complement of **vinden** squares nicely with
the often observed characteristic of this type of construction, viz. that the
temporal interpretation of the embedded clause is totally dependent on the
temporal specification of the matrix verb (cf. De Geest 1973). This may be
illustrated with the following examples.

   (144) a. dat ik zag dat de prunus bloeide
            that I saw that the cherry tree blossomed

       b. dat ik de prunus zag bloeien

In (144) the moment of perception does not have to coincide with the moment of blossoming of the tree: that the tree had its blossom may be deduced from other circumstances that are perceived. In (144b), on the other hand, it is necessary that the visual perception coincides with the moment of blossoming. If INFL is regarded as the node that dominates the temporal specification of the proposition denoted by the V", the difference between (144a) and (144b) is explained on the assumption that in the structure of (144b) no INFL is present.

It will be observed that the structure in (143) is still in violation of the UCC, since a V-projection is in the government domain of the verb. Therefore, the rule of V-raising applies in order to save the structure from the UCC. In this way, the obligatory effect of V-raising is immediately accounted for. Two questions suggest themselves at this point. First, why is the structure saved by means of V-raising and secondly, how is the distribution of INFL-projections versus plain V-projections accounted for?

As for the first question, part of the answer would be provided if it could be argued that it is impossible to save the structure by placing the complement clause in postverbal position as is done with INFL-projections. There are at least two ways in which this result can be achieved. One approach is taken by Evers (1982) who argues that each verb must receive an AUX-index. Translated into our terminology, each verb must be associated with an $INFL^o$. Postverbal complement clauses contain their own AUX-index (i.e. in our terminology, have INFL), but V-raising complements lack it. Therefore, the verb of these V-raising complements must be attached to the matrix verb in order to become associated with an AUX-index.

I would like to present an alternative to Evers' analysis. The entire set of V-raising complements may be divided into three different types. This typology is set up only for expository purposes and has no theoretical significance, as will become clear as we proceed. The first type has already been illustrated by the example in (142), and the type is also instantiated in the complement of the perception verbs (cf. (144b)) and the causative verb **laten**. A common feature of these complements is that they contain a lexical subject without having Tense. Therefore, as we argued above, this subject must be licensed, i.e. Case marked by the matrix verb under government. As government holds to the left for verbs in Dutch, this subject NP must precede the matrix verb, as can be seen in (145).

(145) $[_{V'} \ldots [_{V''} NP_{lex} \ldots] V^o]$

Case

It should be noted that all verbs that take tenseless complement clauses with lexical subjects are V-raising triggers.

The second type of preverbal clausal complement is found with the so-called subject raising verbs like the verbs **schijnen, blijken, lijken** etc. These are the traditional pseudo-copula verbs. It will be argued in the fourth chapter that many more verbs should be added to this class. In the discussion of subject raising above (cf. example (124)), it was made clear that the trace left behind by the operation of subject raising must be properly governed by the matrix verb in order to satisfy the ECP. Therefore, this subject must precede the matrix verb as well, as is clear from the diagram in (146).

$$(146) \quad [_{V''} \; NP_i \ldots [_{V'} \; [_{V''} \; t_i \; \ldots] \; V^\circ \;]]$$

$$\text{government}$$

It should be noted again that all subject-raising triggers are V-raising triggers as well. Before turning to the third type, then, it is important to establish at this point that the first two types share the feature of having a complement the subject of which must be governed by the matrix verb. Therefore, if our claim that government is leftward in Dutch is correct, the fact that these complements cannot as a whole be placed in postverbal position follows from the requirement that the subject should be governed. It should be noted that under different theories of V-raising the obligatory preverbal position of the complement is not explained and in fact, no explanation is given for the facts, noted above, that all subject-raising triggers and all verbs taking AcI-complements are V-raising triggers as well.

The third type of V-raising structure causes a problem for the hypothesis presented above. This type of structure does not take a lexical subject, nor does it trigger subject-raising. An example is given in (147).

(147) a. dat ik $[_{V''}$ **e** $[_{V'}$ de krant lezen]] wil

   b. dat ik de krant wil lezen
      that I the newspaper want read
      "that I want to read the newspaper"

(147b) exemplifies the surface form of (147a), which in turn represents the structure before the application of V-raising. What is the subject of the preverbal complement? The general assumption is that it is PRO. Then, if PRO is a pronominal anaphor as it generally assumed, it must be ungoverned (cf. Chomsky 1981). This is at odds with the hypothesis spelled out above, i.e. the hypothesis that these preverbal complements must precede the verb because their subject must be governed. Quite the contrary would be the case if e in (147a) was PRO: it would then be required that the structure is S', given my definition of government, in order to prevent the matrix verb from governing this alleged PRO subject.

Conceptually, this position is less attractive in that it involves contradictory requirements: the clause would have to be transparent in the first two types, in order for the matrix verb to govern the subject position as well as to allow extraction of the verbal head by means of V-raising, whereas it would have to be opaque with respect to the subject in the third type, but transparent at the same time with respect to the possibility of extracting the head.

What I would like to do, therefore, is to reconsider the assumption that the subject in (147a) is a pronominal anaphor. It should be noted that the PRO-theorem (i.e. PRO is limited in its distribution to ungoverned positions) can only be obtained by assuming that PRO as an invisible NP is different in nature from any type of lexical NP, i.e. among the lexical NP's there are anaphors and pronominals, each differing in their binding conditions, but there are no lexical pronominal anaphors[41]. While it is true that some invisible NP's that are PRO equal lexical pronominals in having no local antecedent, while some other invisible NP's look like anaphors in having an obligatory local antecedent, no instance of PRO has both characteristics at the same time. On the assumption that there is only a single type of empty category that can be subdivided in terms of its contextual or functional properties, one would expect a complete match between visible and invisible NP's. Whereas the theory assumes the existence of a class of empty categories that is identical to anaphors in terms of their binding requirements (NP-trace) as well as the existence of a class of empty categories that is identical in their binding requirements to names (WH-trace, but see section 2.6.), there is no class of empty categories that is similar to lexical pronominals in terms of their binding requirements. Moreover, if there is a complete match between visible and invisible NP's, there is no a priori reason why there would not be an invisible anaphor comparable to lexical reflexives, i.e. an empty anaphor with an antecedent that has an independent θ- role. It is important to note that the empty subjects in examples like (147a) are always bound by a uniquely determined antecedent. It might be hypothesized, therefore, that these subjects are anaphoric rather than pronominal anaphors such as control PRO. If this e is indeed an anaphor, there is no conflict in binding requirement that leads to the requirement that this subject be ungoverned. This subject would then be characterized as an invisible anaphor, locally A-bound by an antecedent with an independent θ-role. The claim that there is a set of governed PRO's that are essentially anaphoric is also made in Koster (1981), although the distribution of these governed PRO's within Koster's analysis differs slightly from what I have suggested above. I conclude therefore that an empty category in a θ-position that is governed is always anaphoric. It is a trace, if its antecedent does not have an independent θ-role.

If this analysis is correct, we can maintain the hypothesis that extraposition of these preverbal clauses is impossible due to the requirement that the subject is governed.

Turning now to the second question raised above, viz. how selection of a plain V-projection vs. a INFL-projection is accounted for, we note that the choice of the category of complements is usually regarded as an idiosyncratic matter, which is dealt with in the lexical specification of the individual items. Therefore, the selection may be handled by positing an INFL" complement in the subcategorization frames of the verbs that take postverbal complements, but a V" in the case of the verbs that induce V-raising. However, if the above hypothesis is correct, a more principled explanation may be given for the distribution, an explanation that involves both the semantics of the governing verb and the temporal relation between the proposition denoted by the embedded clause and the proposition in which it is embedded. I shall not go further into this matter.

Above it was mentioned that the effect of V-raising under Evers' (1975) analysis is that the entire V-projection is pruned by a general pruning convention. It should be noted that this is required under the UCC, since, if the V-projection is retained, with a trace in the position of the extracted verb, the structure would still violate the UCC. Evers (1975) offers considerable support for his claim that the embedded clausal domain no longer exists after the application of V-raising, whereas Hoeksema (1980) argues that the hypothesis that a trace is left behind by V-raising causes a number of problems for the theory of trace binding[42].

The analysis of V-raising presented here corroborates our claim that government is unidirectionally to the left in Dutch. We shall now proceed with an additional piece of evidence that directly relates to the previous discussion.

Dutch does not appear to have any raising adjectives such as English **certain, likely** etc. It is rather unattractive to assume that the fact that Dutch does not have raising adjectives is a mere coincidence: it is a priori more desirable if it could be shown that Dutch could not have any raising adjectives. It seems to be possible to present such a principled account for their absence.

Raising constructions with adjectives are not without problems within the framework of GB-theory. Consider the following examples.

(148) a. it is likely that John will go
      b. John is likely [$_{S'}$ [$_S$ e to go]]

The empty category in (148b) must be properly governed in order to satisfy the ECP. The problem is how this can be achieved. It must be assumed that S' can be deleted in the complement of some adjectives, but not in others, just as S' can be deleted in the complement of some verbs but not in others. However, Kayne (1981a:109) notes that the claim that only V (and possibly P)is a structural governor in the sense of being able to govern an NP that it does not θ-mark is at odds with the assumption that in (148b) the empty category is governed by the raising adjective. Kayne suggests, therefore, that in these cases a rule of reanalysis applies which combines the matrix verb and the adjective, such that a complex verb governs the empty node. Let us assume that Kayne's suggestion is correct and turn to the situation in Dutch.

It should be noted first that there are adjectives in Dutch that take sentential complements without assigning a θ-role to their subject. An example is found in (149).

(149) dat het zeker is dat Piet het museum zal bezoeken
      that it certain is that Peter the museum will visit

The sentential complement, which is finite in this case, is in postverbal position as expected. However, if the complement is a tenseless sentence, there is no possibility of raising the subject to the position of the matrix subject, i.e. both (150a) and (150b) are ungrammatical.

(150) a.*dat **Jan** zeker is [e het museum te zullen bezoeken]
      b.*dat **Jan** [e het museum te zullen bezoeken] zeker is

In our account the reason for the ungrammaticality of (150a) is quite straight-forward: the trace in subject position of the postverbal complement must be properly governed, which it cannot be, because the possible governor precedes it. Therefore, (150a) violates the ECP. Let us therefore turn to the structure in (150b). Suppose first that there is no rule of reanalysis. Then the structure is rejected by the ECP as well, as adjectives are incapable of governing across a

maximal projection boundary, because they are not structural governors. Suppose
alternatively that there is a rule of reanalysis as suggested by Kayne. The
structure would then violate the UCC, just as (141) did, i.e. because there is a V
or INFL projection that is governed by V. (150b) would differ from (141),
however, in that the structure cannot be saved by applying V-raising, as the
ungrammaticality of (150c) shows.

(150c) *dat Jan het museum zeker is te zullen bezoeken

I would like to propose that the reason for the impossibility of V-raising is
the fact that the alleged verbal complex, created by reanalysis, branches internally. It was observed by Evers (1975), Nieuwenhuysen (1976) that V-raising is
generally impossible if the verbs are non-adjacent to each other. This is the
case with verbs that select particles: Evers shows that these do never induce V-
raising, and hence that they never take preverbal clauses either. Van Riemsdijk
(1978a), however, convincingly argues that there must be a rule incorporating
particles into their governing verbs, his rule of P-shift (cf. Van Riemsdijk
1978a:108). Hence, after this incorporation, the verbs would be adjacent as is
shown in the following diagram.

(151) a. $[_{V'} ..[_{V''} ..V^O]$ Prt V^O]   P-shift $\Longrightarrow$

b. $[_{V'} ..[_{V''} ..V^O] [_{V^O}$ Prt $V^O]]]$

In spite of the fact that the matrix and the embedded verb become adjacent as a
consequence of P-shift as in (151b), V-raising remains impossible. The explanation for this may be the same as for the impossibility of V-raising in the case of
A-V combinations, i.e. that internally branching verbs are not suitable recepta-
cles for raised complement verbs.

It appears, then, that the difference between Dutch and English with respect
to the absence vs. presence of raising adjectives can be traced to the directionality of government, which lends further support to the correctness of this
requirement.

At this point, it will be convenient to summarize the main points of this
section. The discussion in section 2.7. aims at deriving the relative ordering of
complements from a number of more principled assumptions. In 2.7.1. it is claimed
that one relevant principle is that government is unidirectional and that in
Dutch, verbs govern to the left, whereas they govern to the right in English.

Various pieces of evidence for the correctness of this claim are adduced in section 2.7.2. where it is argued that the distribution of sentential complements, both in extraposition and in V-raising constructions, can be derived from this unidirectionality hypothesis in conjunction with a further principle, the Unlike Category Condition.

These two hypotheses not only account for the obligatory position of some clausal complements and for the obligatory nature of V-raising, they also account in a principled fashion for the complementary distribution of these two complement types. The fact that all subject-raising triggers and all verbs taking AcI-complements induce V-raising is also explained. From the account given for V-raising it immediately follows that Dutch cannot have raising adjectives. Moreover, the analysis of V-raising explains why V-raising structures can never have a complement clause with a PRO subject that receives an arbitrary interpretation: since the subject is always governed, the empty category must be anaphoric.

It turns out, then, that as far as the distribution of sentential complements is concerned, no recourse need be had to PS-rules. The two natural principles that we have proposed above take care of this distribution and have several consequences beyond that. In the following subsection we shall examine whether the distribution of other phrase types can be explained in similar fashion, i.e. without invoking the descriptive tool of PS-rules.

2.7.3. The distribution of other phrase types

After having established the principles that determine the distribution of sentential complements, the relative position of other phrase types will not be very problematic, although a number of questions have to be addressed.

Let us first direct our attention to NP's. The basic assumption is that NP's must receive Case. Therefore they may appear in the complement of the [-V] categories V and P. Due to the different orientation of government of these categories, NP complements precede verbs, but follow prepositions. There is one difference between these categories, however. Whereas the NP complement is always immediately adjacent to the preposition, it may be separated from the verb by other constituents. It was mentioned earlier that the distribution of object NP's in English is accounted for by Stowell (1981) on the assumption that the assignment of Case is subject to an adjacency requirement. Stowell is aware of the fact

that this adjacency requirement runs into problems in other languages, of which
he discusses Italian and Dutch. If it is assumed that the adjacency requirement
is part of the innate knowledge of grammar, it is imperative that the violations
of this requirement found in these languages are explained in some way or other.

As for Italian, Stowell notes that some adverbials may intervene between
the verb and its object at S-structure, notably manner adverbs, but not place and
time adverbs. In order to accommodate these instances of non-adjacency at S-
structure in Italian, Stowell proposes that the adjacency requirement may be met
either at S-structure, as in English, or at the level which he calls argument
projection (cf. Stowell 1981:114). The notion of argument projection, which
Stowell does not formalize, should be understood in the same way as the notion of
vowel projection used in modern theories of phonology (cf. Halle & Vergnaud
1978). A projection is essentially a representation of specific elements of
another representation. So, a vowel projection is a representation of the vowels
occurring within a certain domain. The argument projection of a certain domain is
supposed to include the verb and the object, but not the intervening manner
adverb. Hence, at the level of argument projection the adjacency requirement is
met. Of these two options, adjacency at S-structure or at the level of argument
projection, the former is assumed to constitute the unmarked one. The reason to
adopt this conclusion derives from considerations relating to language acquisition. From that point of view, a marked choice requires positive evidence. If the
choice of the argument projection is the marked one, an Italian sentence with a
manner adverb intervening between the verb and its object would provide the
required positive evidence.

For the situation in Dutch Stowell presents a different analysis, which is
rather unsatisfactory. In Dutch, the object NP can be separated from the verb in
VP-final position by all sorts of constituents. A typical example is found in
(152).

(152) dat Jan zijn vriendin gisteren in Amsterdam ontmoette
      that John his girl friend yesterday in Amsterdam met

The proposal that Stowell develops is apparently motivated by the consideration
that "the order of complements in Dutch is comparatively strict. It is not just
that the object is allowed to appear at the beginning of VP; it actually must
appear there" (Stowell 1981:117). Stowell then goes on to exploit the difference
in position of the verb in main and subordinate clauses. As is well known, Dutch
has a verb-second constraint in main clauses. A typical example is given in
(153).

(153) a. dat Peter John naar Amsterdam stuurt
         that Peter John to Amsterdam sends

      b. Peter stuurt John naar Amsterdam

From examples like these Stowell concludes that the finite verb occupies either
the final or the initial position within VP. On this basis, he assumes that the VP
in Dutch is double-headed, even when only one of the positions in which the head
may be found is filled. The structure of (153a) would be as in (154) under these
assumptions.

(154)   dat Peter [$_{V'}$ [$_{V}$ —] John   naar Amsterdam [stuurt]]
                                   [acc]

The accusative Case of **John** is then assumed to be assigned under adjacency by the
empty head in initial position. It will be clear that this assumption is at odds
with our claim that Case is assigned under government and that government is
leftward looking for V in Dutch.

It turns out, however, that the two assumptions that Stowell makes about
Dutch clause structure are incorrect, which makes his proposal entirely untena-
ble. First of all, the claim that the object must occur in VP-initial position is
clearly false, as the examples in (155) demonstrate.

(155) a. dat Jan gisteren zijn vriendin in Amsterdam ontmoette
         that John yesterday his girl friend in Amsterdam met

      b. dat Jan in Amsterdam gisteren zijn vriendin ontmoette
      c. dat Jan in Amsterdam zijn vriendin gisteren ontmoette

Unless the object NP is a clitic, it has a great mobility within VP. Secondly,
Stowell's claim that in main clauses the finite verb occurs in VP-initial
position is due to a mistaken interpretation of the verb-second constraint.
Essentially, his interpretation of Dutch main clauses seems to be that they
exhibit SVO order, which is blatantly wrong. Almost any constituent may appear in
sentence initial position, followed by the finite verb. If the constituent in
initial position is not the subject, the subject follows the finite verb. This is
illustrated by the examples in (156).

(156) a. Gisteren ontmoette Jan zijn vriendin in Amsterdam.
      b. In Amsterdam ontmoette Jan gisteren zijn vriendin.
      c. Zijn vriendin ontmoette Jan gisteren in Amsterdam.

Here the object **zijn vriendin** is either separated from the verb by the intervening subject or it is in sentence initial position itself. These facts are of
course well-known from the literature (cf. Koster 1976, Thiersch 1978). The most
generally adopted analysis to describe this situation is that a rule of V-
movement moves the finite verb in main clauses into the sentence-initial COMP
(this position is filled by the lexical complementizer in embedded clauses)[43].
Furthermore, one constituent of the clause is attached to the right of the finite
verb, which may be the subject or any other constituent that can be moved there
without violating constraints on possible movements.

Stowell's theory of a double-headed VP must therefore be rejected. We also
have to conclude that the object receives Case from the verb in VP-final position. The question then arises whether the adjacency requirement as a universal
principle for Case assignment can be maintained in the light of the phenomena
found in Dutch. It should be stressed, however, that it would be counterproduc-
tive at this moment just to dismiss the adjacency requirement, since then we are
left with no explanatory principle at all. Let us therefore try to find an
alternative to reconcile the phenomena in Dutch with this adjacency requirement.

One way to tackle this problem would be to adopt Stowell's notion of argument
projection, but this step is a priori rather unsatisfactory in that it requires
the postulation of a new kind of representation which is not motivated independently. There is an alternative approach, however, that does not introduce any
new rules or requirements. In fact, this alternative is already available, and it
will be seen that it raises some problems for those languages in which adjacency
is observed.

First we have to make a distinction in Dutch between those constituents that
may intervene between the verb and its object and those constituents that must
intervene. Amond the latter we find predicative complements and inherent adverbials of place and direction. These constituents will be dealt with in the final
chapter where it will be seen that the fact that they must intervene between the
verb and its object is a consequence of the formation of a verbal complex.
Constructions involving these types of constituents will not be discussed here,
therefore. Among the former constituents we find all sorts of adverbials and
predicative adjuncts. These constituents may precede or follow the object and
they are typically optional.

Before proceeding to the way in which these phenomena should be treated, we
have to say something about the way in which adverbial modification should be
handled in a framework that dispenses with PS-rules. In older studies of phrase
structure (e.g. Jackendoff 1977), a special level of structure was assumed to be
projected by the base rules to accommodate adverbial constituents within the
predicate. In Jackendoff's X'-theory, this is the level of V". Within our
system, the geometry of phrases is determined by the θ-criterion and the
Projection Principle which require that a phrase has a head, a projection level
containing the complements and, depending on the properties of the head, a
projection level containing the subject of the phrase. Jackendoff (1977:61)
characterizes V" complements (in his sense of complement, i.e. material following
the head) as "the expressions of manner, means, accompaniment, instrument,
purpose, and other so-called VP adverbials. Semantically, they map predicates
into predicates of the same number of arguments, and they contribute to the main
assertion of the sentence". In a certain sense, this characterization is a bit
odd, given the fact that Jackendoff places all these adverbials at the level of
VP. Because of this syntactic position, these adverbials will always map one-
place predicates into one-place predicates, the single argument being the syntactic subject. However, his semantic characterization does not require that
all these adverbials are VP-adverbials. It would also allow that e.g. a manner
adverb modifies a transitive verb, yielding another, complex transitive verb
(phrase). The main reason to assume that VP-adverbials are attached at a higher
level of structure than argument expressions (apart from the subject) seems to be
that the relative ordering of the object and the adverbial falls out from the
level of attachment. However, this relative ordering is precisely a consequence
of the adjacency requirement on Case assignment in Stowell's theory.

How should adverbial modifiers be accommodated within a theory that dispenses
with PS-rules? The following strategy seems to be promising. The semantic characterization of adverbial modification given above states that the semantic type of
the predicate is preserved when it is modified by an adverbial. A theory of
syntactic adjunction of modifiers would give a parallel syntactic preservation.
So, if (157) is the basic syntactic structure of (159) as determined by the
Projection Principle and the θ-criterion, (158) could be taken as the structure
of (160), where the adverb is Chomsky adjoined to V'.

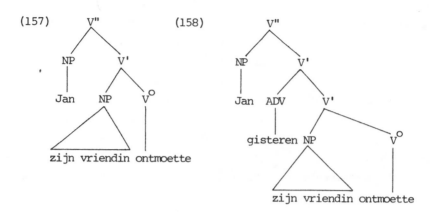

(159) (dat) Jan zijn vriendin ontmoette
      that John his girl friend met

(160) (dat) Jan gisteren zijn vriendin ontmoette
      that John yesterday his girlfriend met

There is of course no principled limit to the number of adjunctions that can be
created. The result of repeated adjunction is a stacked structure of V', a
structure that is impossible under Jackendoff's theory of phrase structure. It
turns out that stacking of V' under repeated modification yields correct results
under constituency tests proposed by Jackendoff. As for membership of V' vs. V"
in his theory, Jackendoff makes use of the so-called "do so" replacement (cf.
Jackendoff 1977:58). The phrase **do so** is considered to be a pro-V' as it cannot be
followed by expressions that are considered to belong to V', i.e. arguments and
inherent phrases. This behaviour is illustrated with the following example.

(161) a. Joe bought a book on Tuesday, but Sam did so on Friday
      b.*Joe put a book on the table , but Sam did so on the chair

"The ability of **on Tuesday** to follow **did so** indicates that it is a V" or a V"'
complement in this sentence; the inability of **on the chair** to follow **do so**
indicates that it must be inside V' in the antecedent sentence" (loc. cit.). The
do-so test in English is equivalent to the **doe-dat** test in Dutch: this test is
also used to discriminate between V' and V" complements (cf. Kraak & Klooster
1968). The rationale behind the observed behaviour of **doe dat** is of course that
dat satisfies the subcategorization of the verb **doen**. Therefore, any expression
accompanying **doe dat** must be construed (hence be construable) as a modifier of

this expression. Now it appears that it is not true that **doe dat** (and similarly **do so** in English) can only be interpreted as a "pronominal replacement" of a verb plus its complements, i.e. as referring to the V' in Jackendoff's sense in the antecedent expression. It may also be interpreted as referring to this V' and a modifier. Consider the following example.

(162) Jan heeft gisteren in de garage zijn auto gewassen en
      John has yesterday in the garage his car washed and

      Piet heeft dat vandaag gedaan.
      Peter has that today   done.

The expression **heeft dat gedaan** in the second conjunct can be interpreted both as "has washed his car" and as "has washed his car in the garage". This is predicted under the analysis according to which repeated modification creates a stacked rather than a flat structure of modifiers. Similar remarks can be made about adjectival modification of nouns. These modifiers are assumed to be generated at the N" level in Jackendoff's system, but data involving 'pronominal replacement' show again that a stacked structure makes better predictions. Just like **do so** is assumed to be a pro-V', **one** is considered to replace N'. Similarly, Blom (1977) argues that **er** in Dutch is a pro-N'. It turns out, however, that both English **one** and Dutch **er** can refer to a combination of a noun and an adjectival modifier. Consider the following examples.

(163) Jan bouwde twee grote stenen huizen en
       John built two large stone houses and

       Piet bouwde er drie
       Peter built there three

(164) They only bought the blue cotton trousers and
       we only the red ones

The preferred interpretation of the second conjunct in (163) is that Peter built three large stone houses. For independent reasons, **er** cannot be combined with a quantified NP without the nominal head but with an adjective[44]. However, if the verb is deleted in the second conjunct, the second conjunct might read as in (165) where the interpretation is that Peter built three small stone houses.

(165)   (en) Piet drie kleine
        and Peter three small

Similarly, in the English example in (164) **ones** is interpreted as cotton trousers
and not as trousers (cf. also Hornstein & Lightfoot 1981:20).

We conclude, therefore, that adverbial modification should be handled by
adjunction of the adverbial phrase to the relevant projection. Let us now return
to our initial problem, i.e. to account for the non-adjacency between the verb
and its object under the assumption that there is an adjacency requirement on
Case assignment. It should be observed that if this requirement is correct, it
would forbid the adjunction of a modifier prior to the combining of the verb and
its object, at least if no linear rearrangements are carried out before the
application of Case assignment, i.e. before S-structure. It should be noted that
given the freely operating rule MOVE α, which can either involve substitution or
adjunction, there is nothing in the theory to prevent the object from being moved
out of its base position and being attached by adjunction to a higher level of
structure. Consider the following example.

(166) dat Jan zijn vriendin gisteren ontmoette (cf. (160)).
      that John his girl friend yesterday met

(166) constitutes an apparent violation of the adjacency requirement in that the
NP object is separated from its Case assigner by the intervening adverb. It is
also a counterexample to the claim that modifiers always occur peripheral to
complements (cf. (3)v. above). The structure of (166) might, however, be represented as in (167).

(167)

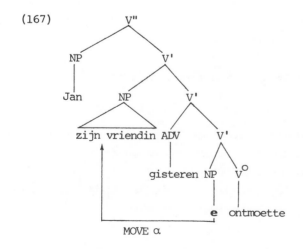

The highest V' node in this structure is created by Chomsky-adjunction of the NP **zijn vriendin,** which has been moved out of the position adjacent to **ontmoette** by application of MOVE α. Since the landing site of **zijn vriendin** is created by adjunction, it is an A'-position. Its extraction site is of course an A-position to which a θ-role is assigned by the verb. Therefore, the empty NP in (167) is a variable, i.e. an empty category, locally A' bound and in an A-position. The chain (**zijn vriendin, e)** is visible for the θ-criterion, because Case is assigned to it via the empty category. Case assignment of this empty category observes the adjacency requirement. Therefore, no violation of this requirement occurs, not even in those cases where it appears to be violated.

It may be noted that the effect of the operation of moving the object to a structurally higher position has the same effect as the rule of NP-placement proposed in De Haan (1979). For a discussion of the merits of this proposal, the reader is referred to Verhagen (1981). The problems with De Haan's rule pointed out by Verhagen do not carry over to the present analysis.

The most important aspect of the analysis presented here is that it comes for free within the framework of GB-theory. At the same time it reveals a problem for this theory, since the analysis proposed here is available for those languages that seem to observe the adjacency requirement in a more direct way, e.g. in English. The question, then, is why the object cannot be moved from its base position to be attached to a structurally higher position. Another, possibly related question, is why the adjunction of the NP object should be on the lefthand side of V' in Dutch and not on the opposite side, or at a higher structural level.

The fact that adjunction must be to the lefthand side of V' in Dutch suggests that the NP should remain governed by the verb, if our hypothesis that government is unidirectional to the left in Dutch is correct. Given our definition of government, the object in adjoined position is indeed still governed (see also the discussion in Belletti & Rizzi 1981 on the position of the inverted subject in Italian). One may wonder why the operator-variable structures created by WH-movement are not restricted to the locality determined by the government domain of the head. A speculation from a functional point of view would be that the greater distance created by WH-movement is counterbalanced by the morphological or formal identification of the relation by the feature [+wh] (cf. Van Riemsdijk 1978a:44,45 for similar suggestions to motivate base-generated landing sites that are not motivated in terms of being input to deep structure projection rules).

If the idea that the moved constituent must remain within the government domain of the head is correct, one would expect for English that an NP object

which is moved out from its position adjacent to the verb, is adjoined to the
right of V'. This expectation would be correct if Heavy-NP-shift is analyzed as
an instance of Chomsky-adjoining heavy NP's to the right of V'. In similar
fashion, free inversion of the subject in PRO-drop languages may be taken to be an
instance of Chomsky adjunction of the subject NP to V', resulting in a configuration in which the inverted subject is governed by the verb.

There is still another alternative approach to account for the non-adjacency
of the verb and its object found in Dutch. It might be claimed that the adjacency
requirement is met at S-structure, but that the linear order is changed by rules
of scrambling applying in the left-hand component of the grammar. Suggestions to
this effect have been made in the literature quite frequently. This approach
strikes me as rather unsatisfactory, however, in that the phenomenon is basically
dismissed as irrelevant as long as no concrete and testable proposals are put
forward concerning the properties of these so-called rules of scrambling. Moreover, it appears to be the case that the hypothesis that the order of objects and
adjuncts is permuted by means of rules of scrambling makes a number of incorrect
predictions. Consider the following examples.

(168) a. dat hij **de kinderen** aan **elkaars** ouders toevertrouwt
         that he the children to each others parents trusts

      b.*dat hij aan **elkaars** ouders **de kinderen** toevertrouwt

(169) a. dat hij **de gasten dronken** weg bracht[45]
         that he the guests drunk away brought

      b.*dat hij **dronken de gasten** weg bracht

(170) a. dat ik **die mensen** met **elkaars** hamers heb vermoord
         that I those people with each others hammers have murdered

      b.*dat ik met **elkaars** hamers **die mensen** heb vermoord

(see Hoekstra 1981a,1981b for discussion). What these examples illustrate is that
the relative ordering of the object and an adjunct (adverbial adjuncts in the
examples (168) and (170), a predicative adjunct in example (169)) determines
possible construals, in the a. and c. cases a binding relation, in the b. case a
control relation. These construals are accounted for by the theory of binding and

the theory of control. There are two possibilities. Either these theories apply at the level of LF or they apply at S-structure. Under the first option, the judgements in (168)-(170) cannot be accounted for since the construal rules and the scrambling rules are insensitive to each other, as they apply in different components of the system. Under the second option, the rules of scrambling could be made sensitive to construals established at S-structure, but that would require at least that a theory of scrambling rules is formulated that can account for this sensitivity. In the absence of such a theory, relegating these observations to the left-hand component of the grammar is mere handwaving. Moreover, the adjunction analysis proposed above is available anyway.

It was noted above that the adjunction of the NP object to a structurally higher position has the same effect as the rule of NP-placement proposed by De Haan (1979:58 ff.). The arguments that De Haan adduces in support of his rule carry over to the present proposal, therefore. An interesting piece of evidence put forward in De Haan will be repeated here. It is argued in Verhagen (1979) that a certain class of adverbs attach to focus, or put differently, determine which part of the sentence is interpreted as the focus. So, in (171) the italicized portion is the focus of the sentence as it follows the adverb **waarschijnlijk** (probably), which is a member of the relevant class of adverbs. Adjunction of the object to the left of **waarschijnlijk** has the effect of extracting the object from the focus. This is demonstrated by the data in (172). The PP in postverbal position is linked to the NP in preverbal position by the rule Linking to Focus, proposed by Guéron (1980). Since the NP **de fiets** is not part of the focus in (172b) because it precedes the adverb **waarschijnlijk,** the PP in postverbal position cannot be linked to it. Hence the sentence is illformed.

(171) a. dat Harry waarschijnlijk **de fiets met het vlaggetje**
         heeft gekocht
         that Harry probably   the bicycle with the flag
         has   bought

      b. dat Harry de fiets met het vlaggetje waarschijnlijk
         heeft gekocht

(172) a. dat Harry waarschijnlijk **de fiets heeft gekocht**
         met het vlaggetje
      b.*dat Harry de fiets waarschijnlijk **heeft gekocht**
         met het vlaggetje

These data illustrate the same point as made above, i.e. the rule of focus assignment is part of the derivation from S-structure to LF, therefore, the ordering difference in (171)-(172) cannot result from the application of scrambling rules in the left-hand component of the grammar.

Let us now return to the difference between verbs and prepositions that we mentioned at the beginning of this subsection, viz. that the object is always adjacent to P but not to V. We are now in a position to explain this difference. Accepting Stowell's adjacency requirement, I have argued that instances of apparent violations of this requirement in the case of the verb and its object can be explained by assuming that an operator-variable relation is created by adjoining the NP object to a higher position. The chain that is created receives Case via the empty category that is adjacent to the verb as required. If the hypothesis that prepositions do not license empty categories is true, the reason why there no apparent violations of adjacency in the case of PP is evident: the empty category left behind by MOVE α violates the ECP.

More problematic within the present theory is the occurrence of NP complements to adjectives. According to the theory of Case, only the [-N] categories Verb and Preposition are able to assign Case. Therefore, it is predicted that no NP's are found in the complement of adjectives. This problem has been discussed for German by Van Riemsdijk (1981a). I shall adopt his proposal for the situation in Dutch, noting, however, that the phenomenon seems to be much more restricted in Dutch than it is in German. It was also more widely distributed in Middle Dutch. As in present-day German, the NP complements are marked with genitive or dative Case in Middle Dutch. These morphological Cases are typically inherent rather than structural Cases, the choice being determined by semantic parameters. The fact that the range of adjectives taking NP complements has become more limited in modern Dutch is obviously related to the loss of a viable morphological Case system. Stoett (1923) mentions many adjectives that are constructed with a PP complement in modern Dutch, but with a genitive NP in Middle Dutch. In later stages of Middle Dutch, these complements are sometimes also marked with accusative rather than genitive Case, indicating that the loss of Case had already started by that time. Apparently, NP complements to adjectives in Modern Dutch are to be considered remnants of this earlier period. The phenomenon does not seem to be productive in Modern Dutch.

As for its relative position within AP, the NP seems to have a mobility that is similar to that of NP complement to verbs. It obligatorily precedes the head, which follows from the hypothesis that [+V] categories govern to the left. It need not be adjacent to the adjectival head, however. As in the case of verb

phrases, the head and the NP complement may be separated by optional material.
Consider the following examples.

(173) a. dat hij geheel en al de stad meester was
         that he completely   the town master-of was

      b. dat hij de stad geheel en al meester was

(174) a. dat hij waarschijnlijk zijn werk zat was
         that he probably his work weary-of was

      b. dat hij zijn werk waarschijnlijk zat was

This permutability may be analyzed along the same lines as in the case of the
object of V. It is remarkable, however, that with some specifiers, the NP
complement is obligatorily separated from the head by the specifier, contrary to
the predictions made by the adjacency requirement. A speculation might be that
the adjacency requirement is relevant only for the assignment of structural Case
and not for inherent Case. The following examples illustrate this situation.

(175) a.*dat hij erg zijn werk zat was
         that he very his work weary-of was

      b. dat hij zijn werk erg zat was

(176) a.*dat hij meer dan dat geroddel beu was
         that he more than that gossipping tired-of was

      b. dat hij dat geroddel meer dan beu was

According to Van Riemsdijk (1981a), this is the normal situation in German: the
complement has to occur in a position which is peripheral to the specifier. I have
no explanation to offer for this situation.

    This ends our discussion of the distribution of NP's. I am well aware of the
fact that many issues have been left untouched in the preceding discussion. At
the same time, however, I think that the most central questions have been dealt
with.

    At the end of this chapter, some attention will be paid to the distribution of

AP's. It was already mentioned that adjectives do not take AP complements, a fact that is explained by the Unlike Category Condition. An AP can be a complement to verbs and to the preposition **met**. Starting with the latter, we note that AP's cannot occur in the complement of prepositions in general. Examples of an AP complement to the preposition **met** are found in (177).

(177) a. Met je mond open (zie je er dom uit)
             With your mouth open (you look dumb)

        b. Met de helft van de ploeg dronken (arriveerden we in ons dorp)
             With the half of the team drunk   (we arrived in our village)

The absolute **met**-construction is discussed in Beukema & Hoekstra (1983a). It is argued there that the structure of such constructions is as in (178).

(178)

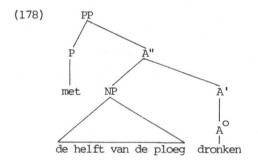

According to this analysis, the subject of the small-clause AP receives Case from the preposition **met**. This is corroborated by the absolute **mit**-construction in German where the subject of the AP receives dative Case, the Case that is governed by **mit**. In order to be able to assign Case to this subject, the preposition must be able to govern across a maximal projection boundary, a property that is not general for prepositions. It must be concluded, therefore, that **met** in Dutch is exceptional in possessing the property of being a structural governor. For further discussion of these constructions, the reader is referred to Beukema & Hoekstra (1983a).

Given the fact that an outside governor for the subject of AP's is required, it is expected that AP's can be a complement to the category verb only, which is indeed the case, pace the absolute **met**-construction. An analysis of these AP complements will be deferred until we have had occasion to go more deeply into the analysis of small clauses in chapter 4.

Apart from functioning as complements, AP's are found as specifiers of nouns and as predicative adjuncts. Attributive AP's obligatorily precede the noun, but follow determiners and numerals, as is the characteristic order in NP's in SOV languages according to Greenberg (1963). Predicative adjunct AP's have more or less the same positional possibilities in Dutch as adverbial adjuncts, i.e. they may precede or follow the object as long as they precede the verb.

Attributive AP's usually precede the noun in English as well. Stowell (1981: 282 ff.) proposes to account for this obligatory position by assuming that rules of word formation are responsible for this ordering, rather than rules of syntax. He suggests several pieces of evidence for this rather remarkable position. First, he mentions the well-known fact that complex AP's tend to follow the modified noun, rather than precede it. To the extent that only simple adjectives may precede the noun, then, the ordering of specifiers within NP could be accounted for by the stipulation that the head of NP occurs in initial position, just like the head of other categories in English. The prenominal adjectives constitute an exception to this stipulation, but this exception would only be apparent if the prenominal adjective is in fact part of the noun, attached to it by means of rules of word formation. As a second piece of evidence, Stowell adduces the fact that strings of adjectives in prenominal position tend to occur in a fixed order. He suggests that this parallels the fixed ordering of clitics to verbal stems in the Romance languages, which he assumes to derive from rules of word formation as well [46].

There are several problems with this approach, however. Some of these are pointed out by Stowell himself. First of all, multiple modification by adjectives would require that the relevant rules of word formation can apply to their own output, thus creating words of infinite length. This is a rather unattractive feature of the proposed analysis. Secondly, the stress pattern of normal adjective-noun combinations in phrase structure differs from the stress pattern in true adjective-noun compounds, cf.:

(179) a. The White House
      b. a white house

Stowell dismisses these data as irrelevant, by stating that "it is known that various morphological affixes have idiosyncratic effects on stress". Although this is true, it should be noticed that in the case under discussion the difference in stress pattern is not introduced by different 'affixes', but rather by one and the same form. In the absence of a concrete and specific proposal, this argument cannot be taken seriously. The most serious problem with his analysis is not mentioned by Stowell. Whereas it is certainly true that adjectives tend to follow the noun when they are combined with a complement, it is not true that complex AP's that are complex due to left recursion have to follow the noun. If the adjective is modified by an adverb, the AP may occur in prenominal position, as in "a very big man". A consequence of Stowell's proposal would be that **very,** an adverb, is analyzed as modifying a noun, albeit a complex noun. This is a rather unnatural situation.

What this last problem shows is that the reason for the prohibition of complex AP's in prenominal position is not directly related to its complexity per se, but rather by the fact that this complexity is due to right recursion. This prohibition follows from the Head Final Filter proposed in Williams (1982). This filter is discussed in section 3.3.3.1. below. The filter states that the head of AP that occurs in prenominal position must occur in final position. Because complements of adjectives obligatorily follow the head, there is a conflicting set of requirements, which precludes a complex AP in prenominal position.

The situation in Dutch differs from English in only one respect: since most complements of adjectives in Dutch may precede the adjective, no conflict arises with the Head Final Filter. Therefore, not only simple AP's precede the noun that they modify, but the same is true for complex AP's. The only adjectives that cannot occur in prenominal position with a complement are those adjectives that exceptionally take an obligatory complement to their right. An example is the adjective **dol** in the sense of 'fond', as is illustrated with the following example.

(180) a. (dat Jan) dol op kinderen (is)
        that John fond of children is
    b.*(dat Jan) op kinderen dol (is)
    c.*een op kinderen dolle man
      a of children fond man
    d.*een dolle op kinderen man

What this means is that the relative position of specifiers of the category N depends on the category of the specifier: postnominal if the specifier is a PP or an S', prenominal if it is an AP.

In the case of the category verb, this categorial asymmetry was accounted for in terms of the requirement that NP's must receive Case, unlike PP's, whereas clausal complements are not allowed in preverbal position due to the UCC. What we should find out, then, is whether AP's have a property comparable to the property of requiring Case that NP's have, in terms of which their distribution can be explained. Stowell (1981:142) claims that such a property does exist, viz. that AP's require Case just like NP's. How this Case requirement fits in with the adjacency requirement is not discussed by Stowell. In any event, constructions with an AP following an NP would be rather problematic if both constituents require Case and if Case assignment is subject to adjacency. This seems to be an immediate problem for which I do not see a solution. Whereas it is not exceptional for adjectives to exhibit Case paradigms, this Case is generally determined by agreement with an NP rather than by direct assignment by some Case assigning category (e.g. a verb). Stowell cites the instrumental Case that is assigned to predicative AP's in Russian, but it seems to me that this is the exception rather than the rule. I want to suggest, therefore, that the property that we are looking for is agreement rather than Case assignment. If we look upon Case assignment as an identificational strategy for the NP to which the Case is assigned, as we have done throughout, it makes sense to assume that agreement of adjectives is the analogue of Case assignment to NP's, i.e. AP's are identified as related to a particular NP in terms of agreement. Speculating further along these lines, we might assume that agreement is a relation that falls under the theory of government as well. Both the theory of Case assignment and of agreement would then fall under the same formal theory.

It is evident that the fact that predicative adjuncts must precede the verb, falls out as a consequence from the hypothesis that the AP must be governed. If we continue along this line, the obligatory prenominal occurrence of attributive AP's would be accounted for if the AP must be governed by the noun it modifies in order to be identified by agreement. This would require that nouns govern to the left. Earlier we suggested that the orientation of government for various categories is subject to an evaluation metric that assigns a higher markedness value to some distributions than to others. If it is possible to draw any conclusions from quantitative data, i.e. if we may assume that an option is less marked when found in the majority of languages, the data in Greenberg (1963) indicate that the cooccurrence of Adj-N and OV ordering is the unmarked choice. From this perspective, Dutch falls nicely into place. The fact that English is somewhat indeterminate with respect to the position of attributive AP's fits in with the general change from OV to VO where English has developed much farther than Dutch and German, but not as far as French and Spanish where attributive AP's usually follow the noun.

At present I have nothing more to offer on the distribution of AP's. As I

already announced, a full discussion of some issues concerning AP's is deferred
until chapter 3, specifically a discussion of predicative complement AP's and the
internal structure of AP's with respect to the Head Final Filter.

2.8. Concluding remarks

In this chapter I have presented an overview of the basic principles of the theory
of Government and Binding, suggesting a number of modifications along the way.
Specifically, I have argued that the ECP can be reduced to the requirement that
empty categories are properly governed by a lexical governor, thus dispensing
with the option of licensing empty categories by a local antecedent. The requirement of a local antecedent for traces in general, i.e. for both NP movement traces
and WH- movement traces, follows from the Binding Theory, which was generalized
from a theory of A-binding to a theory of A and A'- binding along the lines of
Aoun's proposal. Aoun's further suggestion that WH-movement traces are not only
subject to the binding requirement of anaphors but also to the binding requirement for names was argued to be unnecessary, since the requirement that variables
are A-free follows independently from the θ-criterion and the Projection Principle. In order to subsume A'-binding under the binding requirement for anaphors,
it was necessary to change the definition of accessible SUBJECT slightly, a
change that is motivated independently. It could then be argued that the principle of Subjacency could be dispensed with because most of its empirical content
follows from the ECP and the Binding Theory. A number of problems that were
problems for Subjacency as well remain, however.

I suggested that these problems might be solved by pragmatic rather than
syntactic principles. Against the background of the principles of GB-theory as
discussed in the first subsections of this chapter, the ordering of complements
in Dutch was investigated. Stowell's approach that this ordering is not explained
by PS-rules and that therefore other principles are needed for the distribution
of phrases was adopted. One of the principles proposed in the preceding discussion is the Unlike Category Condition. Another hypothesis that plays a central
role in the account of the distribution of the major phrase types is the notion of
asymmetric government. In combination, these two hypotheses account for a vast
range of facts, some of which are rather subtle.

The next chapter is devoted to a discussion of passives, ergatives and the analysis of small clauses. In the preceding discussion, we were forced to anticipate the analyses to be presented in the next section on a number of occasions. This might have led to some confusion or scepticism with respect to the analyses in the present chapter, which I hope will be cleared away as we proceed.

Chapter 3

The Nature of Transitivity

3.1. Introduction

Although this chapter is concerned with the nature of transitivity, a large part of it is devoted to passive constructions and the various analyses of these constructions within different frameworks. The motivation for this is that a comparison of different points of view gives us a clear picture of the essential properties of the constructionS on the one hand, while the properties of these various frameworks can be compared on the other hand. In section 3.2. a historical review of the various analyses is presented. Four major different conceptions of the phenomenon of passive can be distinguished. First of all, the transformational analysis proposed within the Standard Theory (Chomsky 1965) and the changes that this analysis has undergone in the course of the development of generative theory. A discussion of the passive analysis within GB-theory will be deferred until section 3.3. More or less as an alternative within the Extended Standard Theory (EST), a lexical analysis of the passive was developed which is also discussed below. The third analysis that we discuss is the so-called phrasal analysis defended in Bach (1980) and adopted by others working within the tradition of Montague Grammar and closely related frameworks. Historically, a fourth analysis was developed before the phrasal analysis, viz. the analysis within the framework of Relational Grammar. A discussion of the Relational Grammar approach is presented after the discussion of this phrasal analysis to get a better correspondence with section 3.3., where we shall extend the scope of our discussion beyond the passive phenomenon.

Section 3.4. is the core of the third chapter. On the basis of the analyses in that section, a different conception of transitivity is proposed and it is demonstrated that this leads to a classification of verbs that is superior to the traditional one. It is argued that the passive construction is a manifestation of a more general phenomenon. Various empirical problems in the grammar of Dutch will be shown to find straightforward solutions within the conception that is proposed below.

3.2. The passive: a historical survey of different approaches.

3.2.1. The transformational analysis

The passive construction has played a prominent role in the development of generative grammar. In this section, this historical development will be reviewed in order to make the essential characteristics of the passive construction stand out more clearly. The passive construction constituted one of the motivations for the level of transformations in the model proposed in Chomsky (1957). It was argued there that it is impossible for a context-sensitive rewriting system to introduce the subclass of transitive verbs in both active and passive construc- tions by means of a single rule. Consequently, two distinct rules would be needed to introduce one and the same formative, e.g. the formative **use** in two different constructions, thereby missing the generalization that the selectional proper- ties of these two formatives **use** are in fact identical and the subcategorizatio- nal properties predictably different. In order to capture this generalization, the analysis of passive sentences is mapped out into two different structures, related to each other by means of the level T, i.e. the transformational compo- nent. At one level, passive sentences are represented as structures which are similar to actives. If the introduction of the relevant formatives is to take place at this level, the same context-sensitive rule can introduce them in structures leading to both active sentences and passive sentences. Since the entities to be related by means of level T are full sentential syntactic structu- res, the function that relates these entities must of course be formulated in structural terms as well, and the function has to apply to sentential structures.

As Heny (1979) notes in his review of **The Logical Structure of Linguistic Theory**, LSLT (Chomsky 1955), the kind of motivation for the passive transforma- tion crucially depends on the nature of the assumptions about the organization of the grammar made in LSLT, more specifically, on the assumption that formatives are introduced by means of the same rules that generate hierarchical structures.

This conception of the grammar, which undoubtedly was heavily influenced by the prevalent distributionalism of the time, drastically changed with the innovations in **Aspects** (Chomsky 1965) in which the task of the PS-system of the LSLT-model was divided over two subcomponents, a set of context-free rewriting rules which generates syntactic deep structures and a lexicon in which all lexical items are listed with a full representation of their unpredictable features. The operation of introducing formatives into syntactic phrase structures is no longer performed by the PS-rules, but by a general insertion procedure. Of the two variants considered in **Aspects,** the transformational procedure became generally adopted. In order for this transformational procedure to function properly, lexical items are provided with a context specification in their feature set. This context specification functions as the structural index of the transformational insertion operation that must enter the item in question.

Given this new conception of the grammar, it is far from self-evident that, since it was based on a different conception, the original motivation for the passive transformation carries over to this new theory. However, the level of transformations seemed to be included in the **Aspects** framework "as if by nature" (Heny 1979). This might in part be due to the inclusion of a semantic component in **Aspects** and the Katz-Postal law that derived from the organization of the grammar[47] : because passives were assumed to be semantically identical to their corresponding actives, they ought to be derived from the same deep structure.

A more prominent motivation for maintaining the passive transformation might have been the assumption that each lexical item is associated with only a single structural index for the context into which it can be entered. As far as I am aware, this assumption has never been explicitly justified in the literature, but it undoubtedly served as a working hypothesis for much of the work within generative grammar. This should not cause much surprise given the methodological priority attributed to transformational explanations (cf. Newmeyer 1980). Upon closer scrutiny, however, it is very clear that the principle of a single subcategorization feature is not and cannot always be fully adhered to. To see this, let us examine Chomsky's remarks on the passive in **Aspects.** He argues that the passive transformation is restricted to verbs that allow a manner adverbial (p. 103-104) and the manner adverbial with these verbs is optional (p.166 ff). Passive is sometimes prohibited (e.g. with **resemble, cost, weigh),** sometimes it is obligatory (e.g. with **allege, rumour),** but generally it is optional. This three-way distinction can be expressed in the lexicon on the assumption that passive is obligatorily triggered if a **by**-phrase, as an expansion of Manner, is present in deep structure. Verbs like **allege** should then be subcategorized for an

obligatory **by**-phrase, whereas the option of a **by**-phrase should be excluded from
the subcategorizational feature of verbs like **resemble**[48]. The main group of
transitive verbs takes an optional Manner adverbial, thus accounting for the
optionality of passive with these verbs. This optionality is expressed by means
of a syntactic redundancy rule of the form [+ -- Manner]-> [+ ---]. Note that
this redundancy device merely says that for any element X to be associated with
a structural index P, it will be the case that X is also associated with a
structural index Q; which is to say that X is associated with two distinct
subcategorization features. Since such a redundancy function is in fact a
mapping of one structural index onto another -by deletion in this case- it a
formally a transformational operation[49].

As Heny (1979) points out, the possibility of stating relations between
subcategorization frames in the lexicon basically undercuts the arguments for the
need of the level T in Chomsky (1957) based on passivization. One can only wonder
why this possibility was not exploited to the full at that time.

Chomsky's use of base-generated receptacle positions for the postposing of
the subject NP in his analysis in **Aspects** is in fact a prelude to Emonds' theory
of structure preservation (Emonds 1969,1976). Emonds observed that the derived P-
marker of passives could be accounted for in terms of substitution transformations. Ultimately, this insight enlarged the explanatory role of the Base Component. If it is assumed that the postposing part of the passive rule is in fact a
substitution operation for an NP contained in a base-generated PP-position, it is
explained e.g. why the passive **by**-phrase follows all NP's and AP's within VP, but
precedes all sentential complements. Even though Emonds' theory was successful in
capturing a fair number of generalizations, the question is whether it can be
derived from more basic principles of the grammar or whether it should be taken as
a primitive concept of the theory as a whole. It is obvious that the former is the
most desirable. First of all, the structure-preservation requirement leans on the
specific PS-rules that a language happens to have, but it is not clear why a
specific language has that set of PS-rules in the first place. Secondly, if
transformations are defined as structure-changing rather than structure-genera-
ting operations, why should they preserve structure rather than change it?
Thirdly, if a major group of transformations must observe the structure-preservation requirement, why should there be a class of root transformations that do
change structure? Some of the discussion below is contingent on these questions,
which I think are of great importance.

The analyses mentioned so far all regard the passive process as a monolithic
operation that is only involved in the derivation of passive sentences. This

construction-specific approach to transformations was abandoned, which ultimately led to the formulation MOVE α, under which the relevant aspect of the passive
process is subsumed. We shall proceed by surveying the relevant steps that have
led to this result.

The first step was the generalization of passive over both verbal and nominal
structures in Chomsky (1970), a consequence of the lexicalist hypothesis. The
NP's of the type in (1b) used to be derived from the sentential structure in (2b)
by means of a nominalization transformation, applying to a passive structure,
while it applies to an active structure like (2a) to derive a nominal construction like (1a) from it.

(1) a. the enemy's destruction of the city
    b. the city's destruction by the enemy

(2) a. the enemy destroyed the city
    b. the city was destroyed by the enemy

Notice at this point that Chomsky's argumentation in **Remarks on Nominalization** is
flawed in at least one respect. One of his arguments against a transformational
treatment of derived nominals like (1) is that there are no derived nominals
corresponding to transformationally derived structures. As an example he cites
the well-known opposition between (3a) and (3b), where (3a) would be a nominalization of (4a), which is derived by **tough-**movement from a structure underlying
(4b), whereas (3b) is a nominalization of a transformationally non-derived
structure, like (5a).

(3) a.*John's easiness to please
    b. John's eagerness to please

(4) a. John is easy to please
    b. It is easy to please John

(5) a. John is eager to please
    b.*It is eager to please John

The fact that we do not find nominalizations of transforms is an accident if
nominalization is a transformational operation. If, on the other hand, nominalizations are derived from their corresponding verbs in the lexicon, their absence

is explained by the organization of the grammar. This line of argumentation gave rise to the so-called feeding criterion for the status of lexical rules (cf. Wasow 1977). The argument is without force, however. Notice first of all that "the easiness to please John", which could be a nominalization of (4b),is equally ungrammatical, suggesting that the reason for the ungrammaticality of (3a) might be something else. But more important, the argument is misleading, since after having established a lexical theory of nominalization, Chomsky argues that transformations must be generalized to apply crosscategorially, so as to allow passive to apply both to (1a) and (2a) to derive (1b) and (2b), respectively. This led to the introduction of the feature theory of categories. However, (1b) might also be construed as an example of a nominalization of a derived structure, i.e. if (1b) is not considered to be derived from (1a), but rather from (2b).

However, although the argumentation may be called misleading, I think Chomsky's conclusions are correct. Now that the passive process was taken to generalize over both verbal and nominal constructions, the process had to be split up into two steps, Agent Postposing and Object Preposing, since the latter is optional in nominal structures to which the former has applied as in e.g. "the destruction of the city by the enemy".

A brief digression is in order here. Notice that there is a remarkable difference between the possibilities of 'Object' Preposing in verbal structures and corresponding nominal structures with respect to the scope of application. Later, it will be seen that 'Object' Preposing is impossible with small-clause complements and Exceptional Case-Marking constructions. Here, we will limit ourselves to the difference with respect to so-called pseudopassives as is illustrated by the following examples.

(6) a. the desired result was arrived at
    b. the war was prayed for by the military industrials
    c. these children were cared for by a machine

(7) a.*the desired result's arrival at
    b *the war's prayer for by the military industrials
    c.*the children's care for by a machine

This asymmetry between passivization in verbal and nominal structures does not discredit a generalized rule of passivization, however. The existence of pseudopassives in English may be taken to be a rather marked phenomenon. In most languages, preposition stranding by means of NP movement is not allowed, as duly noted by Van Riemsdijk (1978a). The possibility of preposition stranding in English may be taken to result from a marked process, e.g. the process of reanalysis as proposed by Hornstein & Weinberg (1981) which rebrackets the string so as to incorporate the preposition into the verb. The complement of the preposition then becomes a bare NP to this newly created verbal complex and is hence eligible to be moved into subject position. No such reanalysis is possible with other categories, i.e. nouns and adjectives, thus accounting for the ungrammaticality of the examples in (7). In Dutch, pseudo-passives like in (6) are impossible, a difference with English that may be related to the positional difference of the verb, if linear adjacency is a condition on reanalysis processes like the one proposed by Hornstein & Weinberg. Kayne (1981c) has proposed an alternative theory of preposition stranding, which not only accounts for the absence of preposition stranding in Dutch, but also in French where the order of heads and complements is the same as in English. A potential counterargument to this reanalysis proposal or to any alternative that seeks to explain the contrast between (6) and (7) might be derived from the well-formed examples in (8).

(8) a. a never thought-of solution
    b. the badly cared-for children

However, we shall stick to the assumption that the process or principle that makes preposition stranding possible is limited to verbal structures, and take the discussion of the examples in (8) up later.

A second difference between nominal and verbal passives is noted in Fiengo (1981). The examples in (9) and (10) show that Object Preposing is more general in verbal structures.

(9) a. This emotion was expressed by John with great precision
    b. Carthage was attacked by Rome

(10) a.*This emotion's expression by John
     b.*Carthage's attack by Rome

According to Fiengo (1981:45 ff.) the difference in grammaticality between (9) and (10) might be accounted for by assuming that in the usual case the preposition **of** in derived nominals is inserted transformationally, as suggested in Chomsky (1970), whereas the head noun would be subcategorized to take a PP complement in the cases in (10). Under this assumption, the reason for the impossibility of these examples could be the same as for the examples in (7)[50].

Let us return to the main theme. How can we account for the difference in applicability of object preposing in nominal and verbal structures, optional in the former but obligatory in the latter? An answer to this question was provided by the introduction of trace theory (Fiengo 1974, Chomsky 1975). It is assumed that empty categories created by movement are retained in derived structure, a consequence of the hypothesis of structure preservation, and provided with an index identical to the category that formerly occupied the empty position. These indexed empty categories are interpreted as anaphors, i.e. according to this definition of empty categories, movement rules become constrained by the conditions on antecedent anaphor relations. A general property of antecedents is that they must be structurally superior to their anaphors, i.e. c-command them (cf. Reinhart 1976). In accordance with these assumptions, a trace left behind by the application of Agent Postposing would result in a structure that violates this condition on antecedent-anaphor relations, since a trace in subject position is structurally superior to the antecedent. Therefore, in order to arrive at a grammatical output, the trace must be eliminated. According to Fiengo (1974), the obligatory effect of Object Preposing in verbal structures derives from this need to eliminate the improperly bound trace left behind in the subject position by the application of Agent Postposing. The fact that Object Preposing is optional in nominal structures is accounted for by assuming that the improperly bound trace can be eliminated in an alternative way within NP's, namely by a rule called Determiner Spell Out. This rule is restricted to apply in NP's. (See Dresher & Hornstein 1979 for a more general discussion of trace erasure).

It soon became clear that the operation of trace elimination basically undercuts the arguments to have a rule of Agent Postposing at all. If semantic interpretation is done at the level of S-Structure, and if the trace left behind by Agent Postposing may never occur in this representation, there is no reason why Agent Postposing should be applied at all. Moreover, the deletion of the trace essentially constitutes an irrecoverable deletion. Therefore, the thematic role associated with the syntactic subject in active sentences must also be interpretable in the **by**-phrase directly. Hence, it was concluded that there is no rule of Agent Postposing at all, and that consequently, the thematic subject is base-generated in the **by**-phrase.

In conclusion, we see that the transformational operation involved in the generation of passive sentences is limited to the preposing of the object, an operation that may apply both in verbal and nominal structures. The name of this operation, viz. Object Preposing, still suggests that an element is involved in this operation which is essential for passives i.e. an object. However, in standard analyses of passive constructions it is assumed that not only objects of the passivized verb are preposed, but also non-objects, like the subject of a tenseless embedded clause. This point is important with respect to the much debated issue of the existence of a rule of subject to object raising, extensively argued for by Postal (1974). What is at stake in this discussion is not so much the existence of this particular rule, but rather the question of whether passive is correctly characterized as a clause-internal operation, or still more generally, whether linguistic theory should provide the possibility of a distinction between clause-internal and intraclausal rules, possibly among other types. Such a classification of rule types used to be generally adopted and still is adopted within the framework of Relational Grammar, as we shall see below. If the characterization of passive as a clause-internal rule is correct, passives of the type in (11) would indeed require a rule that makes the embedded subject a constituent of the matrix clause, in this case the object.

(11) The commies are believed to be the cause of all troubles

Chomsky's (1973) position is that all transformational rules are unbounded, the bounded effects of specific rules being derived from the imposition of conditions on rule applicability such as the Specified Subject Condition (SSC) and the Tensed-S-Constraint (TSC). In the case of (11), these restrictions would not prevent the embedded subject in underlying structure from being raised in a single step to the matrix subject position. If this is true, the term Object Preposing to refer to the process relevant in the derivation of passives is misleading. It was consequently replaced by NP-movement.

This step opens up the possibility of abandoning the construction-specific approach to passive. The operation of NP-movement can be identified with the operation involved in the derivation of subject-raising constructions, which are exemplified in (12).

(12) a. It seems that John has left
     b. John seems to have left

Ultimately, then, the transformational contribution in the account of the relation between active and passive constructions is reduced to the application of MOVE NP, which in turn is an instance of the general schema to which the core of the transformational component is reduced, MOVE α, in which α is a category.

Other information relevant for the proper functioning of the rule is provided by other principles of the grammar, as our survey above has indicated. The theory of structure preservation and the prohibition of irrecoverable deletions ensure that the landing site of MOVE NP is an empty NP position. Trace theory ensures that the effect of MOVE NP is upgrading, the distance between the landing and the extraction site of the operation being constrained by general conditions on rule applicability or more specifically, by conditions on possible antecedent–anaphor relations.

It may have been noticed that by eliminating the rule of Agent Postposing, we are left without an explanation of the obligatory effect of Object Preposing in verbal passive structures. It has been suggested that something like the empty node filter in the sense of Emonds (1969,1976), which filters out all derived structures that contain empty nodes which have been empty throughout the derivation. This does not explain, however, why the empty subject position cannot be filled with a pleonastic element like **it**. This matter will be taken up again in section 3.3.3.

This concludes our review of the transformational theory of passivization up to 1978.

3.2.2. The lexical analysis.

Chomsky's (1970) Lexicalist Hypothesis that word formation should be handled in the lexicon gave rise to a lexical analysis of passivization, or rather to a number of lexical analyses. Freidin (1975) argues for the lexical nature of passivization by making use of the hypothesis that transformations are unable to change node labels. His basic assumption is that passive participles are adjectives, derived from verbs. The rule to derive these adjectives must therefore be lexical.

This argument is discussed in Wasow's study of the demarcation problem between the lexicon and the syntactic component (Wasow 1977). He tries to draw a dividing line between the domains of the two components by collecting a number of distinguishing criteria that occur in the literature, either implicitly or explicitly.

The first of these criteria relates to Freidin's (1975) claim that transformations are not allowed to change node labels. The second criterion involves the

structure- preservation requirement. Lexical rules are trivially structure preserving in the sense that the contextual property of an item derived by means of a
lexical rule necessarily satisfies the phrase structure of the category to which
it belongs. However, Wasow constructs this criterion as necessary for lexical
rules, but not as sufficient. As for passive, then, this criterion is of no help
in deciding between a lexical or a transformational derivation as the operation
is clearly structure preserving. Wasow's third criterion is the feeding criterion
that has already been mentioned above. In one direction, this criterion states
that lexical rules may not be fed by transformations. The feeding criterion is
very powerful since it can only be countered by giving up certain basic assumptions about the organization of the grammar as a whole. Brame (1975) shows how
powerful such an argument can be by demonstrating that if Equi-NP-Deletion (or
its interpretive variant) is abandoned, a whole range of other transformations
must be given up as well. Wasow observes that there are only two transformations
within the EST tradition that are assumed to feed the passive rule, both of which
having a questionable status. The first is the alleged rule of Raising to Object
mentioned above, the other Dative Movement (cf. Emonds 1972, Jackendoff & Culicover 1971), which was argued by Oehrle (1976) not to exist. Oehrle proposes that
the relationship between the two different contexts in which the relevant class
of verbs that exhibit the dative alternation may appear must be stated in the
lexicon as a rule relating two different subcategorization features in the way
that we discussed above in relation to the redundancy rule for Manner in **Aspects**.
The feeding criterion also works in the other direction. If some rule, of which
the status is unclear, can be argued to feed another rule which is undisputably
lexical, the rule must be lexical as well. This direction of the feeding criterion is exploited by Bresnan (1978) in order to argue for the lexical nature of
not only passivization, but also of unspecified object deletion and medio-
passivization (alternatively called middle formation). Restricting ourselves to
passivization, we cite the following examples.

(13) a. Our products are untouched by human hands
     b. Antarctica is uninhabited by men

It is a general assumption within the EST-tradition that word-formation rules
belong to the lexicon (cf. Jackendoff 1975, Aronoff 1976). This is certainly true
for the rule of **un**-prefixation (cf. Aronoff 1976:70). The examples in (13) are
put forward by Bresnan (1978) to illustrate that the rule of passivization stands
in a feeding relation to the rule of **un**-prefixation, which shows that passiviza-

tion must be lexical as well. Bresnan's argument for the lexical status of passivization is not without problems, however. It is generally assumed that, apart from the passive rule, there is a word-formation rule that forms adjectives that are formally identical to participles (cf. Wasow 1977,1980, Williams 1981a). What is needed therefore, is some principled way to determine the relation between this adjective-formation rule and the rule of passivization. We shall return to this matter in section 3.3.3.1. It should be noted that the problem with the examples in (8), repeated here, is related to this issue.

(8) a. a never thought-of solution
    b. the badly cared-for children

A fourth criterion in Wasow's list involves the possibility of having exceptions: lexical rules may, but transformational rules may not have exceptions. If lexical rules are regarded as redundancy functions over a fully specified lexicon, as argued by Jackendoff (1975), the fact that there is no corresponding output to each suitable input requires no further explanation. It is not clear how a transformational rule could be made sensitive to exception features in the lexical representations of scattered members of a particular category. Restrictive theories of the transformational component, e.g. Lasnik & Kupin (1976) do not allow for it at any rate. From the point of view of language acquisition, it seems to be very implausible to assume that such exception features are acquired, as this would need negative evidence which is unavailable to the language learner. Moreover, given the reduction of passive to an instance of MOVE α, it is hard to see how the process could be made sensitive to an exception feature in the lexical representation of an item that is not even mentioned in the structural description of the rule. It is of course possible to impose lexical restrictions in a different way, e.g. in the framework of GB-theory this can be done in terms of exceptional prohibition of Case assignment etc. In general, however, the criterion of having exceptions seems sensible (cf. Baker 1979).

We now turn to Wasow's final criterion and investigate its impact. This criterion has to do with the blindness of transformational operations. Lexical rules are bounded in the sense that they may only manipulate material contained in the lexical representations of the items to which the lexical rule applies. The localness criterion plays a prominent role in the discussion of the status of passivization. Wasow rationalizes this criterion in the following way.

"In trying to make fully precise the property of "localness" that should

characterize lexical rules, one rather strong hypothesis to put forward is
that the only elements of a verb's environment that may enter into the
statement of lexical redundancy rules are the NP's bearing deep structure
grammatical relations to it (viz. subject, direct object, indirect object).
In an intuitive sense that is hard to pin down, these NP's are the elements of
a verb's environment most closely associated with it. There can be little
doubt that they must enter into the statement of contextual features; indeed,
informal statements of both selectional restrictions and strict subcategorization are typically formulated in terms of these relations .... Thus, I
claim that a natural way of stating the "localness" property of lexical rules
is to insist that they be "relational" in this sense. I assume that transformations, in contrast, are defined in the usual way, in terms of structural
relations of phrase markers". (p.330).

Notice at this point that the restriction imposed on lexical rules to material
that is present in the lexical representation is a necessary one. This is not
true, however, for the more narrow conception Wasow presents in the above
quotation. In his subsequent discussion, Wasow accepts that so-called indirect
object passives like "Mary was given flowers" require a transformational analysis, because he assumes the lexical rule of passivization to operate on "logical"
direct objects only. Although we might in principle agree with Wasow's conclusion, it is worth noticing that this argument for restricting lexical rules in
this way is not compelling, since indirect objects are present in subcategorization frames just like direct objects and hence both are in principle accessible
to lexical manipulation.

In Wasow (1980), a different course is taken to explain the differences
between the two passives distinguished in Wasow (1977), the verbal and the
adjectival. Both types are now assumed to be lexical in nature -a position that is
in agreement with Bresnan (1978), to which we return below-, but the different
properties are now argued to follow from a different distinction, viz. the
distinction between major and minor rules[51]. The class of minor rules is formulated in terms of thematic functions, whereas major rules manipulate the information in the subcategorization frames. The so-called adjectival passive, then, is
restricted in terms of the notion Theme. This conclusion, which is quite generally adopted (cf. Williams 1981a), will be challenged in section 3.3.3.1. The
controversy about the nature of the verbal passive still continues.

Wasow's position differs in a number of respects from Bresnan's approach. As
mentioned above, Bresnan assumes that the constructions which Wasow and Williams

suppose to be derived by means of the adjectival passive rule, are derived via a process called participle-adjective conversion (cf. Bresnan 1980a). This conversion rule is fed by the lexical rule which accounts for the regular verbal passive. The relevant conversion rule is formulated in (14).

(14) Participle-adjective Conversion

morphological change: $V_{[Part]} \vdash [V_{[Part]} \ A]$

operation on lexical form: $P \ (....(SUBJ)...) \vdash$
$$STATE\text{-}OF \ P \ (..(SUBJ)..)$$

condition: $SUBJ = THEME$ of P

The rule in (14) should be read as follows. At the level of morphophonology there is an identity mapping: the adjectives are directly derived from the participial form of the verb. There is also an operation on the lexical form of the verb to which the conversion applies. The lexical form of a verb is basically the set of grammatical relations associated with that verb. It indicates by which grammatical functions the arguments are realized. So, in an active lexical form, the agent argument is expressed by the SUBJ, whereas it is expressed by a BY-OBJ in a passive lexical form of the same verb. Both the active and the passive lexical forms are present in the lexicon, since they are related to each other by means of a lexical rule. Thus, the operation on the lexical form says that the rule maps the possibly complex predicate P of a SUBJ X onto a predicate STATE-OF P of the same SUBJ X, provided that this SUBJ expresses the theme argument of this predicate. This condition ensures that the rule only applies to the lexical forms of those intransitives that are assumed to have Theme SUBJ's, whereas it selects at the same time the passive lexical forms of transitive verbs. Therefore, the rule accounts for such adjectives as in (15) and (16), while excluding such adjectives as in (17) and (18).

(15) a. an undescended testicle (from intransitive **descend**)
     b. a fallen leaf   (from intransitive **fall**)

(16) a. an unsupported claim   (from passive **support**)
     b. a given book   (from passive **give**)

(17) a *a laughed man   (from intransitive **laugh**)
     b.*a danced man   (from intransitive **dance**)

(18) a.*a given woman   (from bitransitive **give, woman**
                                indirect object)
     b *a resembled man   (from transitive **resemble**)

The examples in (17) and (18) are out, either because the SUBJ bears no Theme relation to the predicate, or there is no passive lexical form available as in the case of **resemble.** This shows that the conversion rule must be fed by the rule of passivization, which must therefore be lexical according to the feeding criterion. It should be noted that this way of accounting for the so-called adjectival passives is superior to the approach taken by Wasow (1977,1980) and Williams (1981a), where a separate lexical passive rule is postulated. In that case, a rule more or less similar to Bresnan's conversion rule is needed to account for the adjectives derived from the participles of intransitive verbs. In our own analysis of the adjectival passive, which differs significantly from Bresnan's analysis, we shall be able to capture this generalization without being forced to assume either a separate lexical passive rule for adjectival passives, or a condition on rule application in terms of thematic roles.

Before we go into Bresnan's analysis of verbal passives, it may be interesting to have a closer look at the condition on the conversion rule in (14) which mentions the notion Theme. As noted in the previous chapter, I assume that there is no point in differentiating between the various thematic roles. One consequence of this is that it is impossible to write rules or conditions on rules that are sensitive to particular θ-roles. In general, there seems to be little confidence in the definability of these θ-roles. Williams (1980:207), who exploits the notion Theme in his analysis of predication states: "In the worst case, it will be necessary to specify which NP a VP-dominated predicate modifies. In this worst case, theme is being used as a purely diacritic rule feature. In a large number of cases, though, theme seems to give the correct answer, at least to the extent that the notion theme is clear in the first place"[52]. It will be clear that the danger of circularity looms large here. Let us consider the following examples in more detail.

(19) a. John likes this music
     b. This music is liked by John

(20) a. The music pleases John

b. John is pleased by this music

Bresnan (1980 :34) notes that these verbs "express similar thematic roles in their predicate argument structures, but by means of different grammatical functions.... Both verbs express a relation between an "experiencer" and "experienced", but the experiencer is the SUBJ of **like** and the OBJECT of **please**". Thus, it is assumed that **the music** has the same thematic function in (19) and (20), call it X, whereas **John** has a different thematic function in both cases, call it Y. Since we find the adjective in (21), we may equate X with Theme, given the condition on the conversion rule in (14). Therefore, it is predicted that (22a) is grammatical and (22b) ungrammatical. In fact, the reverse is true.

(21) the generally disliked music

(22) a. *the pleased music

b. a displeased person

In order to accommodate these cases while maintaining the conversion rule as it is, we are forced to analyze these verbs as expressing different thematic functions. It will be evident, however, that in doing so, we determine thematic roles on the basis of the linguistic generalizations that we can capture if these particular thematic functions are assumed. Then, the thematic functions are virtually reduced to the status of diacritic rule features. The intuitive basis for assigning specific thematic functions is thus lost, so that we lose at the same time the epistemological priority assigned to thematic functions (cf. Chomsky 1981:10). In this way, thematic functions cannot be suitable candidates to count as primitives in Chomsky's sense.

Bresnan (1980a) suggests a different way to accomodate the examples in (19)-(22), viz. by extending the condition on the conversion rule so as to allow the rule both with theme subjects and with experiencer subjects. But, whereas this extension correctly allows for (22b) on the basis of the passive lexical form of **please**, it predicts a host of ungrammatical cases. An example would be (23b), if we assume that it is plausible that the subject in (23a) bears the experiencer role to the predicate.

(23) a. The man felt a draught in the room

b *A felt man

It turns out, then, that thematic roles are either related to the overall conceptual structure, in which case they come into conflict with linguistic facts that one seeks to explain in terms of them, or they are used as coding devices in lexical representations to allow the statement of descriptive generalizations.

Let us now turn to a discussion of Bresnan's conception of verbal passives. In her (1978) paper, Bresnan argues that lexical representations should include a functional structure in addition to a syntactic subcategorization feature. Passivization is not regarded as a structural operation, i.e. as a transformation relating different phrase structures or as a lexical rule relating different subcategorization features, but rather as a rule that operates on the representation of functional structure where the logical relations between a predicate and its dependents are stated.This lexical operation, then, is assumed to involve an existential binding of the subject argument which causes the object argument to be expressed as the syntactic subject as defined in Chomsky (1965), i.e. [NP, S]. She argues that "the ability of the NP to passivize depends on its **lexical relation** to the verb, **as expressed in the functional structure**" (Bresnan 1978:22, emphasis mine).

Whereas logical relations between predicates and arguments are expressed in functional structure, the representation of the syntactic structure in the lexicon (i.e. in subcategorization features) merely expresses syntactic dependencies. A specific syntactic relation need not always correspond to the same logical relation. A certain NP can be a verb's syntactic subject without bearing any logical relation to it. Examples of this are the raising verbs, which have the lexical representation as in (24) according to Bresnan (1978:26).

(24)   tend: V, [-- NP to VP] , TEND $((NP_1)$ VP)

NP_1 in (24) is the name for the syntactic subject. Clearly, then, it has a syntactic or grammatical relation to **tend**, but not a lexical relation "as expressed in functional structure" (Bresnan 1978:27).As a matter of fact, it is hard to see how this lexical approach would be capable of handling the **believe** passives, with (25) the representation of **believe** as used in (26a). NP_2 in (25) does not have a logical relation to **believe** as far as functional structure is concerned and hence should not be eligible for passivization. Yet, this appears to be possible, as shown by (26b).

(25) believe: V, [-- NP to VP], NP_1 BELIEVE $((NP_2)$ VP)
(26) a. John believes the hot dog to be dangerous for our health

b. The hot dog is believed to be dangerous for our health

It is clear that the name NP_2 is not of any help here, as NP_2 is the name for the syntactic direct object, i.e. for (NP,VP). It was Bresnan's intention to distin-guish between various NP_2's, viz, between those that do and those that do not bear a logical relation to the verb of which NP_2 is the syntactic direct object. From this perspective, the following passage from Bresnan (1978:35) is hard to inter-pret.

"A question that must be asked is why the passive transformation has been perceived as a structure dependent operation. The answer seems to be that certain noun phrases can be passivized (....) even though they bear no logical relation to the passivizing verb...The logical object of **believe** is the proposition that the hot dog is dangerous to our health. From this it has been concluded that the passive transformation is blind to grammatical functions -that it is purely structure dependent. (....).

As can now be seen, this reasoning confuses grammatical functions with logical functions: it is based on the assumption that if **the hot dog** is not a logical object of **believe,** it cannot have been a grammatical object of **believe.** But the assumption is not necessary".

From this quotation, one must conclude that Bresnan assumes a three-way distinc-tion between syntactic relation, logical relation and grammatical function. In the quotation from p.22 where Bresnan states that "the ability of the NP to passivize depends upon its lexical relation to the verb as expressed in functio-nal structure' the expression "lexical relation as expressed in functional structure" must refer to grammatical function. However, it is entirely unclear how the notion of grammatical function is distinct from (NP,VP) on the one hand and logical object on the other.

Extending her (1978) lexicalist position, Bresnan has developed a somewhat different framework, which is referred to as Lexical Functional Grammar (LFG, see Bresnan 1980a, 1980b). In this framework, there is indeed a three-way distinc-tion, which I assumed was implicit in Bresnan (1978). In LFG, each sentence is provided with a dual representation consisting of a constituent structure and a functional structure. The latter is a representation of the meaningful grammati-cal relations obtaining in the sentence. Grammatical relations are lexically encoded by assigning grammatical functions to the predicate- argument structures of lexical items. These grammatical functions are the universals of the theory in

terms of which rules like passive are formulated. It is clear, then, that this
organization of the grammar makes LFG highly comparable to Relational Grammar.
The syntactic encoding of grammatical functions is regarded as a language particular matter (see Bresnan 1980a:5). The formulation of passivization within this
system is given in (27).

(27)   The passive in English

Functional change: $(SUBJ) \vdash \emptyset \, / \, (BY\ OBJ)$

$(OBJ \ ) \vdash (SUBJ)$

Morphological change: $V \vdash \quad V_{part}$

Before we come to the end of this overview of the lexical analysis of passive, one
aspect of Bresnan's (1978) position deserves to be mentioned. We noted above that
Wasow construed his structure-preservation criterion in such a way that structure
preservation is a necessary but not a sufficient condition for lexical rules.
Therefore, this criterion is not able to decide between a lexical or a transformational approach if we are dealing with a structure-preserving process.
Bresnan (1978) takes the stronger position that structure preservation is a
sufficient condition for lexical status. If this is true, Emonds' theory of
structure preservation is reduced to a theorem, since lexical rules are structure
preserving by their very nature. In Hoekstra, Van der Hulst & Moortgat (1980a), a
further conceptual advantage of the lexical status of passives and of structure-
preserving rules in general is put forward, viz. their bounded character. Within
transformational analyses in the EST-tradition, the bounded effect of rules like
passive is derived from conditions on rule application like the Specified Subject
Condition and the Tensed S Constraint. These conditions have the status of
primitives, however. The boundedness of passivization follows automatically from
a lexical treatment, because lexical rules can never manipulate material beyond
their domain of application, which is limited to the clause (viz. the locality
condition). Since the locality of subcategorization and selection follows from
independent considerations, boundedness of lexical rules has the status of a
theorem as well.

    In Hoekstra, Van der Hulst & Moortgat (1980b), another conceptual advantage
of the lexical treatment of passivization is suggested. It is a common point to
make that whenever a different analysis is put forward within generative grammar
nothing is gained by moving the complexity from one component to another. Such a
move is profitable only if it reduces the class of potential grammars. Now, it

should be noted that lexical rules are available in both a lexical and a transformational framework. Besides lexical rules, a transformational framework also has transformations. Therefore, in the latter framework, both a transformational and a lexical analysis are available, which may lead to indeterminacy, unless there are principles that determine a choice between the two alternative treatments. As long as such principles are lacking, the indeterminacy can be resolved by eliminating the transformational solution, because the lexical solution cannot be eliminated. As Gazdar (1980) puts it: "The strongest way to constrain a component is to eliminate it". In section 3.2.5., the passive in Dutch will be considered against the background of the lexical and transformational approach.

3.2.3. Phrase-structural approaches to passive

Recently, various analyses of the passive have been put forward in which passive is neither conceived of as a sentence-level rule (e.g. a sentence-level operation like a transformation) nor as a strictly lexical rule, but rather as a rule that operates on the phrasal category TVP (transitive verb phrase). The category TVP includes both basic expressions that combine with an NP to give an intransitive verb phrase, as well as complex expressions with the same combinatorial property. Keenan (1980) defends such a phrasal analysis of passive by pointing out that the domain which is relevant for passivization, specifically for the correct interpretation of passives, exceeds the domain of the word, whereas sentence-level treatments typically exceed the relevant domain. The insufficiency of sentence-level approaches to passivization is claimed to be illustrated by the fact that unlike the marking of e.g. question formation and similar operations, passive is never marked at the sentence level. In general, subjects of passive sentences do not appear to be any different from subjects of active sentences and the application of passive is always signalled at the verb phrase level, according to Keenan. I would like to point out in passing that the **ne**-cliticization in Italian and the rule of **en**-avant in French[53] can be construed as counterexamples to Keenan's conjecture that subjects of passives are never treated differently from subjects of actives, at least when the ergative analysis, which is discussed in section 3.3.3., is taken into account.

In his defense of passive as a phrasal operation, Bach (1980) notes that the category TVP is not easily accommodated by phrase-structure grammars of the usual type, because in English the parts of complex TVP's occur discontinuously. In Hoekstra (1981a), it is pointed out that this is not true for Dutch. The examples below illustrate that the categories out of which the category TVP is built up in Dutch are usually linearly continuous. Gazdar & Sag (1981) demonstrate moreover that within the more elaborate system of generalized-phrase structure grammar (c.f. Gazdar 1980), a category TVP can be accommodated for the grammar of English as well.

Below, I shall consider Bach's proposal for the analysis of passive in some detail. First, however, the notion of TVP is introduced with a number of examples from Dutch. A number of arguments in favour of the category TVP are put forward.

In the examples in (28)-(30), the parts printed in bold face can be consider-ed TVP's. As mentioned above, the internal parts of these TVP's in Dutch are continuous.

(28) dat Jan zijn boek **op de plank legde**
     that John his book on the shelf put

(29) dat Jan zijn vriend **van verraad beschuldigde**
     that John his friend of treason accused

(30) dat Jan zijn broer **vervelend vond**
     that John his brother boring found

The phrase-structure rules in (31) project the required structure. The categorial properties of the XP are determined by the subcategorization of the basic expressions, e.g. **legde** is subcategorized as TVP/PP, i.e. it gives a TVP in combination with a PP. Other verbs, like **vinden**, allow expressions of various categories to take the position of the XP.

(31)   VP -> NP   TVP
       TVP -> XP   V/XP

In support of the category TVP, the following syntactic evidence may be put forward. First, the distribution of adverbials demonstrates that the constituent parts of TVP's function syntactically as unanalyzable, i.e. impenetrable units. In Hoekstra (1978b), it is argued that the adverb **niet** should be regarded as an expression that combines with members of various categories, including adjectives, numerals and manner adverbs. The examples in (32) illustrate that **niet** is placed to the immediate left of the category with which it combines.

(32) a. een niet tevreden mens
         a   not satisfied person

     b. niet veel pijlen
        not many arrows

     c. hij loopt niet hard
        he walks not fast

As for verbs, the position of **niet** supports the thesis that the verb must be generated in clause-final position. In embedded clauses, i.e. in clauses that display verb final order in surface structure, **niet** occurs to the immediate left of intransitive verbs, whereas it comes in clause-final position if the verb is in second position in root clauses. This is shown by the examples in (33).

(33) a. dat Jan niet lachte
        that John not laughed
     b. Jan lachte niet
        John laughed not

With transitive verbs, the situation is a bit more complicated. Usually, the negative adverb **niet** is placed to the immediate left of the verb, except when the object has a non-specific reading. In that case, the negation is fused with the indefinite article.

(34) a. dat Jan de auto niet zag
        that John the car not saw

     b. dat Jan een auto niet zag
        that John a car not saw

     c. dat Jan geen auto zag
        that John no car saw

We would expect, then, that **niet** occurs to the immediate left of the verb in the

negative counterparts of the examples in (28)-(30). This expectation is not borne
out; **niet** is placed to the immediate left of that part of the clause which is
assumed to be a TVP.

(28') dat Jan zijn boek **niet** op de plank legde

(29') dat Jan zijn vriend **niet** van verraad beschuldigde

(30') dat Jan zijn vriend **niet** vervelend vond

What has been just illustrated with **niet** above is true for adverbial modification
in general: TVP's cannot be penetrated by modifiers.

A second piece of evidence in favour of the category TVP comes from idiomatic
expressions. Let us make a distinction between basic and derived or complex
linguistic expressions. The meaning of the former invariably belongs to the idiom
part of the grammar[54], whereas the meaning of complex expressions is generally
determined on the basis of the meanings of the constituent parts, in accordance
with the principle of compositionality. It is the role of function-argument
structure (which I assume is isomorphic with syntactic structure, unless there is
strong evidence to the contrary) to indicate the way in which the meaning of
complex expressions is built up from the meanings of the constituent parts.
General schemata of function-argument structure, then, will determine the notion
"possible idiom", on the quite reasonable assumption that only constituents in
function-argument structure can be possible idioms, i.e. have a non compositional
meaning (cf. Hoekstra 1981a for more discussion of this issue). If this is
correct, idiomatic expressions can be used as an argument in favour of a specific
constituent-type in function-argument structures. Idioms like 'kick the bucket'
would then argue for the existence of a constituent in function-argument structure equivalent to VP. Given the thesis of isomorphy, this requires the existence
in syntactic structure of a category corresponding to this VP-like constituent in
function-argument structure. Turning to our category TVP, we notice that we do
find quite a few idioms that combine with an NP to give a VP. The examples in (35)
bear this out. The parts in bold face printing in (35) are idiomatically bound. It
is impossible to have an adverbial modifier inside the idiomatic part of the
sentence.

(35) a. dat wij iemand **bij de neus nemen**

         that we someone at the nose take (=to fool someone)

     b. dat wij iemand **over de hekel halen**

         that we someone over the hackle get (=to criticize someone)

   c. dat wij iemand **over de kling jagen**
      that we someone over the blade chase (=to put to the sword)

A third, more delicate argument in favour of the category TVP is discussed in
Hoekstra (1981b). We shall briefly review the argument here. As discussed in
chapter 2, there are two types of tenseless complement clauses, those that are
found in postverbal position and those that occur in preverbal position and
undergo V-raising. Some verbs always take postverbal complements, others always
take V-raising complements, while there is also a set of verbs that allows for
both complement types. A relevant example from this class is the verb **proberen**
'try'. Consider the examples in (36).

(36) a. dat Jan probeerde de krant te lezen
        that John tried the newspaper to read

     b. dat Jan de krant probeert te lezen
        that John the newspaper tries to read

In the classic analysis of sentential complementation (Evers 1975), (36a) is
described as resulting from sentential extraposition, where the infinitival
clause is moved to postverbal position as a whole. (36b), on the other hand, is
assumed to derive from V-raising applied to a preverbal complement clause, from
which the head is extracted. There are also constructions like the one in (36c)
which cannot be described in terms of these rules, since the postverbal part is
more than a verb, although it is not the entire clause either, since the object of
leggen occurs before the matrix verb.

(36) c. dat Jan zijn boek probeert op de plank te leggen
        that John his book tries on the shelf to put

In Hoekstra (1981b) such examples are analyzed as having a TVP in postverbal
position.
   A final piece of evidence comes from considerations concerning subcategorization. In general, subcategorization frames refer to phrasal categories that
appear as sisters of the subcategorized element. In some cases, however, it is
required that subcategorization imposes more specific requirements on the internal make-up of the sister phrases, e.g. in the case of prepositional objects,
where the preposition is selected in terms of a specific lexical item. In

Hoekstra, Van der Hulst & Moortgat (1980a), the head constraint (not to be
confused with a restriction on movement rules proposed under the same name in Van
Riemsdijk 1978a) is formulated which restricts the depth of analysis of subcategorization. It states that subcategorization can only impose restrictions on the
internal make-up of sister phrases as far as the head is concerned. Notice,
however, that such a selection in terms of a specific lexical item is quite
commonly necessary for the XP-part of TVP's, but not in other cases. The following examples illustrate this type of selection in the case of XP's in TVP's.

(37) a. dat wij iemand **tot** ridder slaan
        that we someone to knight hit (=to knight someone)

     b. dat we iemand **als** de dader beschouwen
        that we someone as the offender consider

     c. dat we water **in** wijn veranderen
        that we water into wine change

Together with the fact that these XP's cannot be separated from their verbs, the
specific selectional requirements that can be imposed on the internal make-up of
the XP suggests that the XP and the verb constitute a close unit. More or less the
same kind of argument can be adduced in favour of a category TVP in English.

    Let us now turn to Bach's analysis of passive based on the category TVP. Bach
(1980) defines a phrasal rule which maps TVP's into a special passive category
PVP (Passive Verb Phrase). His central claim is that all TVP's have good passives, at least in English, and that none of the non-TVP's have good passives. The
claim, then, is clear. If the statement just given is correct, a generalization
that can be expressed if the notion of TVP is exploited is missed otherwise. Bach
(1980:302) himself notes the most important caveat: "if we let the passive facts
determine our classification, the analysis is circular". Bach uses a categorial
grammar. Within such a system, the category of expressions is determined in terms
of the elements with which they combine and the result of the combination. So, VP
can be defined as a category that results in a sentence when combined with an NP,
i.e. S/NP. As mentioned above, TVP is syntactically defined as an expression that
yields a VP when combined with an NP. The semantic category should be a function
of the syntactic category, i.e. the semantic category of a TVP should be a
function from NP denotations to VP denotations. What this means is that there is
in fact little room for variation in the assignment of either syntactic or

semantic categories. A problem may arise in such well-known cases as the examples
in (38)-(39).

(38) a. John persuaded Mary to go
     b. Mary was persuaded to go

(39) a. John promised Mary to go
     b.*Mary was promised to go

At first sight, **promise** and **persuade** seem to require the same syntactic complement structure, either NP S'as assumed by Chomsky and others or NP VP as assumed
by Bresnan, Brame and others. But, whereas **persuade** in (38b) has a good passive,
promise has not, as can be seen in (39b). It must be concluded, therefore, that
persuade to go in (38a) is a TVP,but that **promise to go** in (39a) is not. Bach
follows Thomason (1976) in assigning **promise** the category (VP/VP)/NP. The structure in (41) represents the internal structure of (39a), whereas (40) represents
(38a).

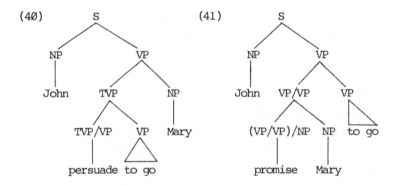

Since the different categorization of **persuade** and **promise** cannot be motivated in
terms of their differential behaviour under passivization, other evidence supporting the distinction must be adduced. Bach provides four pieces of evidence,
of which he notes (p.302) that "these facts are only weakly suggestive of the
difference". We shall now discuss these four pieces of evidence. They involve a.
control properties, b. unspecified object deletion, c. heavy-NP-shift and d.
conjunctions.

    The control facts, more extensively discussed in Bach (1979), seem to corro-
borate the distinction between the two categories: **promise** takes subject control,

whereas **persuade** takes object control. The data are well-known:

    (42) a. I persuaded John to love himself/*myself

           b. I promised John to love myself/*himself

This is Visser's generalization (cf. Wasow 1980), which states that predicative complements are associated with the subject if the matrix verb is intransitive, but with the object if the matrix verb is transitive. The same generalization is expressed by Rosenbaum's (1967, 1970) Minimal Distance Principle and Koster's (1978a) Locality Principle. For these principles, the cases like **promise** are the exception. Within the system of Bach, the verb **promise** itself is not intransitive, but its NP complement is not an object either. The relevant generalization here is that controllers cannot be left out in general, i.e. the generalization is independent of subject or object control. Therefore, the control facts in (42) are not independent of pasivization. Since passivization suppresses the argument that is realized in subject position, applying passive to a verb that takes subject control will always yield an ungrammatical result[55]. This means that the ungrammaticality of (39b) is accounted for independently by the requirement that controllers should be present, irrespective of the categorization of **promise**. In fact, since the approach taken by Bach and Thomason requires a categorization different from TVP, it is necessary to assign a totally different category to **promise** in (43) and (44), where **promise** takes two NP's or an NP and a tensed clause as complements, which I find very undesirable. Since the explanation for the impossibility of passivizing in (39b) is independent of the categorization, a more similar categorization of **promise** in its various uses is a priori more satisfactory.

    (43) a. I promised Mary a rose garden

           b. Mary was promised a rose garden

    (44) a. I promised Mary that the car would be there in time

           b. Mary was promised that the car would be there in time

Turning to Bach's second piece of evidence, we see that this too is related to the generalization concerning control. Verbs of the **persuade** category, i.e. those that combine with some category to yield a TVP, never allow unspecified object deletion, whereas those like **promise,** which as a basic (lexical) expression combines with an NP to form a complex expression in general do allow this NP to be deleted.

(45) a. *I persuade to go

b. *I regard as crazy

c. *I put in the closet

(46) a. I promised Mary to go

b. I promised to go

Bach argues that this difference with respect to the possibility of unspecified object deletion follows from the given classification on the assumption that unspecified object deletion operates in the lexicon as advocated by Bresnan (1978) and Dowty (1978, 1981). The verbs **persuade, regard** etc. themselves do not take objects and hence no rule can apply to them to delete this object in the lexicon. It will be clear, however, that the data in (45)-(46) follow immediately from the generalization mentioned above that controllers may not be left unexpressed. Since the verbs in (45) all take object control, this object may not be deleted. Apart from the fact, then, that in this case too the facts can be accounted for in a different and in my view, more appealing way, it seems to me that Bach's argument is conceptually wrong. Whereas it is true that the verbs in (45) do not combine with an NP directly, there is as far as I know no restriction on a lexical rule that would map items of the category TVP/VP into the category VP/VP. Bach's explanation seems to require the existence of such a principle. I assume that if such a principle is stated, it would essentially have the content of the explanation that we propose for the contrast in (45)-(46), viz. the condition that controllers cannot be deleted.

Bach's third observation to motivate the differential categorial assignment involves heavy-NP-shift. The object of **persuade,** or rather of **persuade to VP** can be shifted to the right when it is heavy, but applying this shift to a heavy object NP of **promise** yields worse results, as is illustrated in (47).

(47) a. I persuaded to leave the house all the little

boys in the basement

b.?I promised to leave the house all the little boys

in the basement.

Bach argues that these judgements can be explained if **promise NP** is syntactically more coherent than **persuade NP,** in accordance with the structures in (40)-(41). We return to this observation below.

The last piece of evidence is based on the assumption that only expressions

of the same syntactic category can be conjoined. Given the unquestionable transitivity of **visit,** the grammaticality of (48) argues for the transitivity of
persuade VP. However, in order for these facts to substantiate the categorial
distinction between **persuade** and **promise,** it ought to be the case that **promise NP**
can be conjoined with verbs like **try,** as both are of the category VP/VP. Hence,
(49) should be grammatical as well. This prediction is not borne out.

(48) I visited and persuaded to vote for me a man that I
     met in the grocery store

(49)*I promised John and tried to go

Moreover, the conjunction of complex TVP's and basic expressions of that category
is subject to various constraints that are not well understood. Consider e.g.
(50). It appears that a conjunction in which a complex TVP precedes a simple one
leads to ungrammaticality. The ungrammaticality of (50) suggests that the relatively good result in (48) is related to the applicability of heavy-NP-shift.

(50) *I persuaded to vote for me and left a friend

Heavy-NP-shift itself is not without problems either. This is illustrated by the
fact that (52) is unacceptable, although the expression **give a book** must be
considered a TVP, given the grammaticality of (51). The reason for the relatively
bad results in (47b) and (52) may therefore very well be related to a different
factor, e.g. to their semantic role of being recipient.

(51) Mary was given a book (by John)

(52) *John gave a book all the little boys in the basement

After this review of Bach's evidence in support of a categorial distinction
between **persuade** and **promise,** it must be concluded that passivization is the only
firm evidence for the proposed distinction. It is suggested above that the
ungrammaticality of the passive of **promise** in (39b), the initial motivation for
the distinction, can be explained in terms of a much more general principle, viz.
the principle that controllers may not be left unexpressed. The difference in
grammaticality between the examples in (53) indicates that it is indeed this
principle rather than a different categorization that explains the ungrammaticality of (39b) and (53b).

(53) a. John was promised to be allowed to leave

   b *John was promised to leave

The phenomenon that the controller changes if the infinitival complement is passive is also found with verbs like **ask** (cf. Chomsky 1981:76 for discussion). In the light of the foregoing discussion, it should be concluded that there is no sufficient evidence for the claim that **persuade** and **promise** belong to different syntactic categories. Therefore, the central claim of Bach's proposal, viz. that all and only TVP's have good passives is not substantiated.

There are other problems with Bach's TVP approach as well, as Bach himself notes. Notice that the grammaticality of the passive in (54b) forces us to analyze **believe VP** as a TVP, an analysis that is supported by the possibility of applying Heavy-NP-Shift, if this is adopted as a criterion (cf. (54c)).

(54) a. John believes the hot dog to be dangerous

   b. The hot dog is believed to be dangerous

   c. John believes to be dangerous every hot dog that
      you find in the street

However, if **believe** with an infinitival complement is assigned to the same category as verbs like **persuade,** no distinction is made between traditional control and raising verbs. The raising verbs of the type of **believe** are discussed in Bach's section "Problems and Prospects", and clearly, this class of verbs belongs to the first category mentioned in that title.

Bach suggests two possible solutions to this problem, both of which run into problems. The first would be to assume that verbs like **believe** take two arguments: **believe** would then be categorized as VP/ NP to VP. The problem with this categorization is that the category departs from the usual practice in Montague Grammar in which only monadic functions are used (i.e. all categories are binary branching) and, more important for the present discussion, the combination of **believe** and the **to VP** would still not constitute a TVP. Accordingly, (54b) remains anomalous for Bach's approach. Bach's second suggestion meets with the same problem. According to this suggestion, **believe** would be categorized as VP/ to S. This category would be ad hoc as well and would not solve the problem with (54b), as no TVP is created. Moreover, if a category like this is set up, a more obvious candidate for membership of this category would be a verb like **want** as in (55), which does not allow passivization, nor Heavy-NP-Shift.

(55) a. I wanted Bill to win

    b.*Bill was wanted to win

    c.*They would want to win any candidate who would take the
       trouble to run in every primary

(example (55c) is taken from Chomsky 1981:70).

The problems with the TVP approach to passivization increase if it is generalized to other languages. First of all, passivization in various languages is not restricted to transitive verbs. Thus, in Dutch, but also in German and Latin and many other languages, passivization on intransitives is possible as well. A second problem is that so-called "indirect object passives" which are found in English, are generally impossible in Dutch. This is somewhat surprising from the point of view of the TVP approach. Bach (1980), following Dowty (1978), assumes that **give a book** in (56a) is a TVP, which is necessary in view of the passive in (56b). The assumption that **give a book** is a TVP squares with the observation that in English complex TVP's usually form a kind of brace construction around their NP argument, the left member of the brace being the basic verbal expression, while the rest of the complex follows the NP[56]. As noted before, the internal parts of TVP's in Dutch are continuous, following their NP argument as a whole. One would be tempted, therefore, to consider **bloemen geven** in (56c) a complex TVP, taking **Marie** as its NP argument. However, the passive corresponding to (56c) is not (56b), but rather (56e).

(56) a. I gave Mary a book

    b. Mary was given a book

    c. dat ik Marie bloemen gaf

    d.*dat Marie bloemen werd gegeven

    e. dat Marie bloemen werden gegeven

To account for this asymmetry between Dutch and English, one could of course assume that verbs like **geven/give** are both categorized as TVP/NP, the NP argument being the notional indirect object in Dutch, but the notional direct object in English. It will be clear, however, that then the categorization does not reflect any deeper logico-semantic properties of the verbs in question. In fact, the categorization would merely be ad hoc in as far as it is not related to any other property that differentiates the two languages. A priori, it would be preferable if the distinction between Dutch and English could be shown to follow from other differences, or that various differences can be related to a single, more fundamental difference. As for the function- argument structure of bitransitive verbs, I have argued that in Dutch the combination of the basic verb and the notional direct object constitutes a complex function, taking the notional indirect object as its argument (cf. Hoekstra 1981a). I see no reason why these arguments should not carry over to English. Therefore, it seems reasonable to conclude that the differences in passivizability should be made contingent upon something other than function-argument structure.

A further problem for the TVP analysis follows from cases like (57), where we find a so-called inversion predicate. This class of verbs is extensively discussed in section 3.3. below.

(57) a. dat zij hem opviel
         that she him struck

     b.*dat hij door haar werd opgevallen
         that he by her was   struck

As mentioned above, the syntactic categories are defined in terms of the categories with which they combine and the resulting expressions. Clearly, the verb **opvallen** 'strike' combines with an NP argument to yield a complex expression that in turn must combine with an NP to form a sentence. Therefore, given the way in which categories are defined, verbs like **opvallen** should be categorized as TVP's. Nevertheless, they fail to passivize. The account of this impossibility that will be discussed below is not available within the surface-oriented approach of Montague Grammar which does not have transformations of the usual type, nor anything similar in function.

At an abstract level, I think that Bach's defense of a general rule of passive is in a sense a variant of the early transformational approach to passivization. The proposed rule can be so general because problematic examples are resolved by assigning a category distinct from TVP to expressions or complex expressions that fail to undergo the rule. Above, we have pointed out a number of problems with this approach. It may be the case that other phrasal approaches to passivization do not meet with these problems, e.g. the analysis of passivization within Gazdar's Generalized Phrase Structure Grammar presented in Gazdar & Sag (1981) does not meet with the problem of the **believe** passives. This is possible because the correspondence between syntactic category and semantic translation is less strict than in Bach's analysis. Here I shall not pursue this line of investigation any further.

3.2.4. Summary of results

In the preceding sections several proposals have been reviewed to account for the phenomenon of passive within frameworks that are different in varying degrees. We can distinguish between the transformational approach based on MOVE α, two types of lexical approaches, and the phrasal theories of passivization.

From a certain point of view, these approaches can be considered as differing in the scope or the domain in which the operation of passive is supposed to apply (cf. Keenan 1980). Within lexical approaches, the level relevant for passive is the word, as passive is regarded as a rule that applies to items of a specific category in the lexicon. Phrasal analyses take the relevant domain to be the domain of a specific type of phrase,viz. the domain of TVP. Transformational analyses (as well as analyses within the framework of Relational Grammar) are regarded as analyses that apply at the sentential level. It was noted above that this domain is too wide according to Keenan (1980), while he argues that the level of the word is too limited.

Although such a scope distinction between the various approaches indeed seems to exist, it is not clear whether this distinction properly characterizes the most fundamental difference between these approaches. It seems to me that the matter of scope is fundamental in differentiating between lexical and phrasal analyses, but that there is a more fundamental difference between these two on the one hand and the transformational approach in terms of MOVE α on the other. For linguists like Keenan, Bach, Bresnan and those working within the framework of Relational Grammar and related frameworks (e.g. Functional Grammar), passive is a fundamental linguistic category, both formally and functionally, both in specific languages and in languages in general. Thus, in Bresnan (1980a), it is held that the theory of grammar should "explain the universal semantic effects of rules like passivization" and that passivization "can be universally characterized" as a rule that makes the OBJ (a universally relevant grammatical relation) into a SUBJ (id.) and either removes or demotes the SUBJ to OBL (=oblique, also a universally relevant grammatical relation). These grammatical relations are comparable to the grammatical relations of Relational Grammar. Within Bresnan's Lexical Functional Grammar, a level of representation is defined in terms of these universal grammatical relations, which mediates between predicate-argument structures and surface syntactic structures. The variable manifestations of passive across languages follow from language particular encodings of grammatical functions in syntactic or morphological categories.

Similarly, analyses employing the category TVP treat the passive phenomenon as a homogeneous one: passive is regarded as a rule mapping TVP's into the category VP (or PVP in Bach's analysis), the translation rule guaranteeing that the subject of the derived VP is interpreted as the object of the corresponding TVP.

Within recent transformational theories, on the other hand, the notion of passive is merely used as a descriptive term, referring to a functional rather than a formal category. It appears to be the case that within this framework these functional categories are of little interest. Since passive is not a formally homogeneous category, then, the conception of passive differs radically from the other approaches mentioned above. Passive structures, i.e. structures that can be thought of as serving a similar functional role (e.g. of suppressing the subject argument) are regarded as the result of various interacting rules and principles, none of which is specific to the phenomenon of passive. Since there exists a certain amount of parametrical variation among languages, the formal means used in passive structures as well as the scope of the phenomenon in one language may very well be quite distinct from those in other languages.

Since the theory of passive within the EST framework regards passive structures as the result of rules operating on and being sensitive to syntactic structures of the individual language, and lexical and phrasal analyses tend to favour an approach that is less based on the particular syntactic structure of specific languages, the predictions made by the two approaches are also distinct: the transformational approach predicts that language-particular structural factors will enter into the explanation of the scope of the phenomenon, whereas the other approaches do not predict this. As will be clear from the above characterization, this holds true particularly of Bresnan's (1980a) approach: surface syntactic (and morphological) manifestations of passive depend on language particular encoding properties, whereas passive itself is defined as a rule that changes universal grammatical relations. This organization, then, predicts that there will be no interaction of the rule of passivization and the surface syntactic properties of a particular language.

In the discussion in section 3.3., several observations are made that suggest that rather the opposite is the case. We shall argue that a number of differences between Dutch and English with respect to the scope of passivization follows from the positional difference of the verb, a fact that was traced to a different orientation of government in chapter 2.

Much of the discussion in the following sections will concern the passive in Dutch. In order to provide insight into the nature of the relevant facts and in

order to make the foregoing discussion of different approaches more concrete, we
shall discuss two of the most explicit analyses of the Dutch passive that are
available in the literature in the final subsection of 3.2.

3.2.5. Passive in Dutch

In Hoekstra & Moortgat (1979a), an analysis of Dutch passives is proposed, which
is based on the rule typological approach of Wasow (1977) and formulated in terms
of Bresnan's (1978) lexical theory. It is argued there that passive participles
in Dutch are verbal rather than adjectival, as was assumed to be the case in
English by Freidin (1975). Therefore, the criterion involving a category change,
as used by Freidin to argue for the lexical status of the passive in English,
cannot be employed to establish the lexical nature of passive in Dutch. Nevertheless, it is concluded that passive is lexical in Dutch according to the criteria
formulated in Wasow (1977), specifically according to the locality criterion in
the sense in which Wasow himself construed this notion (cf. section 3.2.2.
above). This conclusion seems to follow logically, since there are no passives
in Dutch analogous to the English passives in (58)-(61), i.e. indirect object
passives (58), raising passives (59), pseudo-passives (60) and passives based on
idiom chunks like in (61).

(58) The girl was given very many dolls
(59) The hot dog was believed to be dangerous
(60) This bed was slept in by Napoleon
(61) Advantage was taken of the man's ignorance

In short, it appears that only direct objects in a thematic sense can become
subjects of passive sentences. Koster (1978a) suggests that the fact that Dutch
has passives based on intransitives indicates that passive in Dutch is lexical,
as there are passive-like effects, without the application of MOVE α.

Let us first demonstrate that the passive participle in Dutch is verbal
rather than adjectival. The first argument involves the traditional test to
distinguish between verbs and adjectives in Dutch, viz. their position relative
to the finite verb in embedded clauses. Adjectives must obligatorily precede the
finite verb, whereas non-finite verb forms may follow it. Therefore, both orders

are permitted in (62), but in (63) only the order with the adjective preceding the verb is permitted[57].

(62) dat we daar gespeeld hebben/hebben gespeeld
     that we there played have /have played

(63) dat Jan daar ziek werd/*werd ziek
     that John there ill became/became ill

Passive particles are like non-finite verb forms in that they may both precede and follow the finite verb. This property is quite significant, as can be seen from the following observation. If a participle is prefixed with **on-** ('un'), it must be an adjective, since **on**-prefixation is restricted to adjectives. The contrast between (64a) and (64b) then strongly suggests that the passive participle is indeed verbal.

(64) a. omdat hij in dat vak getraind is/is getraind
        because he in that job trained is/is trained
     b. omdat hij in dat vak ongetraind is/* is ongetraind
        because he in that job untrained is/ is untrained

A second argument to support the claim that passive participles are verbal can be deduced from the different orientation of complements of adjectives and verbs. Whereas PP complements are assumed to have their base position in front of the verb, genuine adjectives take their prepositional complements in post-head position. This difference is most clearly demonstrated by preposition stranding. A stranded preposition must precede its governing verb, but it usually precedes the adjective. This is illustrated in the following examples.

(65) a. dat Piet zeker goed in wiskunde is
        that Peter certainly good in mathematics is

     b. dat Piet er goed in/* in goed is
        that Peter there good in/in good is

(66) a. dat Piet zeker op jou gerekend heeft
        that Peter certainly on you counted has

    b. dat Piet er zeker op gerekend heeft/* gerekend op heeft

        that Peter there certainly on counted has/counted on has

The examples in (67) will suffice to confirm the hypothesis that passive participles are not adjectives: leftward stranding of the preposition is only possible
if the participle is not prefixed by **on-**, i.e. it is excluded if the form is
undoubtedly adjectival.

    (67) a. dat Peter er zeker in getraind wordt

          that Peter there certainly in trained is

      b.*dat Peter er zeker in ongetraind is

          that Peter there certainly in untrained is

      c. dat Peter er zeker ongetraind in is

          that Peter there certainly untrained in is

As the categorial status of the participles cannot be used to argue for the
lexical status of passive in Dutch, a prominent role is assigned to the locality
criterion, i.e. to the fact that passive in Dutch does not seem to be a rule that
is strictly sensitive to configurational information. A rule like (68), when
adapted to Dutch, would clearly overgenerate enormously[58].

    (68) X-np-VY-NP-Z

$$\text{X-np-VY-NP-Z} \Longrightarrow 1\text{-}4\text{-}3\text{-}t_4\text{-}5$$

       1 2 3 4 5

(with np indicating an empty NP position). The rule would be both too weak and too
strong: too weak in that it is incapable of accounting for impersonal passives
and too strong in that not any NP in a specified structural position may be moved
into an empty subject position. As an example of such overgeneration, consider
(69), which does not seem to differ structurally from cases like (70).

    (69) a. dat dat meisje hem bevalt

          that that girl him pleases

      b.*dat hij door dat meisje wordt bevallen

          that he by that girl is pleased

(70) a. dat dat meisje hem zoent
         that that girl him kisses

     b. dat hij door dat meisje wordt gezoend
        that he by that girl is kissed

It must be kept in mind, though, that it is always possible, at least in
principle, to construct an analysis in which these overgenerating effects are
accounted for by principles that are not directly related to passive. This is the
course taken by Den Besten (1979) in his challenge of the lexical analysis of the
verbal passive in Dutch. Accepting Wasow's rule typology, he questions the
empirical generalization made in Hoekstra & Moortgat's (1979a) analysis. According to Den Besten, there is no reason to assume that MOVE NP is not responsible
for the generation of verbal passives in Dutch, as indirect object passives,
raising passives and idiom chunk passives do occur, though on a rather limited
scale. Pseudo-passives are fully absent.

    The evidence presented by Den Besten is rather slender. As for raising
passives, Den Besten cites the verb **achten** as the single verb that allows a
raising passive.

(71) dat jij wordt geacht t dat te weten

However, this verb is not only exceptional with respect to passivization. First
of all, the verb is exceptional in having no active counterpart. Secondly, it was
pointed out in chapter 2 that raising verbs and verbs that take an AcI complement
have to take these complements in preverbal position for principled reasons and
that they therefore induce verb raising from this complement. Therefore, if
achten is the only example to argue for the existence of raising passives in
Dutch, the conclusion seems to be unwarranted[59]. In section 3.3., however, it
will be seen that raising passives are in fact abundantly present in Dutch, given
a particular analysis of specific types of construction. It should be noted here
that the apparent absence of raising passives in Dutch is obviously related to
the following observation. First of all, there are hardly any verbs that take
infinitival complements with lexical subjects. This implies that the set of
possible inputs for the generation of raising passives is in fact very small.
Secondly, the few verbs that do allow lexical subjects in infinitival complements
all induce verb raising, as noted above. This might be related to the explanation
of their failure to undergo passivization.

The situation with so-called indirect object passives is a little more encouraging. Although it is in general impossible to passivize on indirect objects in Dutch, there appears to be a definable subset of such passives that are in fact possible. The example cited by Den Besten is worth considering in some detail.

(72) er werd ons verzocht weg te gaan
      there was us requested away to go

(73) wij werden verzocht weg te gaan
      we   were   requested away to go

Although (72) shows that with the verb **verzoeken** the indirect object need not be moved into subject position (or at least receive nominative case), (73) with an underlying indirect object in the nominative is perfectly grammatical, in spite of vehement normative opposition, as Den Besten notes. Everaert (1982) cites a fair number of similar examples with verbs like **aanraden** 'advise', **verbieden** 'forbid', **beletten** 'prevent', **verwijten** 'reproach' etc. The possibility of having an indirect object is is clearly related to the categorial status of the direct object. If the direct object is nominal, passivization of the indirect object is impossible.

(74) a. Men heeft het ons verzocht
        One has it us requested

     b. Het is ons verzocht
        It is us requested

     c.*Wij zijn het verzocht
        We are it requested

Furthermore, tenseless direct object clauses make the phenomenon of passivization on indirect objects more readily possible than tensed object clauses and judgements about the felicity of indirect object passives vary from speaker to speaker. Thus, (75b) is ungrammatical according to Den Besten (1979), whereas (76b), which is entirely parallel to (75b), is grammatical according to Everaert (1982).

(75) a. Men heeft hem verboden om daarheen te gaan
      One has him forbidden for there-to to go

   b.*Hij is verboden om daarheen te gaan
      He is forbidden for there-to to go

(76) a. Ik verbood haar het boek te lezen
      I forbade her the book to read

   b. Zij werd verboden het boek te lezen
      She was forbidden the book to read

What the occurrence of these indirect object passives suggests is that the possibility of passivizing on the indirect object is due to a rather superficial property, which has to do with some sort of structural and linear adjacency to the verb. Ultimately, the productive existence of such passives in English must be related to the fact that thematically based Case marking was lost and to the fact that in English, unlike in Dutch, the indirect object is adjacent to the verb. The hypothesis that the loss of thematically based Case marking in English is responsible for the emergence of these indirect object passives is defended in Lightfoot (1980). That the positional difference of the verb in English and Dutch is responsible for the difference between these languages with respect to the passivizability of the indirect object, was also concluded by Den Besten (1979), who implements this view in terms of abstract Case-marking devices. The grammaticality of (73) and examples like it, then, follows from the fact that the indirect object is not separated from the verb by an intervening direct object if the direct object is sentential. Under those circumstances, the indirect object is construed as the closest antecedent in the sense of Den Besten (1979).

The preceding discussion illustrates the point made in the previous section that rather superficial syntactic properties determine the possibilities of passivization, and that therefore approaches of passivization that conceive of it as a fundamental category, which must be described in terms of universal grammatical relations as SUBJ and OBJ, are misdirected.

The same point is illustrated by the asymmetry between Dutch and English with respect to the occurrence of pseudo-passives. This, too, follows from the positional difference of the verb. Pseudo-passives like (77) in English are absent in Dutch, as shown by (78).

(77) The desired result was arrived at

(78)*Die oplossing werd over getwijfeld

That solution was doubted about

In the framework of Lexical Functional Grammar of Bresnan (1980a), the possibility of such pseudo-passives is accounted for in terms of a reanalysis, which operates in the lexicon. The rule applies to lexical forms, i.e. the level of representation that is defined in terms of the universal grammatical relations of the framework. Clearly, the rule must apply prior to the rule of passivization, which must also apply to the level of lexical form. However, just as the rule of passivization is not and cannot be sensitive to the language- particular syntactic encoding of the grammatical relations, one would expect that this is equally impossible with the rule of P-incorporation. This rule is formulated in (79) (cf. Bresnan 1980a:64).

(79) V-P incorporation

Operation on lexical form: $(P\ OBJ) \vdash\ (OBJ)$

Morphological change   : $V \vdash [V\ P]_V$

P OBJ is the name of a grammatical relation, just like SUBJ and OBJ etc., and is not a name of a syntactic category. Since grammatical relations are taken to belong to an inventory of universal relations, one would not expect that there is any difference between P OBJ's that are realized with a preposition and P OBJ's that are realized with a postposition, as the distinction seems to be a matter of surface syntactic encoding. Nevertheless, the applicability of V-P incorporation depends on adjacency. Given such an adjacency requirement, the fact that Dutch has no pseudopassives again follows from the positional difference of the verb. This point is illustrated even more clearly by the following observations.

Traditionally, it is claimed that Dutch has both prepositions and postpositions, the latter being a kind of remnants of an older stage, on the assumption that Germanic was more consistently postpositional. Given their marginal occurrence, their status in a synchronic grammar is unclear (cf. Van Riemsdijk 1978a and the review in Hoekstra & Moortgat 1979b). A relevant example is found in (80).

(80) dat wij het kanaal over zwemmen

that we the canal over swim

Is **over** in (80) a postposition, heading a PP with **het kanaal** its complement, or is it a particle with **het kanaal** a bare NP? The following argument by Van Riemsdijk indicates that it can be both.

Pronominal, non-human complements of adpositions take the form of a proform with the feature [+R], which obligatorily occurs to the left of the adposition. The following examples illustrate the contrast between the form of non-human pronouns as bare NP and those of non-human pronouns in the complement of an adposition.

(81) Jan zag een paard en wij zagen **het** ook
     John saw a horse and we saw   it too

(82) Jan keek naar een paard en wij keken **er** ook naar
     Jan looked at a horse and we looked there also at

Now consider the difference between (83a) and (83b): whereas the former suggests that **over** in (80) takes **het kanaal** as complement, which appears with the feature [+R] if it is pronominal, the non-R-pronoun in the latter suggests that **het kanaal** in (80) is a bare NP complement.

(83) a. het kanaal waar wij over zwemmen
        the canal where we   over swim

     b. het kanaal dat wij over zwemmen
        the canal that we   over swim

Given this dual possibility, where in one instance a verb is preceded by a bare NP complement, we may expect to find passives on these bare NP complements as well. Here we enter into a domain where judgements are very subtle and show variation among speakers. Consider first of all the choice of auxiliary. This matter will be dealt with in detail in section 4.4., but at this moment it is relevant to see that in the perfect of (80) there is also a dual possibility of selecting the perfective auxiliary.

(84) a. dat wij het kanaal over zijn/hebben gezwommen
        that we the canal over are/ have   swum

     b. dat we de straat over zijn/hebben gestoken
        that we the street over are/have   crossed

c. dat we de helling af zijn/hebben gelopen
   that we the slope down are/have walked

Let us look at the interplay between these two options, i.e. the option of
selecting **zijn** vs. **hebben** as the perfective auxiliary and the option of having an
NP particle or a postpositional PP analysis. Theoretically, these two options can
give rise to four different situations. It seems to me that only two out of these
four possibilities are correct, i.e. if the non-R-pronoun is selected, the
auxiliary **hebben** is favoured, whereas **zijn** is better in the case of an R-pronoun.
Admittedly, the judgements are subtle, but they seem to me to point in the right
direction.

(85) a. het kanaal dat/*waar we over hebben gezwommen
     b. het kanaal waar/*dat we over zijn gezwommen

(86) a. de straat die/*waar we hebben over gestoken
     b. de straat waar/*die we over zijn gestoken

(87) a. de helling die/*waar we af hebben gelopen
     b. de helling waar/*die we af zijn gelopen

In other words, **hebben** is chosen if we are dealing with a (complex) transitive
verb, as is usual with transitives, but **zijn** is favoured if the verb is intransitive and is accompanied by a postpositional PP. There are other verbs, however,
that for reasons that are entirely unclear to me, do not permit the choice of
hebben as a perfective auxiliary. An example is found in (88).

(88) a.*de helling die we af gegleden hebben
       the slope that we down slid have

     b. de helling waar we af gegleden zijn
        the slope where we down slid are

Let us assume that the preceding argument is correct. It is to be expected, then,
that there is a passive counterpart for the a-examples in (85)-(87), but not for
the b-examples. However, although there is a passive like (89), it is not
immediately evident that it corresponds to (85a) rather than to (85b).

(89) Dat kanaal is nog nooit door iemand over gezwommen
     That canal is still never by anyone over swum

However, the fact that there is no passive corresponding to any of the examples in
(88) strongly suggests that we are on the right track.

(90) *Die helling is nog nooit door iemand afgegleden
     That slope is yet never by anyone down slid

Still more suggestive evidence is provided by the following argument. Consider
the sentence in (91), where we find both a direct object (het schip) and a NP P
sequence, the structure of which may be ambiguous. Since the verb is clearly
transitive, the perfective auxiliary **hebben** must be chosen. The passive of (91)
can only be based on the direct object **het schip,** as is illustrated in (92).

(91) dat de kapitein het schip de haven binnen heeft/* is gevaren
     that the captain the ship the harbour into has/is sailed

(92) a. het schip werd door de kapitein de haven binnen gevaren
        the ship was   by the captain the harbour into sailed

     b.*de havens werden het schip door de kapitein binnen gevaren
        the harbours were the ship by the captain into sailed

Next to (91), however, there is also a construction like (93), without the direct
object **het schip.** Again, there are two choices of the relative pronoun as well as
two choices of the perfective auxiliary.

(93) a. dat de kapitein de haven binnen voer
        that the captain the harbour into sailed

     b. de haven waar de kapitein binnen gevaren is
        the harbour where the captain into sailed is

     c. de haven die de kapitein binnen gevaren heeft
        the harbour that the captain into sailed has

It is to be expected, then, that there is a passive corresponding to (93c), which turns out to be the case. Moreover, there are two possible usages of the participial adjective.

(94) de haven die zojuist binnen gevaren is heet Santa Cruz
     the harbour that right now into sailed is is called Santa Cruz

(95) a. de binnengevaren schepen
        the ships which have been sailed in (i.e. into the harbour)

     b. de binnengevaren havens
        the harbours which have been sailed into

What the preceding discussion illustrates is that the possibility of pseudo-passives found in English depends on the adjacency of the adposition and the verb. If this adjacency holds in Dutch, which is the case with postpositional adpositions, passivization is possible as well.

On the whole, then, the conclusion seems to be warranted that passivization is not really a homogeneous phenomenon in terms of essential categories, but that the possibilities of a general rule, which ultimately is part of Universal Grammar, are determined by rather superficial characteristics of a particular language. We argued that several scope differences between passivization in Dutch and English are related to the positional difference of the verb. There-fore, the hypothesis that the passive rule in Dutch can be properly characterized by its lack of blindness is inspired by observations that can be argued to be determined by factors that have nothing to do with passivization itself, and consequently is unfounded. This suggests that the EST approach, according to which the rule of passive does not even exist as such is on the right track. Rather, there is a rule of MOVE NP, or preferably MOVE α, that is either operative in the language or not. Given the occurrence of subject-raising constructions in Dutch, it would come as a surprise within the framework of EST assumptions if there were no transformational passive constructions in Dutch.

3.3. Extending MOVE NP: unaccusatives

3.3.1. Introductory remarks

In this section, the domain of applicability of MOVE NP will be extended to other construction types than subject raising and passivization. The discussion is focused on specific constructions in Dutch, but many of the arguments carry over to other languages.

We shall begin with a review and criticism of a number of proposals made by Perlmutter within the framework of Relational Grammar, specifically his unaccusative analysis and the analysis of inversion constructions. Then we continue by reformulating these hypotheses within the theory of Government and Binding. It will be seen that this theory attains a high level of explanatory adequacy in this domain. At the same time, various long-standing descriptive problems in the grammar of Dutch will receive a natural explanation within the framework of GB-theory.

3.3.2. No initial subject: two hypotheses about basic clause structure.

In section 3.2.2., a distinction had to be made between two classes of intransitives: those that allow the rule of participle-adjective conversion and those that do not. Adopting Bresnan's terminology, one might say that the former have Theme SUBJECTS, whereas the latter have non-Theme SUBJECTS.

In Perlmutter (1978), a specific hypothesis is put forward concerning a distinction that is similar to the one above. Perlmutter defines the initial stratum as a level of representation at which the predicate with its nominal dependents with their initial grammatical relations to this predicate is represented, and argues that the initial stratum of a monadic predicate either has the structure represented in (96) or the structure represented in (97). A stratum like (97) is called "unaccusative", a name that is significant in the light of recent explorations in the same field within GB-theory. Strata like (96), on the other hand, are called "unergative".

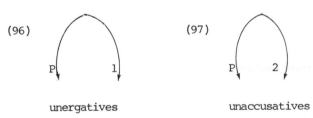

(96)   (97)

    P   1   P   2

       unergatives   unaccusatives

The stratal diagram in (97) embodies the claim that there may be strata without a subject (the 1-relation). This possibility is not open to all strata, however. In Perlmutter & Postal (to appear a:33), a law is formulated to the effect that each final stratum must contain a subject. This law is given in (98).

(98) The final-1-law

If there is a c_kth stratum of b and no c_{k+1} st stratum
of b, we say that the c_kth stratum is the final stratum of b.
Then: If b is a basic clause node, the final stratum of b
contains a 1-arc

Therefore, in order to arrive at a final stratum that observes (98), the initial 2 (direct object) in (979) must be advanced or promoted to subject. This advancement process is referred to as "unaccusative advancement".

Besides the final-1-law, another universal law is relevant for these unaccusative structures as well. This is the 1-advancement exclusiveness law, formulated in (99).

(99) The 1-advancement exclusiveness law

In a relational network in which A and B are neighboring 1-arcs
(i.e. 1-arcs with the same tail), if A is an advancee arc
B is not an advancee arc.   Perlmutter (1978:166)

Informally, the law states that within a single clause only one promotion to subject may take place. In conjunction with (98) and the unaccusative analysis, this law makes a specific prediction. To see this, we have to make a brief digression into the analysis of passive in general and the impersonal passive in particular.

According to Perlmutter & Postal (1977), Relational Grammar characterizes passive as a universal rule that promotes the direct object to subject, with a subsequent demotion of the subject to the status of chomeur. This view of passive seems to conflict with the existence of impersonal passives, which lack a direct object that can be promoted to subject. To maintain their universal characterization of passivization, however, Perlmutter (1978) and Perlmutter & Zaenen (to appear) analyze impersonal passives in Dutch as involving the promotion of a direct object dummy **er** which can be omitted in surface structure, subject to dialectal and other variation.

If the analysis of unaccusatives involves the promotion of the initial direct object to subject by the rule of unaccusative advancement, then, the 1-advancement exclusiveness law in (99) predicts that impersonal passives are impossible with unaccusative predicates.

It will be evident that this prediction cannot be used to determine whether a particular predicate selects an initial unaccusative stratum or not, for this line of reasoning would be circular. Perlmutter (1978) does not provide any specific principle, however, to predict which predicate will select an initial unaccusative stratum, but he notes that the strongest hypothesis would be that "there exist universal principles which predict .....initial unaccusativity. [.....]. The basic idea is that initial unaccusativity is predictable from the semantics of the clause" (Perlmutter 1978:161). In spite of this, Perlmutter limits himself to listing examples of both types of intransitives, noting that predicates that select an initial unergative stratum have a notion of activity in their meaning, whereas the predicates of the unaccusative variety can also be classified into a number of semantically characterizable subgroups (o.c. 162). He notes, however, that nothing hinges on the particular subgroups given in these lists. Personally, I am rather sceptical about the possibility of finding such predictive principles. A perusal of various semantically based classifications of verbs (e.g. Vendler 1967, Dowty 1979, Dik 1978) did not offer any perspective in this direction[60]. I shall not discuss this matter any further now and assume that the distinction between the two classes of predicates is a matter of selection in the lexicon. It is evident, however, that at least some semantic subregularities exist.

3.3.2.1. Unaccusatives in Dutch

The distinction between unaccusative and unergative predicates in Dutch is manifested by the choice of the perfective auxiliary[61], unaccusative predicates selecting **zijn** and unergatives selecting **hebben**. We thus have the opposition between (100) and (101).

(100) a. dat Jan valt
          that John falls

    b. dat Jan gevallen is
       that John fallen is

(101) a. dat Jan lacht
        that John laughs

    b. dat Jan gelachen heeft
       that John laughed has

Not only do unergatives select **hebben** in their perfect, nearly all transitives
select **hebben** as well[62]. As far as I am aware, no explanation has been given for
the difference in auxiliary selection. Traditional grammarians refer to notions
like mutativity and completion (cf. Kern 1912) which would appear to be relevant
in their view. Verbs that we call unaccusatives here would then denote mutations.
De Vooijs (1947) illustrates the relevance of completion by giving the following
examples.

(102) a. dat ik gewandeld heb/*ben
         that I walked have / am

    b. dat ik naar Groningen gewandeld ben/heb
       that I to Groningen walked am/have

Whereas the simple verb **wandelen** selects the perfective auxiliary **hebben,** the
complex predicate **naar Groningen wandelen,** which denotes not only the act of
walking but also the completion of this act, may select either of the perfective
auxiliaries. The selection of auxiliary in the latter case involves a semantic
difference, which corresponds to a syntactic difference. A more extensive discussion of this fact is presented in section 4.2. Here we just point out that the
prepositional complement **naar Groningen** can only occur in postverbal position if
hebben is selected as the temporal auxiliary:

(103) a. dat ik naar Groningen gewandeld heb/ben
         that I to Groningen walked   have/am

    b. dat ik gewandeld heb/*ben naar Groningen

In case that **zijn** is selected, a suitable paraphrase would be "that I went to

Groningen on foot" whereas the sentence with **hebben** is more appropriately para-
phrased with "that I was walking on my way to Groningen'.

The following list gives a representative sample of unaccusative verbs,
although it is by no means exhaustive:

sterven 'die'	emigreren 'emigrate'
blijven 'remain,stay'	groeien 'grow'
komen 'come'	krimpen 'shrink'
gebeuren 'happen'	ontsnappen 'escape'
aanslibben 'silt up'	ontstaan 'come into existence
ontaarden 'degenerate'	ophouden 'cease'
ontwaken 'awake'	opstaan 'get up'
dalen 'land'	rijzen 'rise'
uitgaan 'go out'	slagen 'succeed'
aankomen 'arrive'	verbleken 'fade'
verschijnen 'appear'	verdorren 'wither'
verstrijken 'elapse'	zinken 'sink'
vertrekken 'depart'	zwellen 'swell'
stijgen 'rise'	barsten 'burst'

It is evident that most of these verbs indeed denote a change of state, but as
we shall see in the next section, there is a class of verbs with essentially the
same syntactic properties, which do not denote any mutation. Having set up two
subclasses of intransitives on the basis of auxiliary selection, we notice that
the verbs of the unaccusative class are those that allow participle-adjective
conversion. This is illustrated by the following examples.

(104) a. de kinderen zijn jong gestorven
          the children are died young

      b. de jong gestorven kinderen
          the young died children

(105) a. de kool is snel gegroeid
          the cabbage is fast grown

      b. de snel gegroeide kool
          the fast grown cabbage

(106) a. de man heeft gelachen
         the man has laughed

      b. *de gelachen man
         the laughed man

(107) a. de kinderen hebben gedanst
         the children have danced

      b. *de gedanste kinderen
         the danced children

Another correlation involves the formation of impersonal passives, as was noted
by Perlmutter (1978) (cf. above). Whereas the unaccusative verbs do not allow
the formation of impersonal passives, intransitives that select **hebben** as their
temporal auxiliary freely allow it. The following examples are taken from Perlmutter (1978).

(108) a. *Er werd door de kinderen in het weeshuis erg snel gegroeid
           There was by the children in the orphanage very fast grown

      b. *Er werd door het water snel verdampt
         There was by the water very fast evaporated

(109) a. Er werd de hele avond door een van de kinderen gehuild
         There was the entire evening by one of the children cried

      b. Er wordt in deze kamer vaak geslapen
         There is in this room often slept

As we saw above, Relational Grammar explains the difference in grammaticality
between (108) and (109) by assuming that unaccusative advancement excludes the
possibility of passivization. This assumption is formulated in terms of the 1-
advancement exclusiveness law, stated in (99).

At this point, a brief digression is in order. The stratal diagram in (110) is
a representation of the basic clause structure of (109a), with irrelevant material omitted. Perlmutter (1978:160) defines three types of strata, viz. the
unaccusative (cf. (97)), the unergative (cf. (96)) and the transitive (cf.

(111)below). Given the representation of impersonal passives at their initial
stratum as in (110), it appears to be the case that there are in fact no
predicates that select initially unergative strata.

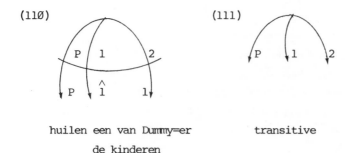

(110)

          P   1   2

          P   1   1

        huilen een van Dummy=er   transitive
        de kinderen

(111)

          P   1   2

Recall that it is claimed that all unergatives allow impersonal passivization and
that impersonal passivization is in fact promotion of a Dummy direct object. This
would imply, it seems to me, that these predicates therefore do in fact select
initially transitive strata (cf. (110) and (111)), in which case it must be
concluded that initially unergative strata are never selected, i.e. are in fact
unnecessary. I leave this matter in the hands of Relational Grammarians.

      I shall now discuss in some detail how the correlations that we have observed
can be captured and explained in terms of Relational Grammar. It was observed in
section 3.2.2. that participles of transitive verbs can be used as predicates
over nouns, provided that the noun corresponds to the direct object of this
predicate, with the further condition that it is the theme of this predicate.
This possibility is shared by participles of unaccusative verbs: they may also be
used as predicates over nouns corresponding to their initial direct object.
Bresnan (1980a) captures this generalization by formulating the conversion rule
in terms of SUBJ in both cases, where the active lexical form of unaccusative
verbs is selected by the condition that this SUBJ is the Theme of the predicate,
whereas this condition selects the passive lexical form of transitive predicates.
The requirement that the SUBJ be the Theme of the predicate also excludes the
application of this conversion rule in the case of unergatives, on the assumption
that their SUBJ's express a non-Theme argument. In Bresnan's account, then, two
distinct notions enter into the statement of the generalization: a grammatical
function (SUBJ) and a thematic role (Theme).

      With the help of the unaccusative hypothesis, Relational Grammar allows the
generalization to be captured in terms of a single notion, viz. initial direct
object, at least if there is a correspondence between initial grammatical rela-

tion and thematic role as Perlmutter suggests (cf. supra). The distinction
between the two types of predicates (unaccusatives and passive transitives)
follows from the different rules involved in the derivation of the two types,
viz. unaccusative advancement and passivization. The relevant generalization can
now be stated informally as in (112).

(112) Participles can be used as predicates over nouns which
     correspond to their initial direct object.

Note that this formulation also excludes a construction like (113a). Although
there is a passive like (113b), the subject of this passive is not an initial
direct object according to Relational Grammar, but rather an initial indirect
object, which has been promoted to the status of direct object by the rule of
Dative Movement, called 3-2 advancement in Relational Grammar. This rule derives
(114a) from (114b).

(113) a. *a given woman
     b. the woman was given a book

(114) a. Someone gave the woman a book
     b. Someone gave a book to the woman

More or less the same can be said about auxiliary selection. Again, there is a
correspondence between passives and unaccusatives in that both select the perfective auxiliary **zijn**. Whereas the formulation in (112) refers to the initial
stratum, an account of auxiliary selection requires that reference is made to the
final stratum and to an earlier stratum. The following formulation seems to be
adequate.

(115) A predicate selects the perfective auxiliary **zijn** if
     one of its nominal dependents is headed by both a
     1-arc and a 2-arc.

It is not necessary to specify in this formulation that the 1-arc must be a final
stratum arc, since if the nominal is also headed by a 2-arc, it can be headed by
the 1-arc only by virtue of a promotion rule having applied to it. The final 1-law
and the 1-advancement exclusiveness law ensure that the 1-arc is a final stratum
arc. Similarly, it is unnecessary and in fact wrong to require that the 2-arc be

an initial stratum arc. This is clear in those cases in which the final subject
is an initial indirect object which has undergone promotion to direct object
first.

It turns out, then, that the framework of Relational Grammar allows a number
of significant generalizations to be captured. From a single assumption about
basic clause structure, a number of interesting generalizations follow: the
distribution of the perfective auxiliaries, the statement of "participle-adjective conversion" and the range of application of impersonal passivization. The
next subsection is devoted to an extension of the idea that initial strata need
not have a subject.

3.3.2.2. Inversion: unaccusativity extended

In the previous section, the hypothesis was discussed that a subclass of intransitives may be analyzed as involving an initial stratum that has no subject.
Supposing that this analysis is correct, we might further hypothesize that the
lack of an initial subject occurs more generally.

This hypothesis would suggest that besides initial strata like (116) for
transitives and (117) for bitransitives, some predicates might select an initial
stratum like (118), i.e. a stratum with both a direct object and an indirect
object, but without a subject.

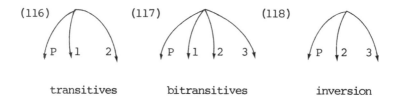

I shall refer to the analysis in (118) with 'inversion', a term that is used in
Relational Grammar for the analysis of the same predicates, though it differs in
an important respect from the analysis presented here. This difference will be
discussed below. As the final-1-law requires that each final stratum has a 1-arc,
we need to assume that some rule applies to (118) in order to provide a final
subject. We shall assume that this is the unaccusative advancement rule.

Given the assumptions made in the discussion of unaccusatives, the predicates

that select an initial stratum like (118) are predicted to have at least the
following properties:
- they will select the perfective auxiliary **zijn,** given that the nominal headed
by a direct object arc in the initial stratum is also headed by a subject arc, due
to unaccusative advancement.
- the participle can be used as an adjective to predicate over nouns corresponding to the derived subject. The participle will be obligatorily accompanied by a
nominal corresponding to the initial indirect object, if the initial indirect
object is obligatorily selected.
- given the 1-advancement exclusiveness law, it is predicted that these predicates will not undergo passivization or impersonal passivization.

Before turning to the predicates that bear these predictions out, we must
sound a note of caution. Besides initial strata like those in (116)-(118) and the
strata discussed in the previous section (i.e. (96) and (97)), there may also be
predicates selecting (119) as their initial stratum.

(119)

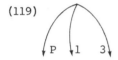

It seems to me that this class is rather small in Dutch. An example is the verb
smaken 'taste', which does not permit passivization, while it selects **hebben** as
its perfective auxiliary, as predicted. The participle cannot be used as in
(120c), nor as in (120d), suggesting that there is indeed no initial direct
object. That the non-subject nominal is indeed an initial indirect object can
also be seen in the nominalization in (120e), where it appears with the preposition **aan** which is the preposition that typically indicates indirect objecthood.

(120) a. dat die maaltijd het meisje gesmaakt heeft/*is
          that that meal that girl   tasted has /is

      b.*dat het meisje door de maaltijd wordt gesmaakt
         that the girl by the meal is tasted

      c.*het gesmaakte meisje
         the tasted girl

    d.*de gesmaakte maaltijd

       the tasted meal

    e. het aan mij smaken van de maaltijd[63]

       the to me tasting of the meal

In German, there seem to be more candidates for the selection of (119). An example is **helfen** 'help'. That the object of **helfen** is indeed an indirect object is clear from the fact that it has dative case, the common marker for indirect objects. That the subject is the initial subject follows from the fact that **helfen** selects **haben** as its temporal auxiliary, at least under the assumption that the distribution of the perfective auxiliaries in Dutch and German is governed by the same principles, which is a quite natural assumption. Given these assumptions, it is predicted that passive is indeed possible with German **helfen,** since there is no unaccusative advancement. However, as passivization is a rule promoting a direct object to subject, the passive will be impersonal, i.e. have a dummy as derived subject, which is a silent one (i.e. a dummy that does not surface) in most cases in German. This prediction is borne out.

    (121) a. Der Jungen hat/*ist mir geholfen

          the boy   has/is me-DAT helped

       b. Mir wird von dem Jungen geholfen

          me-DAT is by the boy   helped

Note that we would expect an impersonal passive with **smaken** in Dutch for similar reasons. This expectation is not borne out, however, for reasons that are unclear to me.

It is worth pointing out that the Dutch equivalent of **helfen** displays all the properties of normal transitives, e.g. it forms a regular personal passive. This casts doubts on the hypothesis that there is a predictable relation between semantic role and initial grammatical relation. Again, it seems to me that the difference between Dutch and German in this respect is related to the fact that German still has a reliable case system, which is absent in Dutch, save for a case distinction in pronouns between subject and non-subject form, as in English.

Let us return now to the inversion analysis in (118). The predicates that appear to have the properties that we predicted are illustrated by the sample in (122).

(122) bevallen 'please', te binnen schieten 'to come to one's mind',
      lukken 'succeed', ontgaan 'elude', opvallen 'strike',
      overkomen 'happen to'

The relevant properties are illustrated in the following examples.

(123) a. perfective with **zijn**
      1. die fout is/*heeft mij opgevallen
         that mistake is/has me struck

      2. die opmerking is/*heeft me ontgaan
         that remark is/has me eluded

      3. die ramp is/*heeft mij overkomen
         that disaster is/has me happened

      4. die som is/*heeft mij gelukt
         that sum is/has   me succeeded

      b. passive excluded
      1.*Ik ben door die fout opgevallen
         I am by that mistake struck

      2.*Ik ben door die opmerking ontgaan
         I am by that remark eluded

      3.*Ik ben door die ramp overkomen
         I am by that disaster happened

      4.*Ik ben door die som gelukt
         I am by that sum succeeded

      c. impersonal passive excluded
      1.*Er is mij door die fout opgevallen
         There is me by that mistake struck

      2.*Er is mij door die opmerking ontgaan
         There is me by that mistake eluded

      d. "participles over derived subject"
      1. de mij opgevallen fout
         the me struck mistake

      2. de mij overkomen ramp
         the me happened disaster

      3. de mij gelukte som
         the me succeeded sum

Notice that the verb **opvallen** is semantically very close to **treffen,** but **treffen**
has all the reverse properties, as illustrated in (124). Once more this is an
indication of the doubtful status of the claim that initial grammatical relations
are predictable on the basis of semantic roles.

   (124) a. de fout heeft/*is mij getroffen
            the mistake has/is me struck

         b. ik werd door die fout getroffen
            I was by that mistake struck

         c. de door die fout getroffen schoolmeester
            the by that mistake struck school teacher

The range of correlations found with these verbs and the fact that these were
predicted on the basis of the assumption that these verbs select an initial
stratum without a subject and that therefore unaccusative advancement is involved
in their derivation constitute strong motivation for the unification of unaccusatives and inversion predicates as we argued.

      In section 3.3.2.1. we showed that unaccusatives share a number of properties
with passives of transitives. We may therefore also expect inversion predicates
to share a number of properties with passives of bitransitives, which indeed
appears to be the case. First, both passive bitransitives and inversion predicates form their perfect with **zijn**. It should be noted that it is by no means
necessary that passives of bitransitives should select **zijn**. In the previous
section, we argued that, given Perlmutter's analysis of impersonal passives as an
advancement of a dummy direct object, there are no genuine intransitive initial
strata. Theoretically, then, the selection of perfective auxiliaries could be

governed by (125) instead of by (115) as we initially assumed.

(125) In final strata with two term arcs (term arcs are 1, 2 and 3)
hebben is selected; otherwise, **zijn** is selected.

A final stratum of a passive bitransitive does indeed contain two term arcs, viz.
the indirect object and the subject. It turns out, however, that our formulation
in (115) yields the correct results.

A second correspondence between inversion predicates and passive bitransitives concerns the phenomenon of what Koster (1978a) calls "indirect object preposing", illustrated in (126)-(127).

(126) a. dat die fout de schoolmeester opviel
         that that mistake the school teacher struck

     b. dat de schoolmeester die fout opviel
        that the school teacher that mistake struck

(127) a. dat dat geschenk de koningin werd overhandigd
         that that present the queen was presented

     b. dat de koningin dat geschenk werd overhandigd
        that the queen that present was presented

Koster (1978a) acknowledged the non-structural character of this phenomenon: in
order to cover the data, his core principle, the so-called Locality Principle,
was augmented by an auxiliary hypothesis (see Hoekstra & Moortgat 1979c) for
extensive criticism). This auxiliary hypothesis formulates a hierarchy of grammatical functions, in the sense of primitive labels, and states that an empty
node may be coindexed with a non-empty node, if the latter is more prominent in
the hierarchy than an intervening node. It is assumed in this hierarchy that
indirect objects are ranked higher than direct objects, which is required in
order to accommodate these cases.

The phenomenon of "indirect object preposing" is extensively discussed in
section 3.3.3.2. below. Here I want to point out that it is never possible to have
an object preceding the subject if it is an initial subject, at least in embedded
clauses. Therefore, the inversion of NP's as in (126) and (127) is impossible in
normal transitive sentences like (128).

(128) a. dat de jongen een auto zag
　　　　 that the boy　a　 car　saw

　　　 b.*dat een auto de jongen zag
　　　　　 that a car　 the boy　 saw

It should be noted that the contrast between (126b) and (128b) would be problematic if no distinction was made between transitive and inversion constructions. It
should also be noted that in active bitransitives the indirect object may not
precede the subject either as is illustrated by (129).

(129) a. dat de ouders die jongen een auto gaven
　　　　 that the parents that boy a　car　 gave

　　　 b.*dat die jongen de ouders een auto gaven
　　　　　 that that boy the parents a　 car　 gave

The phenomenon of "indirect object preposing", then, suggests a fundamental
similarity between passive bitransitives and inversion constructions.

　　　In addition to the property that the subject of the inversion construction
may be preceded by the indirect object, this subject may not occur in the
nominative form if it is preceded by the indirect object. The following examples
illustrate this:

(130) a. dat zij de sjeik wel beviel
　　　　 that she the sheikh quite pleased

　　　 b.*dat de sjeik zij wel beviel

(131) a. dat zij hem gegeven werd
　　　　 that she him given was

　　　 b.*dat hem zij gegeven werd

This property demonstrates that the phenomenon of "indirect object preposing"
cannot be assumed to result from a "normal" preposing, i.e. although the unmarked
order in embedded clauses with a pronominal subject is such that the subject
appears in initial position, an adverbial phrase may precede it with emphatic

stress on the subject pronoun as in (132).

    (132) dat om die reden zij niet naar huis wilde
          that for that reason she did not want to go home

This property, then, sets the constructions with preposed indirect objects off
against constructions which show a preposing of a non-indirect object. In fact,
the only reason to look upon these subjects in constructions with preposed
indirect objects as the subject of the clause is the fact that they possess the
property of determining the verb agreement. In this respect, these alleged
subjects show the same behaviour as demoted subjects in existential constructions. We return to a discussion of this correlation below.

    At the beginning of this section we remarked that the analysis presented in
(118) differs in an important respect from Perlmutter's (1979) analysis of
inversion. Perlmutter's analysis is summarized in the stratal diagram in (133).
He assumes that the final-stratum indirect object originates as a subject in the
initial stratum, which is reranked by a rule of inversion. In our analysis, no
such rule is postulated: the final-stratum indirect object is an initial-stratum
indirect object as well.

(133)

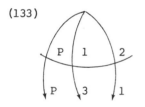

inversion according to
Perlmutter (1979)

Since the analysis presented in (118) and Perlmutter's analysis agree as to the
final stratum relations and the unaccusative part of the derivation, we shall
concentrate on the motivation of adopting the initial subjecthood of the final-
stratum indirect object, the nominal that Perlmutters refers to as the inversion
nominal.

    Anticipating the reformulation of Perlmutter's hypotheses in terms of GB-
theory, it is evident that Perlmutter's conception of these constructions requires an operation that is undesirable from a methodological point of view.
Rephrased in phrase structure terms, the inversion analysis of Perlmutter would
require that the NP in subject position is downgraded into the VP to the position
of the indirect object, resulting in a configuration as indicated in (134). The
trace in this structure would be improperly bound by the NP in the position of the

indirect object as this NP does not c-command the subject position.

(134)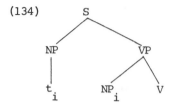

From this point of view, then, Perlmutter's rule of inversion would require an important weakening of linguistic theory. This is not only true with respect to a trace-theoretic interpretation, but holds equally well for Relational Grammar. Apart from this inversion rule, the only types of downgrading or lowering rules proposed are lowerings to chomeur as a result of usurpation, i.e. a promotion. In fact, the only convincing lowering is the demotion of the subject due to the advancement of the object in passives. There has never been a proposal to the effect that subjects retreat to direct object, or direct objects to indirect object[64]. We consider this not to be a coincidence, but rather a phenomenon that should be explained. Within Relational Grammar, this could be stated in terms of the following law.

(135)   A nominal bearing a grammatical relation can only
        be demoted to a chomeur, but not to any other
        position on the Relational Hierarchy

Given the undesirable status of the rule of inversion, then, let us investigate the empirical arguments that are adduced in support of it. It turns out that all the arguments involve control phenomena that are accounted for in terms of the notion working 1. This notion is defined in Perlmutter (1979) as in (136).

(136)   Working 1 (definition)

        A nominal is a working 1 of clause b if and only if:
        (i) it heads a 1 arc with tail b
        (ii) it heads a final stratum term arc with tail b

This notion comprises all and only nominals heading by any of the following arcs:

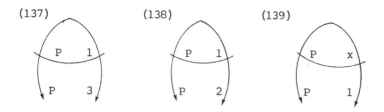

(137)   (138)   (139)

Either we are dealing with an initial subject that is demoted to a final-stratum term arc as in (137) and (138), or the nominal is a final-stratum subject derived from any kind of initial-stratum grammatical relation x, as in (139). Case (139) is of course hardly interesting, since here conditions (i) and (ii) of (136) are fulfilled by the final-stratum subjecthood. Most probably, case (138) does not exist, i.e. as stated above, such an analysis has never been proposed. It appears to be the case, then, that the notion working 1 is relevant only for the inversion nominal. This makes any argument based on the notion of working 1 more or less suspicious.

We shall now review one of Perlmutter's arguments for the initial subjecthood of the inversion nominal. The following example, taken from Perlmutter (1979), involves the **-nagara** construction in Japanese, a construction that is comparable to an infinitival adjunct in English. The sentences in (140) and (141) show that subjects, but not objects or indirect objects can be interpreted as controllers of the understood subject of the **-nagara** clause.

    (140) Arukinagara, daitooryoo wa gamu o kande ita
          walk-while   president TOP gum ACC chewing was
          "While he was walking, the president was chewing gum"

    (141) Sono koto o kangaenagara,   Tanaka-san ni denwa sita
          those things ACC think-while, Tanaka-mr. DAT telephoned
          "While I was thinking about those things, I phoned mr. Tanaka"

In (140), the final (and also initial) subject is doing the walking, not the direct object. Similarly, in (141) **Mr. Tanaka** cannot be construed as the understood subject of the **-nagara** clause, but it is **I** who does the thinking. The second step in the argument illustrates that it is not the initial subject that is construed as the controller. In passives, then, the final subject is the controller of the **-nagara** clause, not the initial subject. So, one would be tempted to conclude that the relevant rule should be formulated in terms of the notion of

final subject. In that case, however, it is wrongly predicted that in the
inversion construction it is the final stratum subject that controls the subject
of the **-nagara** clause. In (142) it is the final indirect object **roodoosya** that
acts as the controller.

(142) Sutoraiki o yatte inagara,   roodoosya ni subete   ga
      strike ACC doing be-while   workers   DAT everything SUBJ

      muzukasiku omoete kita
      difficult seem   came

      "While on strike, everything began to seem difficult to the
      workers"

Perlmutter therefore arrives at the conclusion that the control rule must be
stated in terms of the notion working-1, which requires the initial subjecthood
of the inversion nominal.

  The argument seems ingenious, but it is without force. It is based on the
behaviour of indirect objects in inversion constructions and in active bitransitives. The argument merely shows that these constructions have different
properties. But it is clear that the differential behaviour of the indirect
objects in these two types of structures with respect to control may also be
related to a difference between the constructions that was already motivated,
viz. the presence vs. absence of an initial subject. If we want to show that the
argument is indeed fallacious at the point just noted, the inversion construction
should be compared to a construction type that has a greater similarity to it.
This is what we shall do.

  The argument for the notion working-1 could also be based on the following
Dutch data. First, example (143) shows that it is the final subject and not the
final direct object that acts as the controller for the subject of an infinitival
adverbial adjunct. Example (144) confirms that it is not the initial, but rather
the final subject that is relevant in this respect. Example (145) then shows that
the notion of working-1 is required, since here it it the inversion nominal that
controls the interpretation of the subject of the infinitival adjunct.

(143) *Na van het uitzicht genoten te hebben reed de bus ons weer terug.
       After of the view enjoyed to have   drove the bus us again back

(144) Na van het uitzicht genoten te hebben, werden we terug gereden
       After of the view enjoyed to have   were we back driven

(145) Na van vakantie te zijn terug gekeerd, bevalt dit baantje mij beter
       After from vacation to be back returned pleases this job   me better

The crucial test for the correctness of the argument involves, of course, the
passive bitransitive: in that construction, the final indirect object is also the
initial indirect object, so that it does not qualify as a working-1. The essenti-
als of the analysis of passive bitransitives are represented in (146).

(146)
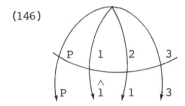

The only nominal that qualifies as a working-1 is the initial direct object that
is promoted to subject. The grammaticality of (147) clearly indicates that an
indirect object can control the subject of an infinitival adverbial adjunct
without ever having been a subject. The conclusion, then, that the final indirect
object in (145) must be an initial-stratum subject thus seems unwarranted.

(147) Na van vakantie te zijn terug gekeerd werd mij een nieuwe baan
       After from vacation to be back returned was me a   new   job

       aangeboden
       offered

Since the crucial support appears to be missing, Perlmutter's inversion analysis
must be rejected in favour of the analysis presented in (118). Therefore,
inversion constructions do not violate the law in (135), i.e. when reconstructed
in terms of trace theory, they do not violate the requirement of proper binding.

    It is interesting to see that the control phenomena above indicate that the
indirect object is in some sense more prominent than the direct object, even when
the latter is promoted to subject. A similar claim is made by Koster (1978a) as
noted above. Although I have no explanation to offer for this, it seems reasona-

ble to conjecture that in the instances of control that we discussed in this
section the relevant control is pragmatic rather than syntactic in nature, given
also the fact that under no analysis the indirect object will c-command the
infinitival adjunct. Since indirect objects usually denote persons and persons
are pragmatically speaking more prominent than non-human referents, the promi-
nence of the indirect object in these cases should not cause great surprise.

3.3.2.3. Summary and evaluation

The previous subsections have reviewed the hypothesis of Relational Grammar that
initial strata may lack a subject. We argued that this hypothesis might be
generalized to cover both unaccusative structures and inversion structures. This
generalization is depicted in the diagrams in (97) and (118), repeated here.

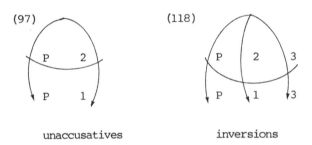

(97)   (118)

        P   2   P   2   3

        P   1   P   1   3

      unaccusatives   inversions

We argued furthermore that the rule of inversion, proposed by Perlmutter, which
maps initial subjects into final stratum indirect objects should be rejected.
This allows us to formulate a law as in (135), which has the effect of considera-
bly reducing the class of possible relation-changing rules.

    It was also concluded that the unaccusative hypothesis allows us to capture a
number of generalizations and make a number of predictions that are borne out.
Specifically, we pointed at a number of similarities between passives and unaccusatives on the one hand and bitransitive passives and inversion constructions on
the other. These similarities follow from a number of laws within the framework
of Relational Grammar such as the final-1-law and the 1-advancement exclusiveness
law.

    In spite of this, I am inclined to have serious doubts about the validity of
the approach. The status of the laws as well as the status of the relational

notions employed is unclear. I think it is a priori more desirable to derive the
predictions made by these laws from structural principles. In the next section we
shall argue that this is indeed possible. In our discussion above, we already
showed how the law in (135) is in fact a consequence of a configurational
requirement, viz. the c-command requirement for binders. This constitutes a
desirable reduction. As for the notion of unaccusative stratum, i.e. a level of
representation that does not contain a subject, it is unclear what this would
mean within a phrase structure grammar. Such an approach would seem to make it
necessary that not all S's are rewritten as NP followed by VP. A question then
arises whether the rule of unaccusative advancement is supposed to build the
required structure.

Another question relates to the connection between the various construction
types. It was shown that unaccusatives resemble passives of transitives whereas
inversion constructions share a number of properties with passives of bitransitives. However, the unaccusatives and inversions involve the rule of unaccusative
advancement, whereas the passive structures are derived by passivization. We
could ask, then, whether these are really distinct rules. If they are, then it
seems to be a coincidence that they is no rule of "dative" advancement to subject,
i.e. would it be possible to have a construction type as in (148)?

(148)

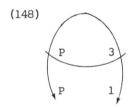

Such an analysis has never been proposed, as far as I know, and I take it that this
is not a coincidence, i.e. that the formal relationship between unaccusative
advancement and passivization (both advancements of 2 to 1) is more direct, e.g.
that they are in fact one and the same rule. If that is the case, the demotion part
of passivization is not a necessary part of the relevant rule, so that in effect
passivization is split up in two separate steps, one of which collapses with
unaccusative advancement (cf. the historical development of the transformational
approach to passivization in section 3.2.1.).

3.3.3. Unaccusativity within GB-theory.

3.3.3.1. The passive in GB-theory

At the end of section 3.2.1. it was concluded that the operation of passive, which is reduced to MOVE NP, is triggered by the empty subject position. It is thus triggered by properties of the landing site. In this respect, the EST-approach is in line with the "spontaneous demotion" analysis of Sadock (1977) and other within the framework of Relational Grammar. The opposite view is held by Perlmutter & Postal (to appear b), according to whom the demotion of the subject to chomeur is universally held to be a consequence of the promotion of a non-subject to subject position. In Bresnan's (1978) lexical approach to passivization, the promotion of the object is again seen as a consequence of the existential binding of the subject argument.

For the paradigm case of passives one might say that it is pointless to ask what the interdependence between the two operations involved is, since they are obviously connected in the sense that both have to take place, which constitutes in fact the reason to assume that they are essentially one operation in the traditional approaches to passivization. However, it was seen above that if one wants to generalize passivization and unaccusative advancement, the process of passivization has to be split up in two separate operations. Given the conception of passivization in Relational Grammar, i.e. that the demotion part is a consequence of usurpation, the unaccusative advancement is triggered by the absence of a subject, i.e. by the final-1-law, whereas the operation of object promotion is not triggered by the absence of a subject. Therefore, a generalization is missed.

Within the framework of GB-theory, there is no rule of passivization, just as there was none in the version of EST with which we ended the discussion in section 3.2.1. There is only the rule of MOVE NP, itself an instance of a general substitution schema. In this sense, then, there are no construction-specific rules in GB-theory.

Consider the following structures.

(149) a. it rains
      b. it seems that John is here
      c. it was believed that John was here

These examples have the subject **it** in common. In none of these cases is it possible to replace **it** by any other expression. It is assumed, therefore, that **it** in these constructions is not a referential expression. As a consequence, no θ-role is assigned to the position occupied by **it,** since otherwise the θ-criterion would be violated, because a non-referential expression would bear a θ-role[65]. It must be assumed, therefore, that the verbs **rain** and **seem** do not assign a θ-role to the syntactic subject position and that the grammar of English has a rule that inserts **it** in a nominatively marked θ'-position (i.e. a position to which no θ-role is assigned).

Given this rule of inserting **it,** it is hard to see how the obligatory effect of NP movement in passives can be derived from the empty node filter, i.e. the question is why (150b) is ungrammatical with **it** occupying the empty subject position.

(150) a. The city was destroyed t by the enemy
       b.*It was destroyed the city by the enemy

Why is it that the insertion of **it** in (149c) yields a grammatical result, but not in (150b)? According to the GB-analysis of passives, this follows from the Case Filter. Unlike S', NP's require Case. Therefore, the S' complement in (149c) can remain in place, but the NP **the city** in (150b) must be moved to subject position on the assumption the no Case is assigned to the object.

According to the Projection Principle, the fact that in passives no θ-role is assigned to the syntactic subject position must be accounted for in terms of a lexical rule, i.e. if a θ-role was assigned to the syntactic position at D-structure, the Projection Principle would require that this θ-role is present in this position at all levels of representation derived from D-structure. In this respect, the GB-approach to passivization resembles the lexical approach, e.g. Bresnan's (1978) approach in which the subject argument is existentially bound by an operation in the lexicon. The obligatory promotion or movement of the object, however, is governed by structural principles. The question then arises to what extent these principles are unique for passivization. It will be seen below that they are not restricted to passives only, but that there is in fact a wider generalization, captured in the formulation in (151). This generalization is generally referred to as Burzio's generalization, as Burzio studied this correlation for Italian in great detail (Burzio 1981).

(151) If the syntactic subject does not receive a θ-role, no
      Case is assigned to an NP governed by the verb which
      fails to assign this θ-role[66].

As for the "absorption" of Case assignment in passive constructions, it is
assumed that this is a consequence of the categorial change that the passive
participle undergoes. The Case-assigning categories are V and P, which share the
feature [-N]. Now, it is assumed that it is this feature that is responsible for
the assignment of objective Case. It is furthermore assumed that passive participles lose this feature, i.e. that these participles are in fact specified as
[+V], a category that can be considered as a neutralization category of verbs and
adjectives. Such a conclusion seems to be required. Consider the possibility that
these participles are indeed adjectives. It was argued in section 3.2.5. that in
Dutch this conclusion is unwarranted. Within the framework of government and
binding, this assumption would predict that instead of moving the object to
subject position in passives, the structure could also be salvaged by the
insertion of the preposition of, i.e. that instead of (150a) we could have (152),
just as (153a) can be salvaged by the insertion of of as in (153b).

(152)*It was destroyed of the city by the enemy
(153) a.*afraid the dog
      b. afraid of the dog

If the claim that passive participles can be considered to be a neutralized
category is correct, it is relevant to reconsider the distinction between a
verbal and an adjectival passive that has been made in some form or other both in
traditional grammar and in various analyses within more recent frameworks (cf.
the discussion in section 3.2.2.).

Wasow (1977) wants to account for the differential behaviour of the adjectival participles and verbal participles in terms of two separate rules of passivization, a rule of verbal passivization which is an instance of MOVE NP, and a rule
of adjectival passivization. In this respect, Williams (1981a,1982) agrees with
him. The arguments for this distinction should be familiar by now. There is no
regular correspondence between prenominal participles and participles in other
syntactic contexts in a number of respects and these differences are argued to
fall out automatically if we are dealing with adjectives in one case and with
verbs in the other.

Bresnan (1980a), while accepting the difference between adjectival and verbal participles, captures the phenomena that Wasow seeks to explain by positing
two separate passivization rules, using a rule that derives adjectives from the
participial form of verbs directly, as stated above (cf. the rule of participle-
adjective conversion in (14)). This way of handling the phenomenon has two

advantages. First, the fact that irregular participial forms are irregular in both their verbal appearance and their adjectival appearance[67] is no longer a coincidence as the latter are directly derived from the former. Within the two-rule approach, there is nothing to ensure that not only the rule of verbal passivization will give rise to a participle such as **broken,** but the rule of adjectival passivization as well. Second, as we mentioned above, the participle-adjective conversion rule generalizes over the formation of adjectival passives and of adjectival participles derived from unaccusative verbs, as in **a fallen leaf.** This is so, since the conversion rule is not a rule of passivization, but rather a rule that applies to all lexical forms that have a Theme SUBJ. This thematic requirement is stipulated in Wasow's rule of adjectival passivization as well, but, since it is a rule of passivization it does not generalize to intransitives that happen to have Theme subjects. Wasow tries to let this thematic requirement on adjectival passivization follow from a general theory of lexical rules in (1977) and from a general theory of major and minor rules in (1980): category-changing lexical rules are supposed to be minor rules and minor rules would be sensitive to thematic relations, unlike major lexical rules like the verbal passive. In Williams' (1981) approach, which is very similar to Wasow's (1977) analysis, the adjectival passive rule is a rule that externalizes the Theme argument, unlike the verbal passive rule which merely dethematizes the syntactic subject by internalizing the external argument. Consequently, the syntactic subject position is a suitable landing site for MOVE NP.

These three analyses, then, agree on two major points. The grammar provides for two different lexical items (either generated by two different passive rules or by one passive rule and one word formation rule) that have different categorial and contextual properties. Secondly, the account of the differences involves a thematic requirement, i.e. the notion Theme plays an important role in all three analyses.

Both aspects of these analyses are in a certain sense undesirable. The use of thematic notions in this way requires an extension of the inventory of primitives with a set of non-structural notions. The undesirability of the postulation of two homophonous lexical items is self-evident, but deserves some comments as well.

The differential properties of adjectival and verbal passives are in large part derivable from the context in which they appear. Let me illustrate this with a simple example.

(154) a. the fund was given a lot of money
      b.*the given a lot of money fund

The contrast in (154) is put forward as support for the distinction: the participle in prenominal position must be an adjective. Adjectives do not take NP
complements, which explains the ungrammaticality of (154b). Alternatively, such
examples are used to demonstrate the sensitivity of the adjectival passive to
thematic relations: **fund** is not the Theme of **give**. By the same token, the
participle **given** in (154a) must be something different from an adjective, because
it does take an NP complement. However, the difference in grammaticality of the
examples in (154) can be accounted for without any reference to the item **given**: as
Williams (1982) has pointed out, the example in (154b) follows from what he calls
the head final filter (HFF), a prohibition of right recursion in specifiers. This
HFF operates independently from participles in cases like:

> (155) a. John is fond of girls
> b.*a fond of girls boy

For discussion of an apparent counterexample in cases like "an easy-to-take
drug", see Nanni (1980). Hence, even if **given** in (154b) was a verb, the construction would be impossible. This point can even be strengthened when we look at
Dutch. In Dutch, the HFF is observed as well. This can be seen in (156).

> (156) a. dat die jongen dol op zijn vader is
>   that that boy fond of his father is
>
> b.*een dolle op zijn vader jongen
>
> c. dat die jongen op Marie verliefd is
>   that that boy with Mary in-love is
>
> d. een op haar verliefde jongen
>   a with her in-love boy

The contrast between (156b) and (156d) clearly shows that what is at stake is not
complexity of the prenominal modifier, but rather right recursion (cf. the
discussion in section 2.7.3.). Given the fact that verbs take their NP complements to the left, a contrast as the one between (154a) and (154b) is not likely
to be found. The following examples bear this out.

> (157) a. dat dat boek haar gegeven werd
>   that that book her given was

    b. het haar gegeven boek
       the her given book

Nevertheless, **gegeven** occurs in prenominal position. Should it therefore be regarded as an adjective? The answer to this question depends, of course, on the extent to which we can derive the differences between the alleged adjectival and the verbal passive from independent properties of the constructions in which the participial forms are found.

    Before going through the motivation of the two distinct passive rules provided in Wasow (1977), we note that there is at least some initial motivation not to consider prenominal participles as plain adjectives. This involves the behaviour of the adverbial modifier **genoeg** 'enough'. This adverb can modify both verbs and adjectives as the following examples illustrate.

    (158) dat dat gat nu groot genoeg is
          that that hole now big enough is

    (159) dat we nu genoeg gevochten hebben
          that we now enough fought have

There is a remarkable difference, however, in that **genoeg** precedes the verb, but follows the adjective.

    (158')*dat het gat nu genoeg groot is
    (159')*dat we nu gevochten genoeg hebben

This positional difference is also found in prenominal position: there the modifier **genoeg** cannot be used with adjectives because of the HFF, whereas it can be used with participles[68].

    (160) *een genoeg grote/groot genoege/grote genoeg jongen
           a   enough big /big   enough /big   enough boy

    (161) een bos genoeg gedroogd hout
           a   bundle enough dried wood

The use of a partitive construction excludes a quantifier reading in (161). This difference between adjectives and participles is paralleled in the case of participles prefixed with **on-** ('un-'). In such cases, we are clearly dealing with an adjective. So, it is to be expected that in those cases the modifier **genoeg** cannot be used either. This expectation is borne out.

> (162) a. twee genoeg getrainde soldaten
>   two enough trained soldiers
>
>   b.*twee genoeg ongetrainde soldaten
>   two enough untrained soldiers

The ungrammaticality of (162b) is not due to a violation of some sort of semantic constraint, since replacement of **genoeg** by the synonymous expression **voldoende** makes it grammatical. What (162) shows is that prefixation with **on-** gives a participle the same status as basic adjectives with respect to the placement of **genoeg.** In section 3.2.5. the same was demonstrated with respect to the position of the stranded preposition. Therefore, there are at least two pieces of evidence that suggest that participles are not plain adjectives, as claimed by Freidin (1975) and Lightfoot (1980). The argument involving Case assignment suggests that they are not plain verbs either.

   Let us therefore explore the consequences of Van Riemsdijk's (1981a) proposal that there may be syntactic neutralizations and assume that participles are lexically specified as the category [+V]. According to Van Riemsdijk's proposal, participles may be inserted in positions that are either specified by the base rules as adjectives or as verbs. This implies that there are no "neutralization projections". However, this proposal is clearly dependent on the idea that there are independent base rules that generate phrase structures, a position that we rejected in chapter 2. Therefore, a participle in prenominal position may be assumed to just project its [+V]-feature. The data involving the modifier **genoeg** can then be accounted for if we assume that **genoeg** includes among its contextual features the statement in (163).

> (163) **genoeg** occurs to the right of [+V,-N] , otherwise it
>   occurs to the left.

(163) is admittedly ad hoc, but the specification is irrelevant for the present discussion. It should be observed, however, that Van Riemsdijk's proposal according to which the neutralized nature of participles is not visible in the phrase structure in which the participle is inserted, would have difficulty in explai-

ning the distributional facts discussed here.

It is now time to turn to the evidence produced by Wasow (1977) and
Williams (1981a,1982) to motivate the distinction between an adjectival and a
verbal passive in order to see whether the neutralization hypothesis can handle
the relevant facts as well. The prediction of the Wasow/Williams theory is that
all participles that must be adjectival for some reason, must have Theme subjects. Therefore, indirect object passives, raising passives, idiom-chunk passives and passives with predicative complements should be impossible with adjectival participles. Wasow has four tests to determine the adjectival status of a
participle: prenominal occurrence, prefixation with **un-**, occurrence in the complement of verbs like **seem, look** and **sound** and modification by **very** instead of by
very much. Of these two tests, the first two can be dismissed as irrelevant.
Consider first the test of prenominal occurrence. As we argued above, everything
that can be explained by the assumption that the participle is adjectival can be
explained by the HFF as well. Given the fact that the HFF is motivated independently, the latter account is superior. The relevant examples are given in
(164).

(164) a.*the given a lot of money fund   (indirect object passive)
      b.*the believed to be a fool boy   (raising passive)
      c.*the taken advantage of boy   (idiom passive)
      d.*the elected president man   (predicative complement passive)

As for the test involving the prefix **un-**, we saw above that these participles
behave as clear-cut adjectives. This is irrelevant for the neutralization hypothesis, however, if we assume that **un-**prefixation applies in the lexicon and
derives adjectives. Hence, if it is assumed that insertion in word formation
rules is restricted by a non-distinctness rather than an identity constraint,
participles of the [+V] category can be inserted in the position of the base of
the word formation rule in (165). The result is adjectival. This assumption
explains the asymmetries observed above between participles with and without **on-**
in Dutch.

(165) A -> $\begin{bmatrix} \\ A \end{bmatrix}$ un + $\begin{bmatrix} +V \\ +N \end{bmatrix}$]

If participles prefixed with **un-/on-** are adjectives, the ungrammaticality of
(166) follows from the Case filter, as adjectives do not assign Case, while the

ungrammaticality of (167) follows from the ECP if it is assumed that adjectives
are not structural governors, i.e. do not have the property of being able to
govern across major boundaries (cf. section 2.7.).

(166)*Bill was untold the story

(167) a.*John was unknown [e to be a communist]
      b.*John was unelected [e president]

Notice that this explanation for the ungrammaticality of (164d) is superior to an
explanation that claims that these preverbal participles are indistinguishable
from adjectives. In Dutch, prenominal participles can occur with a predicative
complement, because these complements occur to the left of the participles and
hence do not violate the HFF. If these participles were adjectival, it should be
expected that they are ungrammatical.

(168) a. de aardig gevonden jongen
         the nice found boy

      b. het geldig verklaarde document
         the valid declared document

The remaining tests involve modification by **very** instead of by **very much** and the
occurrence in the complements of verbs like **seem, sound** and **look**. Let us look at
the first test first. It turns out that the test is rather weak. It predicts that
with the non-thematic passives, **very** should be grammatical. The examples in (169)
illustrate that this is hardly the case.

(169) a. John was very much/ * very sold a bill of goods
      b.*Edward was very (much) ordained deacon
      c.*John is very (much) considered a fool

The most relevant test, then, is the occurrence in the complement of verbs like
seem, look and **sound**. The facts are given in (170).

(170) a. *John seems sold this book (indirect object passive)
      b. *The boy looked thought to be a fool (raising passive)
      c. *Advantage seems easily taken of John (idiom chunk passive)
      d. *John seems elected president (predicative complement passive)

The argument runs as follows. The type of passive found in the complement of these verbs in (170) is verbal. Therefore, the complement itself is verbal, but these verbs do not permit a verbal complement, although they do permit an adjectival complement. I think that this account is correct, but it can be derived in a more principled manner within the framework of assumptions made so far. Let me first present the structure that these constructions would have if the participles were merely specified as [+V]. A relevant example is given in (171).

(171) **John** seems $[_{[+V]}"$ e $[_{[+V]},$ sold] e this book]]

This structure is ungrammatical. The reason for this is clear: the Unlike Category Condition in (107) of chapter 2 forbids the occurrence of a category that is non-distinct from V in the complement of V. A [+V] category is non-distinct from [+V,-N]. Therefore, the structure of constructions like those in (170) must be such that the participial head of the complement is specified as different from [+V], e.g. as [+V,+N]. But under that assumption, the complement structure of the participle cannot be as it is, since this requires a verb or a [+V] category.

It turns out, then, that each of the four tests proposed in Wasow (1977) can be explained by the neutralization hypothesis. Therefore, the generalizations that Wasow captures by postulating two separate rules, one of which is conditioned by a thematic requirement, are in fact spurious. One portion of the facts follows from Case theory, another from the ECP and yet another from the Unlike Category Condition, all of which are motivated independently. (see Lightfoot 1979b for further comments on Wasow's claims).

More recently, Williams (1982) has adduced another argument in favour of the adjectival passive. Since raising passives must be verbal, the ungrammaticality of (172) as opposed to the grammaticality of (173) follows from the assumption that AP's may be fronted, but VP's may not.

(172) *How widely is John believed to have left?
(173) How widely believed is that story?

However, the argument seems to me to be without force. What makes (172) unacceptable is the fact that the ECP is violated. That this violation is not due to the non-adjectival nature of the preposed constituent is evident from the contrast in(174).

(174) a. John is certain to have left
      b.*How certain is John to have left?

In Williams (1982) yet another argument in favour of the claim that there is
both a verbal and an adjectival passive is put forward. This argument leads us to
a question that has not yet been addressed. The argument has the following form.
Adjectival passivization is a lexical rule and therefore does not leave a trace
in post-participle position. Verbal passivization, on the other hand, is an
instantiation of MOVE α and therefore results in a structure that contains such a
post-participle trace. On the assumption that traces are visible for the HFF, the
prediction follows that verbal passives cannot occur prenominally. It should be
recalled that the test of prenominal occurrence was dismissed above as irrelevant, because anything that follows from the assumption that participles in
prenominal position are adjectives also follows from the HFF. Williams (1982:
161), however, presents the following examples as arguments in favour of his
position.

    (175) a. the promised books
          b.*the promised people   (with people as addressee)

    (176) a. the told story
          b.*the told people

Since **people** in (175)-(176) is not a theme, the participle must be verbal
according to Wasow's criteria, which Williams accepts. Hence the structure of
these examples is as in (177), a configuration which is ruled out by the HFF.

    (177) * [[V   trace $_{VP}$] N $_{NP}$]
              <pass. part.>

If we accept this explanation, the distinction between an adjectival and a verbal
passive must be accepted as well. There is an alternative explanation for the
ungrammaticality of the b. examples in (175)-(176), however. It has often been
observed that the notional indirect object argument can more readily be left out
than the notional direct object, i.e. under the required contextual or situation-
al circumstances one can say a sentence like (178), but not (179).

    (178) (it is Susan's birthday. John and Peter are congratulating her)

John gave a Stones record and Peter gave a textbook on
linguistics.

(179) (John and Peter are distributing drinks in a room)
      *Peter gave Mary and John gave Sue.

Why there should be such a difference is unclear to me, although speculations
might be offered. I shall refrain from doing so, however. What is of relevance
here is that the source that is required for a construction like (175b) is itself
ungrammatical.

(180) *The people were promised

(180) is ungrammatical because an obligatory complement is missing. The same is
true of the b.examples in (175)-(176). We can therefore dismiss Williams' argument as irrelevant[69].

    The argument raises an interesting issue, however. If a participle is instan-
tiated as a [+V] category, is there a trace in its prenominal occurrence or not,
i.e. does the structure involve MOVE α? If so, we must also assume, at least for
English, that traces are invisible for the HFF. The structure of "de beloofde
boeken" (the promised books) would then be as in (181).

(181)

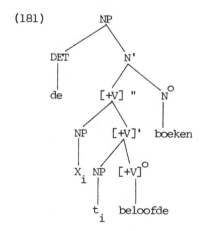

I do not know of any direct evidence in favour of the trace, but the Projection
Principle suggests that the structure in (181) is correct. It will be argued
below that lexical rules are minimal in the sense that they do not manipulate the
mapping of θ-role and grammatical function except for deletion, with some

provisos to be made below. This hypothesis prohibits any rules of externalization discussed by Williams (1981a). Basically, this hypothesis is an extension of the Projection Principle to the lexicon (cf. Finer & Roeper 1982 for similar suggestions). In the absence of arguments to the contrary, then, I maintain the position that (181) is in fact correct.

Let us now turn to the status of X in (181). It has been argued in chapter 2 that government does not exceed the first order projection of the head. Hence, the NP dominating X in (181) is not governed by **beloofde**. Since N is not a structural governor, it must be concluded that the NP is ungoverned. Therefore, the only possible candidate for X is PRO. This conclusion can be supported with the well-known asymmetry between attributive and predicative AP's. Whereas an attributively used AP can be understood as predicating over something else than the head noun that is modified by it, this is never possible with predicatively used AP's. An example is given in (182).

(182) a. een luie stoel
         a   lazy chair (=an easy chair)

      b.*deze stoel is lui
         this chair is lazy

In copula constructions, the subject interpretation of the AP is unique. This follows from the account of copula constructions that will be defended below, according to which the interpretation follows from trace-binding, i.e. the structure of (182b) is as in (182c), with irrelevant details left out.

(182) c. deze stoel $[_{AP} t_i [_{A'} lui]]$ is

The subject of a prenominal AP, on the other hand, is PRO. It is well-known that the interpretation of PRO is less strict. This supports our conclusion that the subject of the prenominal modifier in (181) is PRO.

There is one issue that still has to be settled. Apart from the types of passive mentioned above as instances that require a verbal passive operation according to Wasow, there is one other type of passive that Wasow claims to be transformational, viz. the pseudopassives as in (183).

(183) a. The children were badly looked after
      b. These affairs are cared for by John

c. The plan was talked about

d. The boat was decided on

e. The war was prayed for

In general, these pseudo-passives cannot occur prenominally, apart from a handful of specific combinations, like those in (184), which can also be prefixed by **un-**. These then are exceptional for Wasow as well as for our approach. I shall assume that these are simply listed as adjectives in the lexicon.

(184) a. the badly looked after children

b. the uncared for orphans

(185) a.*the talked about plan

b.*the decided on boat

c.*the prayed for war

How are we to account for the ungrammaticality of the examples in (185)? Notice that the hypothesis that there is an adjectival passive can handle these cases very easily: the subject of the participle or the object of the preposition is not the theme of the verb, hence the participle must be verbal. Then, either verbs cannot occur prenominally (Wasow) or there is a post-participial trace (Williams) which violates the HFF. If our claim that traces are invisible for the HFF is correct, it would seem that we are left without an explanation for the ungrammaticality of (185).

Let us first take a closer look at the analysis of pseudo-passives. According to Hornstein & Weinberg (1981), pseudo-passives in English are possible as a consequence of a rule of V-P reanalysis, a process that rebrackets the string, resulting in a structure where the NP object of the preposition becomes a bare NP object of the newly created complex verb. The ungrammaticality of nominalizations like those in (186) can then be accounted for by assuming that there is no rule operating on adjacent N's and P's.

(186) a.*the plan's talk about

b.*the boat decision on

c.*the war's prayer for

Similarly, there would not be a reanalysis rules that operates on an adjective and an adjacent preposition. If the participles in (185) were adjectives, the ungrammaticality would automatically be explained. However, that conclusion does not square with our hypothesis that these participles are not adjectives.

A more principled explanation for the existence of pseudo-passives in English is provided by Kayne (1981c). His assumption is that in English verbs and prepositions govern in the same way, due to the fact that they both assign objective Case. In this respect, English differs from French and other languages that do not allow pseudo-passives or preposition stranding in general. The fairly general impossibility of preposition stranding follows from the ECP if it is assumed that prepositions are not proper governors. In English, prepositions may license a gap because the verb may transmit its government property to prepositions.

The basic idea, then, is that V and P can be co-superscripted so as to allow an empty category in the complement of the preposition to be properly governed, which is possible if V and P assign the same Case. It should be recalled that the Case assigning feature of V and P is their shared [-N] feature. If it is correct that participles in prenominal position are specified merely as [+V], the participles in (185) lack the crucial correspondence feature with prepositions. Therefore, co-superscripting cannot take place and the structure is ruled out by the ECP. In (183), on the other hand, such co-superscripting is allowed by virtue of the fact that the participle is co-superscripted with a verb, i.e. the copula. This type of co-superscripting is independently motivated in the case of English raising adjectives, where the trace in the embedded subject position must be properly governed, which cannot be obtained on the basis of the adjective alone.

This ends our discussion of the hypothesis of adjectival passivization. I conclude that there is no motivation either for the existence of two rules of passivization or for a constraint on a passivization rule in terms of thematic notions. I therefore maintain the position that a characterization of θ-roles as far as their content is concerned is not only impossible, but in fact unnecessary and therefore undesirable.

The preceding discussion has established two things: the status of the participle as a neutralized category and the status of the passive rule as an operation involving MOVE α. There is also a lexical aspect to the passive derivation, i.e. the absorption of the external θ-role. The formulation of the cooccurrence of θ-absorption and Case-absorption given in (151) does not exclude the possibility that the absorption of Case has no effect. This is found in the case of sentential complements in English and Dutch, but also in the case of impersonal passives in Dutch. If this happens, the nominative position is filled by **er** which can be left out under circumstances that are as yet unclear to me.

3.3.3.2. Inversion and unaccusative

It is easy to see how the analysis of passives in GB-theory carries over to the unaccusative phenomenon, which we have argued comprises both the phenomenon which Perlmutter describes as unaccusativity and the phenomenon which he describes as inversion. In fact, the name used by Perlmutter to refer to this phenomenon is very telling within the framework of Case theory discussed above.

The property of the lack of an initial subject, of which we remarked that its status is unclear, will be formalized with the GB-framework in terms of a Θ'-subject, i.e. a subject to which no Θ-role is assigned. The subject position is present, however, as demanded by the Extended Projection Principle, and it will receive nominative Case if it is the subject of a finite clause. It is therefore a suitable landing site for categories that must be moved from their position because this position does not receive Case. The final subject in unaccusative structures will therefore originate in object position, or rather in a position governed by the verb. This NP position will not receive Case, given the generalization in (151). This analysis brings out in a very straightforward manner the resemblance between passives and unaccusatives that we pointed out above. An example like (187) will have an underlying structure and derivation as indicated in (188).

(187) dat Marie viel

(188)

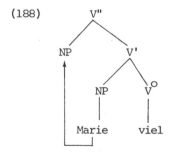

As for inversion constructions, a similar analysis can be given. I shall follow Everaert (1982) in assuming that the NP which is the first NP to the left of the verb receives structural Case, which is absorbed if no Θ-role is assigned to the subject position. This assumption differs from the assumption in Den Besten (1980), who assumes that the verb and its closest argument constitute a small VP which takes the indirect object as its sister, at least in Dutch. I have no particular insights to offer with respect to these different proposals concerning the indirect object NP (see, however, Kayne 1982b for an interesting discussion of the status of the indirect object in French and English). The structure of a sentence like (189) could be as in (190).

(189) dat die ramp mij overkwam
      that that disaster me occurred

(190)

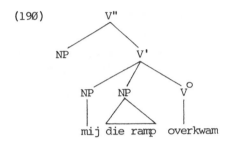

Apart from the arguments for the generation of "unaccusative" subjects in the NP position governed by V which derive from the generalizations that we discussed in section 3.3.2., a major motivation can be derived from the theory of lexical rules. The θ-grid associated with a particular head is a matter that must be lexically encoded. We have taken the position that the association of θ-role and grammatical function is provided in the lexicon. As D-structure is projected from the lexicon, it must be concluded that only lexical rules are capable of manipulating the θ-grid and the association of θ-role and grammatical function. One such lexical rule is the de-thematization operation that deletes or absorbs the external θ-role in the case of passives.

It is of course conceivable that such a lexical rule could manipulate the θ-grid and its association with grammatical functions in a variety of ways. Although the theory of lexical rules presented in Hoekstra, Van der Hulst & Moortgat (1980a) places heavy constraints on possible lexical rules, it is still a rather poorly developed component of the grammar. Chomsky (1981:ch.5 fn.6) correctly observes that given this state of the theory of lexical rules, lexical solutions to problems that were previously accounted for in terms of transformations, while maintaining descriptive coverage, are uninteresting from an explanatory point of view. Efforts should be made, therefore, to further restrict the possible operations in the lexicon. An obvious candidate to limit the variety of operations permitted is the Projection Principle. Without the Projection Principle, the association of θ-grid and grammatical functions could be manipulated by the rule of passive in such a way that not only the external role is absorbed or deleted, but that one of the roles previously assigned to an internal argument is given the status of external θ-role. However, the foregoing discussion suggests that there is no unique θ-role that is assigned to the subject in passive constructions. In the case of impersonal passives it is even impossible that an internal θ-role is assigned to the syntactic subject position by virtue of a lexical operation. What seems to be the relevant generalization is that the expression which appears in the syntactic subject position in passives has the θ -role that is assigned to the NP that happens to be structurally governed by the verb in the active construction. It so happens that there is a range of different roles assigned to these NP's.

The minimal operation that seems to be required in the case of passivization, therefore, is the absorption of the external θ-role. The rest of the θ-grid can be associated with syntactic structure as in the corresponding active. In gene-ral, it seems to be the optimal situation that a particular head that may appear in various construction types assigns the same θ-role to the same syntactic position. Let us suppose, therefore, that lexical operations are limited to absorb or delete the external θ-role. This can be seen as a consequence of the Projection Principle. Much more could be said about this proposal. In any event it is required that lexical operations that involve affixation are allowed to have specific effects on the association of the θ-grid, but I shall not go into a discussion of this matter here.

Consider from this perspective the set of verbs which includes **breken** 'break', **smelten** 'melt', **genezen** 'cure', **ontdooien** 'defrost', **veranderen** 'change', **splij-ten** 'split', **eindigen** 'end', **drogen** 'dry', **afbranden** 'burn down' etc., which can be used transitively with a causative interpretation and intransitively with a non-causative interpretation. A representative example is given in (191).

> (191) a. dat de arts de patient geneest
>   that the doctor the patient cures
>
> b. dat de patient snel geneest
>   that the patient quickly recovers

It is an entirely unpredictable matter whether a particular transitive verb with a causative reading has a non-causative intransitive counterpart and vice versa. Therefore, Jackendoff (1975) and Wasow (1977) argue that, unlike Fiengo (1974) proposed, the relation between the two different uses of these verbs should not be transformationally expressed, but rather by means of a lexical rule. However, the unpredictability of the phenomenon only points to a lexical rule being involved. I want to argue, therefore, that there is a lexical operation which deletes the external θ-role, thus making the syntactic subject position a suitable landing site. The Projection Principle requires that the role assigned to the syntactic direct object in (191a) is assigned to the syntactic direct object in the case of (191b) as well. Because the subject does not receive a θ-role, the object NP does not receive Case and therefore has to move to subject position.

It is relevant to notice that all verbs in this class display the properties of unaccusatives in their intransitive use, i.e. they select the perfective auxiliary **zijn,** do not allow an impersonal passive and the participle can be used to predicate over nouns corresponding to their (surface) subject. This generalization over a subpart of the lexicon now follows from the analysis which is required by principled considerations.

A generalization in the opposite direction may be observed in the case of so-called pseudo-transitive verbs, i.e. verbs that may optionally occur with or without an object. Again, these may enter into different syntactic contexts, which requires some lexical operation on their θ-grid (cf. Bresnan 1978, Dowty 1981). The subject receives the same thematic role in both syntactic contexts, i.e. **Jan** receives the 'eater' role in both (192a) and (192b). The minimal assumption again is that this thematic role is assigned to the same syntactic position in both cases. Accordingly, no movement is involved in the derivation of either (192a) or (192b). This accounts for the fact that pseudo-transitives in their intransitive uses display the characteristics of transitives rather than of unaccusatives, i.e. both select the perfective auxiliary **hebben,** both can be passivized etc.

(192) a. dat Jan om vier uur een appel eet
             that John at four hour an apple eats

      b. dat Jan om vier uur eet
             that John at four hour eats

Therefore, the assumption that the thematic roles assigned by a verb are assigned to the same syntactic positions in different constructions in which the verb may appear supports the unaccusative hypothesis in that the hypothesis allows us to capture generalizations over subparts of the lexicon.

Let us now return to the property of so-called indirect object preposing, a preliminary discussion of which we presented in section 3.3.2. This property signals the basic similarity of inversion constructions and passives of bitransitives, thus supporting the claim that in both cases NP movement is involved. We noted above that the alleged subjects of these constructions, i.e. the constituents that determine number agreement on the verb, may appear after the indirect object, as in the b-examples in (193)-(194).

(193) a. dat die fout de schoolmeester opviel
       that that mistake the teacher struck

   b. dat de schoolmeester die fout opviel
      that the teacher that mistake struck

(194) a. dat een geschenk de koningin werd overhandigd
        that a present   the queen was   presented

   b. dat de koningin een geschenk werd overhandigd
      that the queen   a present   was presented

The difference between the a- and b-examples is reminiscent of the constructions with inverted subjects in Italian. As Belletti and Rizzi (1981) show, a distinction must be made between two kinds of postverbal subjects in Italian. With one class of intransitive verbs, a class that is basically coextensive with the class of unaccusatives in Dutch, a quantified NP without a lexical head noun can occur in combination with the clitic **ne** on the verb, whereas this is impossible with transitive verbs and with the intransitive verbs that we have earlier referred to as unergatives, i.e. the non-unaccusatives. This is illustrated by the following examples.

(195) a. Sono passate tre settimane
        Are   elapsed three weeks

   b.*Sono passate tre Ø

   c. Ne sono passate tre Ø
      Of-them are elapsed three

(196) a. Hanno parlato tre ragazze
         Have spoken   three girls

b.*Hanno parlato tre Ø

c.*Ne hanno parlato tre Ø

In this regard, postverbal subjects of unaccusatives pattern like objects. Burzio (1981) accounts for this by assuming that they indeed occupy the object position. The difference between postverbal subjects of unaccusatives and of non-unaccusatives can then be easily explained. One way to explain it would be to say that the clitic must c-command the empty category that it binds. This requirement would be fulfilled if the quantified NP is in object position, but not if it is adjoined to VP. The b-option in (195) and (196) can be ruled out on the assumption that the NP which is adjoined to VP is governed by the verb and that therefore the empty category in head position of the quantified NP cannot be PRO. For further details, the reader is referred to Belletti & Rizzi (1981) and Burzio (1981)[70].

Direct objects in Dutch possess a property that is comparable to the property of allowing **ne** in Italian. Den Besten (1980) observes that subextraction is impossible with subjects and indirect objects, but allowed with direct objects as shown by the following examples.

(197)   direct object
        Wat heb jij in Italië [$_{NP}$ **e** voor musea] bezocht?
        What have you in Italy   for musea   visited
        "What kind of musea/Which musea did you visit in Italy?"

(198)   indirect object
        ***Wat** heb jij [$_{NP}$ **e** voor mensen] je stuk gestuurd?
        What have you   for people   your paper sent
        "What kind of people did you send your paper?"

(199)   subject
        ***Wat** hebben [$_{NP}$ **e** voor mensen] jou geholpen?
        What have   for people   you helped
        "What kind of people helped you?"

This property of direct objects, then, can be used as evidence for the claim that the alleged subjects in inversion constructions and in passive constructions with bitransitives occupy the direct object position if they are preceded by the indirect object. In general, allowing subextraction may be taken as evidence that the NP from which **wat** is extracted is in the position of the direct object. Consider from this perspective existential constructions. Den Besten (1980) claims that the "demoted" subject in existentials is placed in direct object position. Given the fact that subextraction is restricted to this position, we should expect that it is allowed in the case of existentials. This expectation is borne out by (200).

(200) **Wat** zijn er [$_{NP}$ e voor dingen] gebeurd?
      What are there   for things   happened
      "What kind of things have happened?"

It should be noted, however, that Den Besten's hypothesis concerning the position of the "demoted" subject in existentials cannot be maintained in general. The verb **gebeuren** in (200) is an unaccusative verb. If we take a transitive or a bitransitive verb, however, the direct object position is occupied by the direct object and therefore unavailable for the "demoted" subject. A relevant example is given in (201).

(201) Er hebben enkele mensen mij hun boeken verkocht
      There have some people me their books sold

I shall assume that in these cases the subject is adjoined to V' in the manner indicated in (202), in accordance with our claim that transformations are either substitutions or adjunctions.

(202)

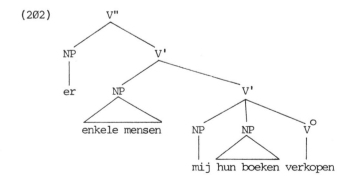

Since the position of the "demoted" subject is not the direct object position, we expect that subextraction is excluded in these contexts. Although judgements are admittedly subtle, I believe that the expectation is borne out.

(203) *Wat hebben er [$_{NP}$ e voor mensen] jou hun boeken verkocht?

Returning to the alleged subjects in the context of "indirect object preposing", we assume that they indeed occupy the position where they are generated at D-structure according to our analysis. Therefore, we expect that subextraction is possible. This appears to be the case.

(204) Wat zijn (er) jou [$_{NP}$ e voor fouten] opgevallen?
      What are there you   for mistakes struck
      "What kind of mistakes have struck you?"

(205) Wat zijn (er) de koningin [$_{NP}$ e voor geschenken] aangeboden?
      What are there the queen   for presents   presented
      "What kind of presents were offered to the queen?"

It should be noted that these subjects possess this property only if they actually occur after the indirect object. In this respect too, this phenomenon resembles the possibility of ne in Italian, i.e. if the subject is preverbal in Italian, ne is also excluded with a quantified NP with unaccusative verbs. This is shown in (206). Similarly, subextraction is impossible if the alleged subjects precede the indirect object. This is demonstrated in (207)-(208).

(206) a. Tre settimane passano rapidamente
         Three weeks elapse   quickly

      b. Tre Ø passano rapidamente

      c.*Tre ne passano rapidamente

(207) * Wat zijn (er) [$_{NP}$ e voor fouten] jou opgevallen?

(208) * Wat zijn (er) [$_{NP}$ e voor geschenken] de koningin aangeboden?

On the basis of these observations, we conclude that the direct object in these constructions remains in its base position, i.e. that no movement is involved in these cases.

Two questions now arise with respect to these "subjects" in direct object position. First, how do these NP's determine number agreement and second, how do they receive Case? It should be noted that the same questions arise with respect to existentials, i.e. in those constructions the NP that receives nominative Case and that determines number agreement on the verb does not occupy the syntactic subject position either. Before answering these questions, we shall discuss a proposal by Den Besten (1980).

Den Besten argues that the presence of **er** in normal existentials is obligatory, which he illustrates with the ungrammaticality of (209). **Er** is optional in the constructions under discussion, however, if the subject is preceded by the indirect object. This is illustrated by (210).

(209) dat *(er) iets raars gebeurd is
        that there something strange happened is

(210) dat (er) mijn oom iets raars gegeven zal worden
        that there my uncle something strange given will be

Den Besten explains the obligatory presence of **er** in (209) in terms of the obligatory nature of the syntactic subject position which may not be left unfilled. He then goes on to claim that the optionality of **er** in cases like (210) can be explained on the assumption that the indirect object optionally moves into the subject position.

This proposal must be rejected for a number of reasons. Firstly, **er** is also optional if the thematic role of the indirect object is not expressed by an NP as in (210), but by a PP headed by **aan** (cf. (211)). This PP cannot be assumed to have moved into the NP slot of the subject.

(211) dat (er) aan mijn oom iets raars gegeven zal worden
        that there to my uncly something strange given will be

Secondly, movement of the indirect object into the subject position would leave a Case marked trace behind. The moved NP itself would receive nominative Case in its landing-site, which would give rise to a Case conflict. The resulting chain would have both a nominatively marked element and an element marked with objective or oblique Case. Den Besten's proposal is tenable only if his solution to the

question regarding the Case marking of the subject in direct object position
which he puts forward (cf. below) is assumed as well. However, I shall argue that
the empty subject position is required in order for the NP in object position to
get Case. Finally, the descriptive generalization that Den Besten seeks to
explain is incorrect, i.e. it is not true that **er** is obligatory in existentials in
general. Although the factors that determine the obligatory presence of **er** are at
present unclear to me, there are perfectly grammatical existential constructions
without **er**. An example is given in (212).

(212) Op die bijeenkomst moesten ($^?$er) om verschillende redenen

    At that meeting must   there for various reasons

    sommige mensen plotseling weg

    some people   suddenly   away

Let us try to develop an alternative analysis, therefore. The basic assumptions
that we shall make are the following. First, number agreement is defined between
the finite verb (or INFL) and the syntactic subject position. This is essentially
Perlmutter & Zaenen's conclusion with respect to existential constructions in
Dutch, where they claim that the dummy **er** is the final 1 (cf. Perlmutter & Zaenen
to appear). The second assumption is that a θ'-position marked with nominative
Case can be optionally lexicalized as **er**[71]. If **er** is not inserted, the position is
identified as pro (cf. Chomsky 1982).

    In existential constructions, it is the "demoted" subject (whether in the
direct object position or adjoined to V' as in (202)) that determines the number
of the finite verb. This kind of agreement is called "Brother-in-law agreement"
by Perlmutter & Postal (to appear b). Chomsky's (1981:87 and 263 ff.) analysis of
there in English can be regarded as a way of formalizing this notion of "Brother-
in-law" agreement. According to this analysis, **there** is lexically specified to
have number, but it has to receive a value for its number feature by means of a
relation with some NP with which it is co-superscripted. The same analysis can be
assumed for Dutch **er,** the difference being that **er** can also occur in subject
position of impersonal passives where there is no suitable candidate to be co-
superscripted with. We shall assume, therefore, that if **er** is not co-superscripted with any NP it takes the unmarked value for number, i.e. singular. The relation
of co-superscripting can be established by means of the following algorithm.

(213) Co-superscripting

    Co-superscribe **er** and an NP c-commanded by **er** if
    this NP has phonetic features and no Case. Copy the
    number of the NP in the feature matrix of **er**.

The NP and **er** that are co-superscripted constitute a chain that is visible for the
θ--criterion by virtue of the nominative Case on **er**. The examples in (214)-(215)
illustrate the operation of co-superscripting: (214) is an example of a construction with an unaccusative verb, where the NP to be co-superscripted occupies the
direct object position, (215) involves an NP that is adjoined to V'.

(214) dat er^i mij [$_{NP}$iets leuks^i] overkwam
      that there me   something funny occurred

(215) dat er^i [$_{NP}$enkele mensen^i] mij hun boek geven
      that there some people   me their book give

In traditional transformational treatments of **there**-insertion it was always
assumed that the insertion rule is restricted by an indefiniteness restriction on
the subject NP. Within a more restricted theory of transformations, it is
impossible to impose such a restriction on syntactic rules, nor is it necessary
to impose such a restriction, because the deviance of existentials with a
definite subject can be accounted for in semantic terms. Barwise & Cooper (1980)
show that the relevant property is indeed a semantic one. They claim that
existentials with a definite "demoted" subject are tautologies, rather than
syntactically ungrammatical. Nevertheless, the appearance of **er** may be taken to
indicate that the constituent that bears the thematic role assigned to the
position occupied by **er** is to be found elsewhere. In this respect, normal
existentials differ from inversion constructions, in that in the latter the
thematic role of the "demoted" subject is assigned to the position that the NP
occupies itself. This might be considered the relevant factor in explaining the
difference in optionality of **er**, at least in as far as there is such a difference.
Although this suggestion may partly explain the distribution of **er**, it is clearly
not the final word.

    The present proposal is an improvement on Den Besten's analysis of the way in
which the subjects in direct object position receive Case. In his analysis, the
node INFL is a sister of the subject NP and the VP (the maximal projection of V)

and nominative Case is assigned to the subject NP under government by INFL. If the "inverted" subject is in direct object position, however, it is not governed by INFL. Therefore, Den Besten has to design an ad hoc device to let INFL govern the NP in direct object position under these special circumstances. This device is called 'chain-government', which is defined as in (216).

(216) A chain-governs B only iff A governs C_1, C_1 governs C_2, C_2 governs ....C_{n-1} and C_{n-1} governs C_n, C_n governs B
$(n \geq 1)$

The notion of chain-government comes into play under the following circumstances.

(217) If an NP (B in (216)) is governed by a category C that may not or cannot assign Case, it receives its Case from the first Case-assigning element by which it is chain-governed.

For the cases under discussion, V is the relevant C and INFL is the first Case-assigning category by which it is chain-governed.

Although this device is capable of solving the Case-marking problem in inversion constructions, it will not help in the case of those existentials where the "demoted" subject is adjoined to V', nor does it account for the number agreement on the verb. Our own proposal accounts for both aspects at the same time in terms of a device of co-superscripting that is independently motivated to handle number agreement in existentials.

It is now time to turn to another difference between the two classes of intransitives that we have set up. This difference again corroborates our claim that the subject of unaccusatives is generated at D-structure in the position of direct object. The relevant difference involves the so-called dative of possession. In western Dutch, this dative only shows up in a number of rather idiomatic examples like those given in (218).

(218) a. Ik zette hem een hoed op zijn/het hoofd
I   put   him a   hat on his/the head

b. De tranen stonden Marie in haar/de ogen
The tears   stood   Mary in her/the eyes

c. Het zweet gutste Piet van zijn/het gelaat
The sweat ran   Peter down his/the face

In eastern dialects of Dutch, the use of the dative of possession has a much wider distribution. This is extensively discussed in Van Bree (1981). The use of such a dative is subject to various restrictions. First of all, it seems that the dative NP must mention the possessor of something mentioned elsewhere in the sentence and is inalienably possessed by the person mentioned in the dative, or at least has a very close relationship with the person mentioned in the dative NP. According to Van Bree, the question as to whether or not the relation that actually exists between these entities satisfies this requirement depends on the imagination of the speaker and can vary accordingly. For the examples in (218), one might say that there is a necessary part-whole relation between the possessed entity (head, eyes, face) and the possessor. The most problematic aspect of the occurrence of a dative of possession is that this occurrence is not licensed by the verb, i.e. the referent of the dative NP does not receive a θ-role from the verb. This is why Van Bree calls these datives non-inherent. Why, then, do these datives not violate the θ-criterion? The answer to this question is connected to the question why there is an obligatory NP that mentions something that is possessed by the person who is mentioned by the dative. Let us assume that the dative NP is licensed with respect to the θ-criterion because it is coindexed with the NP that mentions the entity posssed. Following a suggestion by Guéron (1983), we may say that there is a relation of anaphora between the dative NP and the NP that mentions the possessed entity, perhaps more specifically with the determiner of the latter NP. This would also yield a violation of the θ-criterion, since now there is a chain containing two referential expressions, but only a single θ-role. This violation, however, is resolved if the speaker can interpret these two referential expressions as actually referring to a single entity, of which the dative mentions the "possessor".

Assuming this to be correct, we expect that the normal restrictions on anaphoric relations hold in this case as well. Therefore, it is to be expected that the dative NP must c-command the NP mentioning the possessed entity. This requirement of c-command is fulfilled in the cases where the possessed entity is mentioned in a PP, as in the examples in (218), or if it is mentioned in the NP object as in the example in (219).

(219) Ze heeft me de jurk keurig vermaakt
      She has me the dress beautifully altered

The c-command restriction would furthermore predict that a dative of possession would not be combinable with intransitive verbs, where the subject mentions the

entity of possession, because the dative would not c-command the subject NP.
Although this prediction is correct in as far the unergative intransitives are
concerned (cf. (220)), a dative of possession can easily be combined with
passives (cf. (221)) and with unaccusative verbs (cf. (222)).

(220) a.*Het kind heeft Marie de hele nacht gehuild
      The child has Mary the entire night cried

    b.*De zoon heeft me mooi gezongen
      The son has me   beautifully sung

(221) a. De jurk werd me door moeder mooi vermaakt
      The dress was me by mother beautifully altered

    b. De voeten werden hem altijd op zaterdag gewassen door zijn vader
      The feet were   him always on saturday washed by   his father

(222) a. De oren zijn hem bevroren
      The ears are him frozen

    b. Het huis is hun afgebrand
      The house is them burned down

    c. De vrouw is me gestorven
      The wife is me died

    d. Het oog is me gezwollen
      The eye is me swollen

Again, the subjects of unaccusatives pattern like subjects of passives and like
objects of transitives. This patterning is principally explained in terms of the
unaccusative analysis and the hypothesis concerning the datives of possession put
forth above.

3.4. Transitivity as a subject property

Let us start the final section of this chapter with a short recapitulation of the results of the previous sections. After reviewing several analyses of passives we have concluded that the optimal syntactic approach of passivization is the null hypothesis, i.e. that there is nothing particular in the syntactic component to be said about passivization. One of the reasons for this assumption is that those analyses that employ the notion of direct object presuppose on the one hand that the class of NP's that can become the syntactic subject of passive constructions share some fundamental feature and on the other hand that the "promotion" of this class of NP's is an essential part of the phenomenon of passive. Both these assumptions were argued to be misguided. The existence of impersonal passives and passives of verbs that take sentential complements shows that passivization does not need to involve a "promotion" of any kind. Furthermore, the rule of NP movement that is employed in the derivation of those passives where some non-subject NP is moved into subject position is not unique for passives. This operation can be generalized to unaccusative constructions as well as to subject-raising constructions and the factors that determine its application (e.g. the Case Filter) do not specifically refer to passives either. As for the presupposed homogeneity of the NP's, we have argued that no such homogeneity exists. The optimal grammar for passivization would therefore be limited to a lexical rule that deletes the external θ-role.

In this respect, then, the D-structure of passive constructions is identical to unaccusative constructions. The basic similarity of passives and unaccusatives has been shown by drawing attention to a number of phenomena that find a principled explanation on the basis of the D-structures attributed to them. The difference between passives on the one hand and unaccusatives on the other is that the latter have the property of selecting a θ'-subject on an unpredictable basis, whereas this property is rule created in the case of passives. An intermediate case is formed by the verbs that belong to the class of **breken,** i.e. the class of verbs that may enter into two different syntactic contexts, transitive and non-transitive, with a change in meaning (causative vs. non-causative). Here, too, the unaccusative property is rule created, but obviously the relevant rule is much more restricted than the rule that creates the unaccusative property in the case of passives.

The fact that the Relational Grammar approach can be translated so straight-forwardly in terms of GB-theory does not come as a surprise. Both frameworks are derivational in the sense that dissimilarities at a superficial level are reduced to properties of an underlying level of representation. There are important differences between the two approaches, however. The underlying level is defined

in terms of primitive grammatical relations in the framework of Relational
Grammar. The need for this deviation from the standard structural approach to
grammatical relations was argued to arise from the fact that relevant generalizations could not be captured in structural terms only. "Historically, the RG
abandonment of transformational grammar (TG) was a direct consequence of TG's
failure to provide cross-linguistically viable notions of grammatical relations.
...Transformations, stated in terms of linear order of constituents, made it
necessary to formulate distinct rules for languages with different word order for
what could be characterized in relational terms as the same phenomenon cross-
linguistically" (Perlmutter 1981:3-4). Heny (1981:1-5) lucidly explains what was
the problematic aspect of the theory that gave rise to the emergence of Relational Grammar. Time and time again the grammatical transformations have to repeat
elements both in their structural description and in their structural change that
are irrelevant to the relationship that the grammatical transformation was meant
to express. As this is the case, "then it is not surprising that attempts to ask
questions about the cross-linguistic significance of transformations made little
headway while the classical transformation formed the core of grammatical theory?
(o.c. p. 3). However, the overview of the development of the transformational
analysis has made it clear that the characterization of transformations given in
the above quotation from Perlmutter is no longer correct, now that the transformational component is reduced to MOVE α. The θ-criterion and Case Theory can be
regarded as a means to supply "relational" information over and above the
information supplied by the phrase marker in terms of dominance relations between
categories. The most significant difference, then, between Relational Grammar
and recent generative grammar concerns the question of whether or not the
construction- specific approach is upheld and furthermore how the NP which has to
become subject is identified. In generative grammar, the construction-specific
approach has been abandoned. The characterization of the NP which becomes the
surface syntactic subject is given in terms of a governed NP which fails to
receive Case. The foregoing discussion suggests very strongly that this approach
is superior.

   Turning now to the classification of verbs, we have seen that the category
verb is traditionally partitioned into two subcategories: a category of transitives and a category of intransitives. This distinction is mainly based on the
logically based notion of transitivity, i.e. the notion that a transitive predicate expresses a relation between two arguments, whereas an intransitive predicate can be regarded as a one-place predicate.A more structural approach to these
two subcategories would define transitive verbs as those verbs that combine with

an NP or that are subcategorized for an NP (cf. Chomsky 1965). The classification
of verbs into two classes, then, is based on the presence of an object. I assume
that one has always been aware of the problems that this approach meets with[72]. In
languages that do not exhibit case distinctions, no distinction can be made
between a verb that takes a direct object and a verb that merely takes an indirect
object. Several types of adverbial modifiers can take the form of an NP. Analyses
have been put forth to analyze these adverbial NP's as being really PP's of
which the preposition happened to be deleted. All the problems that the **Aspects**
approach meets with can be defined away in some way or other.

The preceding discussion suggests, however, that a more sensible classification of verbs could be made in terms of the property of selecting a θ-subject.
The traditional class of intransitives can be divided into two subclasses, one of
which displays the properties of transitives, while the other share its properties with passives of traditional transitives. I suggest that transitivity is
regarded no longer as a property of combining with an NP to form a VP (or rather
V'), but rather as having an external θ-role. I propose therefore that the
traditional classification in (223) is replaced by the classification in (224).

(223)   transitive: $[_{V'}, NP \text{ —}]$
           examples: doden 'kill', breken 'break' (causative)
                     opvallen 'strike'

           intransitive: $[_{V'}, \text{ —}]$
           examples: lachen 'laugh', sterven 'die'
                     breken 'break' (non-causative)

(224)   intransitive: θ'-subject
           examples: sterven 'die', breken 'break' (non-causative)
                     opvallen 'strike'.
           transitive: θ-subject
           examples: doden 'kill', lachen 'laugh'
                     breken 'break' (causative)

According to the classification proposed in (224), the subcategory of transitive
verbs includes logically one-place predicates, whereas the subcategory of intransitives includes logically two-place predicates. What this means is that I
claim that the logical nature of a predicate that is expressed by a particular
verb is not a relevant property from a linguistic point of view. The classifica-

tion in (224) expresses a linguistically more significant partitioning of verbs than the classification based on logical properties of the predicates given in (223).

In the following chapter, I shall argue that for each type of transitive verb a parellel intransitive type exists, which suggests that the classification is indeed significant.

Chapter 4

Small Clauses

In the previous chapters, the so-called small-clause analysis was referred to on several occasions and some preliminary discussion of it offered. The idea of small clauses is originally due to Stowell (1981). In this chapter, the small-clause analysis will be subjected to closer examination. Specifically, we shall examine its applicability to Dutch and its relation to the classification of verbs that was proposed in chapter three. This discussion automatically leads to the problem of auxiliary selection in Dutch. It also poses some questions with respect to the adjacency requirement on Case assignment, which we discussed in chapter two. This in turn brings us to the analysis of synthetic compounds.

4.1. The motivation for the small-clause analysis

In chapter two it was argued that the phrase-structure component of the base is to be abandoned for various reasons. It was then argued that the internal structure of phrases is determined by the Projection Principle and the θ-criterion, in combination with the requirement that phrases to which an internal θ-role is assigned must be c-commanded by the head, whereas a possible external θ-role is assigned to the subject of the phrase, defined as the sister of X'. This means, then, that D-structure is essentially a projection of the selectional and subcategorizational properties of lexical heads, possibly further determined by the Extended Projection Principle (cf. Chomsky 1982). According to this approach, a particular head will always assign the same thematic role to the same syntactic position. Consider from this perspective the following examples.

(1) a. John seems to be ill

  b. John seems ill

According to the standard analysis of examples like (1a), the S-structure subject of **seem** is the deep structure subject of an embedded clause, from where it is moved to its S-structure position by means of MOVE α. The motivation for this analysis is that **seem** does not assign a θ-role to its subject, as can be concluded from the fact that it does not take a referential expression in subject position if the complement clause is finite. In the latter case, the subject of the embedded clause can remain **in situ** because it receives nominative Case from Tense. If the complement clause is tenseless, however, no Case is assigned to the subject position from inside the embedded clause. Therefore, the embedded subject, **John** in (1a) should receive Case from **seem**, the matrix verb, but since this verb does not assign a θ-role to its own subject, it does not assign Case to a governed NP either, in accordance with the so-called Burzio generalization. Therefore, in order to receive Case, the embedded subject must be moved to the nominatively marked subject position of the matrix clause. It can be moved into this position, because no θ-role is assigned to this position. In this position it receives nominative Case from TENSE.

  If we accept the claim that verbs which enter into different syntactic contexts assign the same thematic roles to the same syntactic positions, it must be assumed that **seem** in (1b) does not assign a θ-role to its subject either. Therefore, **John** in (1b) cannot be generated in its S-structure position, but must have arrived there through an application of MOVE α. The question then arises from which position it is extracted. It must be assumed that **John** receives its θ-role from **ill**. On the assumption, then, that θ-roles are assigned within the phrase projected around the head that assigns the θ-roles, **John** must originate in the AP. Therefore, the underlying structure of (1b) must be as in (2).

(2) [$_{NP}$ e] seems [$_{SC}$ John ill]

In (2), the label SC stands for small clause. The question is what the category of the small clause is: is it a projection of some lexical category? If not, what could determine the label? Stowell's answer to this question is that it is an AP, i.e. that the maximal projection of the adjective **ill** includes a subject NP. The analysis can be generalized to other categories than AP, i.e. it may be assumed that not only NP's and S's have subjects, but that AP's and PP's can have subjects as well [73].

According to this analysis, **seem** is the basic unaccusative counterpart of verbs like **believe**. This supports our claim that for each type of transitive verb, there is a parallel intransitive, i.e. unaccusative type of verb. I shall come back to this point later. An example of a transitive counterpart of (1) is given in (3).

(3) a. I believe John to be capable of anything
   b. I believe John capable of anything

In (3b), then, the verb **believe** is followed by a small-clause AP, the subject of which receives Case from the governing verb, which is possible here because **believe**, unlike **seem**, assigns a Θ-role to its subject.

The considerations that lead us to assume a small-clause analysis in (1b) also demand that in (1a), **John** receives its Θ-role from **ill**. It follows that the copula **be** must be analyzed as an unaccusative verb as well. What is true for **be** and **seem**, then, is true for copula verbs in general, i.e. all traditional copula verbs are unaccusatives or raising verbs. The same assumptions carry over to Dutch. Moreover, the fact that there are also small-clause PP's suggests that there is no real difference between the traditional copula **zijn** and the traditional main verb **zijn**. So, I assume that the underlying structure of (4a) and (4b) is as in (5a) and (5b), respectively, with the same verb **zijn** appearing in both structures[74].

(4) a. dat Jan ziek is
      that John ill is

   b. dat Jan in de tuin is
      that John in the garden is

(5) a. $[_{V''} [_{NP} e] [_{AP}$ Jan ziek] is]

   b. $[_{V''} [_{NP} e] [_{PP}$ Jan in de tuin] is]

The most obvious transitive counterpart of the verb **zijn** is the verb **hebben** 'have', which we also find with small-clause complements. An example is given in (6).

(6) dat ik $[_{PP}$ een auto in mijn garage] heb
      that I   a car   in my garage   have

There are two questions that suggest themselves at this moment. First, are there any arguments in favour of the small-clause analysis beyond the motivation that derives from the Projection Principle and the θ-criterion? Second, can we motivate the assumption that the label of the small clause is considered to be determined by the predicative element, i.e. by the head of the small clause?

Starting with the latter question, we could wonder what kind of alternative there is for labelling the small clause. A suggestion might be that this label is S, considered as a clause without an INFL. The main reason for rejecting such an alternative is that the choice of category for the small clause is determined by the governing verb or governing category in general. To see this, we should compare the verbs **zijn** en **hebben**. We saw above that the verb **zijn** can take both a small- clause AP and a small-clause PP. The verb **hebben,** however, does not permit a small-clause AP in western dialects of Dutch, whereas it does permit PP's and AP's in eastern dialects of Dutch (cf. Van Bree 1981). So, the examples in (7) are unacceptable for speakers of western dialects, but accepted by speakers of eastern dialects of Dutch.

(7) a. dat ik de vrouw ziek heb
       that I the wife ill have

    b. dat ik mijn band lek heb
       that I my tire flat have

    c. dat ik de knie kapot heb
       that I the knee in pieces have

Similarly, the preposition **met** takes small-clause AP's and PP's, as is shown by the examples in (8), whereas the preposition **zonder** only allows PP complements. This is more extensively discussed in Beukema & Hoekstra (1983a).

(8) a. met [$_{PP}$ een das om je nek]
       with a tie around your neck

    b. met [$_{AP}$ het raam open]
       with   the window open

(9) a. zonder [$_{PP}$ een hoed op je hoofd]
       without   a   hat on your head

b.*zonder [_{AP} de trainer dronken]
  without the trainer drunk

Many more examples could be added to illustrate this point. Therefore, we shall
assume in the remainder of this chapter that the category of the small clause is
determined by the head that supplies the θ-roles inside the small clause.

Turning to the former question, viz. the motivation for the small clause
analysis, we have to consider several aspects. A general consideration that
suggests the correctness of the small-clause analysis is presented in Kayne
(1981b).   In this article, Kayne proposes that the notion of c-command should be
replaced by the notion of unambiguous path. Without reviewing his proposal in
detail, we mention here the result of his hypothesis. The notion of an unambiguous path can informally be defined as a path "such that in tracing it out, one
is never forced to make a choice between two (or more) unused branches, both
pointing in the same direction" (p.146). If the unambiguous-path requirement is
imposed on the government relation, then there must be less n-ary branching, n>2,
than is often thought, i.e. according to the unambiguous-path requirement, most
nodes in a tree should be binary branching. This suggests that those constructions which are usually assumed to have a structure with a head accompanied by two
complements should be reconsidered. The constructions that involve small clauses
are traditionally regarded as constructions with two complements, i.e. it is
generally assumed that a verb like **verklaren** in (10) is subcategorized for both
an NP and an AP complement. Accordingly, the structure of the V' would be as in
(11), where the V' is a ternary branching node. According to the small-clause
analysis, however, the structure of the V' is as in (12), in which we have only
binary branching nodes.

(10) dat ik het document geldig verklaar
     that I the document valid declare

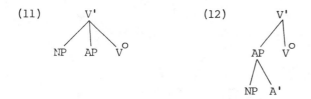

(11)   V'   (12)   V'

      NP   AP   V°   AP   V°

                                       NP   A'

The structure in (12) is not only selected by the θ-criterion, then, but also by
the unambiguous-path requirement. The same is true for the so-called absolute

with/met construction in Dutch and English. Examples like (8) were assigned a structure like (13) by Van Riemsdijk (1978a), which violates the unambiguous-path requirement. The small-clause analysis of the complement of **with/met** is shown in Beukema & Hoekstra (1983a) to be superior for a number of reasons. The structure assigned to these constructions according to this proposal is as in (14), which again is in accordance with the unambiguous-path requirement.

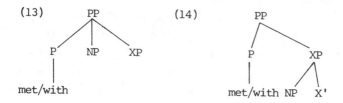

Several arguments thus converge to arrive at the conclusion that (14) is to be preferred over (13), some of which were briefly mentioned in the previous chapters. McCawley (1983) presents other arguments in favour of the claim that the NP and the following predicative expression in the absolute construction form a constituent. The combination of the two items serves as antecedent of a pronoun, can undergo right-node raising and can be the locus of conjoining. McCawley refers to what we would call a small clause as a nexus constituent, which recalls Jespersen's (1940) analysis, which is basically identical to ours.

Another type of construction which the unambiguous-path requirement suggests should be analyzed as involving a small clause are those constructions headed by a verb that selects not only a direct object, but also an inherent adverbial of place or direction. So, whereas (16) represents the structure that would normally be assigned to the V' in (15), the unambiguous-path requirement suggests that its structure should be as in (17). This brings us to another argument in favour of the small-clause analysis.

(15) dat Jan het boek in de kast zet
     that John the book in the bookcase puts

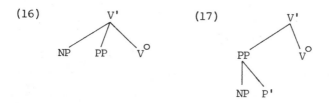

In Dutch, PP's can occur on either side of the verb. In chapter two we provided a principled reason for this. Traditionally, it was assumed that PP's are generated in preverbal position from which they could optionally be moved to postverbal position by means of the rule of PP-over-V (cf. Koster 1973). Not all PP's may be moved to postverbal position, however. In particular, those PP's which we would argue to be part of a small clause may not be moved to postverbal position. This is nicely demonstrated by the following examples.

(18) a. dat Jan een auto in zijn garage heeft
        that John a car in his garage   has

     b. dat Jan een auto heeft

     c. dat Jan een auto heeft in zijn garage

(19) a. dat Jan de zon in zijn gezicht heeft
        that John the sun in his face has

     b.?dat Jan de zon heeft

     c.*dat Jan de zon heeft in zijn gezicht

I would like to maintain that (18a) is ambiguous. In one reading, it is asserted that John owns a car and that this car happens to be in his garage. In the second reading, it is not asserted that John owns a car, but merely that there is a car in his garage. In (18b) only the possession of a car is asserted. The first reading is strongly preferred for (18c). This is confirmed by the examples in (19). The only sensible interpretation of (19a) is not that John owns the sun, but that the situation is such that the sun shines in his face. Therefore, (19b) is ungrammatical, or at least very strange. The PP **in zijn gezicht** may not be placed in postverbal position. Similarly, the phrase **in de kast** in (15) may not be placed in postverbal position as is shown by the ungrammaticality of (20). This corroborates the claim that the structure in (17) is to be preferred over structure (16).

(20) *dat Jan het boek zet in de kast

Why is it impossible to move this PP to postverbal position? The answer to this question is provided by the hypothesis of unidirectional government which we

defended in chapter two. If the structure in (17) is correct, movement of the PP
would also involve movement of the NP subject of the PP to postverbal position.
This subject NP, **het boek,** must receive Case from the matrix verb, however. Since
Case is assigned under government and since government of V is to the left in
Dutch, movement of the entire PP to postverbal position would yield an ungrammatical result, because the subject NP of this PP cannot receive Case. That the
subject NP of the PP receives its Case from the matrix verb **zetten** is clear if we
consider the passive counterpart in (15), which is given in (21). The NP must be
moved into the subject position of **zetten.** According to the analysis of passives
presented in chapter three, this follows from the fact that this NP cannot
receive Case in its base position, due to the absorption of the external θ-role
in the lexical representation of **zetten.**

(21)   dat het boek (door Jan) in de kast werd gezet
       that the book by John   in the bookcase was put

If this account of the ungrammaticality of (20) is correct, it is predicted that
small-clause PP's in the complement of raising verbs may not be placed in
postverbal position for the same reason, i.e. the trace in subject position of
the small-clause PP would not be governed by the matrix verb. The structure would
then be ruled out by the ECP. This prediction is correct. Consider the contrast
between (22) and (23).

(22) a. dat Jan in de tuin wandelt
        that John in the garden walks

     b. dat Jan wandelt
     c. dat Jan wandelt in de tuin

(23) a. dat Jan in de tuin is
     b.*dat Jan is
     c.*dat Jan is in de tuin
        that John is in the garden

The verb **wandelen** assigns a θ-role to its subject as is evidenced by the grammaticality of (22b). **Wandelen** is not an unaccusative verb: it selects the perfective
auxiliary **hebben** and allows an impersonal passive. Therefore, the subject of the
small-clause PP **in de tuin** is not a trace, nor is it a lexical expression. In

(23a), however, **Jan** receives its θ-role not in its S-structure position, but forms part of a chain that also includes the subject of the small-clause PP. The θ-role of this chain is provided by the phrase **in de tuin**. **Zijn** itself does not assign a θ-role to its syntactic subject and therefore, (23b) is ungrammatical. (23c) bears out the correctness of our prediction that a small-clause PP cannot be moved into postverbal position. In (22c), on the other hand, we see that a small-clause PP can be moved to postverbal position. This is to be expected, since the subject of the small clause in that case is neither lexical nor a trace. Rather, the subject position of this small-clause PP is ungoverned and therefore it is PRO. Its interpretation is an instance of control, rather than of trace binding. In this respect, then, the example in (22a) is similar to raising constructions, whereas the example in (23a) is similar to control constructions. It turns out that the differential behaviour of the PP's in these examples(and in the other examples that will be discussed below) with respect to the possibility of PP- over-V supports the small clause analysis.

Turning to another piece of motivation for the small-clause analysis, we look again at the asymmetry between verbs on the one hand and other categories on the other with respect to the possibility of governing into a sister projection. Kayne (1981b) points out that the small-clause analysis of examples like (3b) in conjunction with the hypothesis that nouns cannot govern into sister projections, predicts the ungrammaticality of (24) and similar examples in (25).

(24)   *my belief (of) John capable of anything
(25) a. *their assumption of John dangerous
     b. *the psychiatrist's judgement of the student well-adjusted
     c. *their consideration of Mary a genius

If **John** in (3b) were just the object of the verb **believe,** there is no reason to expect the ungrammaticality of (24) as opposed to the grammaticality of examples like (26).

(26) a. the destruction of the city
     b. their consideration of this proposal

Under the small-clause analysis, (24) is ungrammatical because in general, prepositions may not govern across a maximal projection boundary, unlike verbs. Similarly, the ECP accounts for the ungrammaticality of (27) under the assumption that nouns may not govern across a maximal projection boundary either. In chapter

two, this was used to explain the restricted distribution of V-raising structures.

(27) *Jan's schijn [e te winnen]

It was also noted in chapter two that AP's cannot occur as complements of N. This
cannot be explained in terms of the absence of an AP option in the expansion of
N', for reasons that were discussed there. However, the present discussion
provides a principled answer to the question of why AP cannot occur as a
complement of N. Consider the following examples.

(28) a. dat ik Jan vervelend vind
        that I John boring find

     b.*dat ik vind Jan vervelend

     c.*mijn vondst van Jan vervelend
        my finding of John boring

Jan in (28a) is licensed because the small clause precedes the verb and the verb
may assign Case to this subject NP under structural government. (28b) shows that
the small-clause AP may not occur in postverbal position, which is explained by
the unidirectionality of government. This explains at the same time why AP
complements may never occur in postverbal position, unlike PP's. Example (28c)
shows that a small-clause AP cannot accompany a derived nominal. The preposition
van is incapable of governing across a maximal-projection barrier. The noun
vondst itself is equally incapable of governing structurally. Since this is the
case in general, no N may occur with an AP complement.

Apart from the considerations that pertain to the Projection Principle and
the θ- criterion, the small-clause analysis can thus be supported by general
considerations involving the theory of government and the hypothesis of unambiguous paths. Moreover, there are several empirical arguments that support the
correctness of the small-clause analysis.

An alternative to the small-clause analysis is provided in Williams (1980,
1983). However, some of the arguments that can be given in favour of the small-
clause analysis militate against Williams's predication analysis. According to
this analysis, the subject-predicate relation that holds between the phrase that
is considered the subject of the small clause and the predicative part of the

small clause can be captured by means of predication, which is the operation of coindexing a subject and a predicate. According to Williams' theory the subject relation which a particular NP bears to a particular predicate need not be configurationally defined in such a way that the subject is a specifier of the predicate projection. Therefore, the syntactic structures that are assigned to the various constructions discussed thus far are unnecessary under the predication analysis and accordingly, the structures provided under the small-clause analysis are replaced by the structures that would traditionally be assigned to them. Therefore, every argument which directly argues in favour of the particular structures assigned under the small-clause analysis is at the same time an argument against Williams' theory. One such argument has just been discussed, i.e. if no distinction is made between the NP **John** in (3b) and regular NP objects, there is no basis to account for the difference in grammaticality between (24)-(25) and the NP's in (26).

Another argument against Williams' theory can be derived from the absolute **with** construction. Siegel (1983) observes that it is impossible to extract the NP following **with** in these constructions. This is illustrated by the following examples.

(29) a. She left with the kitchen dirty
b. Jill was performing with a funny hat on
c. Grace was sitting with a very warm coat on
d. We always stay home with Dick Cavett on television

(30) a.*What did she leave with dirty?
b.*What was Jill performing with on?
c.*What was Grace sitting with on?
d.*What do you stay home with on television?

Although Williams has not presented an analysis of these constructions, the structure in(31) would be in line with his theory of predication. In Beukema & Hoekstra (1983a), we argue that the structure should be as in (32).

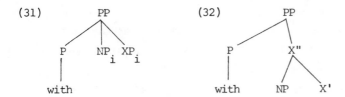

The subscripts in (31) are the result of applying the coindexing rule which expresses the subject-predicate relation existing between the two sisters of **with**. The subject-predicate relation is expressed syntactically in (32). In Beukema & Hoekstra (1983b), an account is given of the impossibility of extraction of the subject NP which presupposes the correctness of the structure in (32) and which is not available if the structure in (31) is adopted. According to that analysis, the impossibility of extraction from these absolute constructions is an instance of the general restriction on empty categories in subject position, i.e. (30) is assimilated to cases like (33) and (34a).

(33)   ***Who** did they think that **e** came in
(34) a. ***Which actress** does John think that a picture of **e** was found by Bill?
     b. **Which actress** does John think that Bill found a picture of **e**?

Kayne (1983a) has argued that the relation between a gap and its antecedent is subject to a general configurational requirement which he calls the Connectedness Condition (CC). Disregarding the parasitic gaps phenomenon and related issues, we can describe the following tree structures as relevant to the CC.

(35) a.   b.   c.

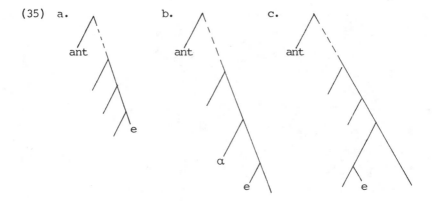

The CC requires that the gap is connected with its antecedent by what Kayne calls a g-projection, which is basically defined as the set of maximal projections constituting the path from the gap to the antecedent, with the further requirement that all maximal projections on this path as well as the gaps have their governors on the same side. For a language like English, this amounts to saying that this path must be uniformly right branching. This is the case in   (35a)

which can be taken to represent the structure of (34b). (34a) is ungrammatical because the gap is contained within the NP **a picture of e,** which is on a left branch. Thus (34a) is an instantiation of the structure in (35c). If the gap is not contained within a maximal projection on a left branch, but constitutes the left branch itself, as in the diagram in (35b), the CC is not violated. Sentences that can be considered to instantiate (35b) are given in (36).

(36) a. **Who** do you believe [e to be the best candidate]
     b. **Who** do you consider [e angry with Mary]
     c. **Who** do you think [$_{S'}$ e [$_S$ e came in]]

However, for (35b) to yield grammatical sentences, α must be a proper governor for the empty category, i.e. α must either be a local antecedent, as in (36c) where the trace in COMP licenses the gap in subject position[75], or a lexical category capable of governing into a sister projection. Verbs have this capacity, as can be seen in (36a) and (36b) in which the verbs **believe** and **consider** occupy the position of α in (35b). Contrary to Kayne (1981c), we claim that prepositions do not qualify as proper governors, at least that they may not license an empty category in the subject position of a sister projection. This is evident from the ungrammaticality of (37b), and the contrasts between (38a) and (38b) on the one hand and between (39a) and (39b) on the other.

(37) a. **What** did they hope [$_{PP}$ for e]?

     b.*__What__ did they hope [$_{S'}$ for [$_S$ e to happen]]?

(38) a. They'd believe [e to be foolish [**any candidate who would take the trouble to run in every primary**]]

     b.*They'd want [e to win [**any candidate who would take the trouble to run in every primary**]]

(39) a. **Who** does John remember [e eating fish] ?

     b.*__Who__ did John talk to Mary about [e eating fish]?

Returning now to the ungrammaticality of the examples in (30), we see that this proposal neatly accounts for this ungrammaticality on the assumption that the structure of **with-** absolutes is as in (32). Only in this structure is there a gap on a left branch. Therefore, Williams would not have a principled way to account for the difference in grammaticality between (40a) (=(30a)) and (40b).

(40) a.*What did she leave with dirty?
     b. What did she leave with?

This concludes the discussion of the motivation for the small- clause analysis.

4.2. Extending the class of verbs taking small-clause complements

Sofar we have considered two classes of verbs taking small- clause complements. On the one hand, there are verbs that are intransitive according to the definition of intransitive adopted in chapter three. This class includes the traditional copula verbs. Since they are intransitive, they are incapable of assigning Case to the subject NP of their small-clause complement, which for this reason must be moved to the θ'-subject position in the projection of these intransitive verbs. The second class of verbs, the transitives, consists of two subclasses. On the one hand there are the verbs that were traditionally assumed to take both a direct object and an adverb of place or direction. Examples of this type are presented in (15), (18) and (19). On the other hand, there are verbs that were traditionally assumed to select a direct object and a predicative complement. A representative set of examples is given in (41).

(41) a. dat ik Piet vervelend vind
        that I Peter boring find

     b. dat Marie haar man ziek meldt
        that Mary her husband sick reported

     c. dat de beambte het document geldig verklaarde
        that the employee the document valid declared

     d. dat wij deze gebeurtenis geheim houden
        that we this event   secret keep

    e. dat zij hem gevangen houden
       that they him captive keep
       "that they keep him in custody"

Each of these can be passivized, showing that "raising" passives are in fact present in Dutch.

In the preceding subsection, we have established the rationale for the analysis of these complements as small clauses in the sense of Stowell. From this discussion, a number of criteria have arisen with which we can determine for a particular situation whether or not we are dealing with a small clause. In the case of an obligatory AP or PP with a verb, this AP or PP must be a small clause, with the exception of the type of PP that we have called argument PP's (cf. chapter 2), and in fact, this small clause may not have a PRO subject. Therefore, the subject of the small clause is a trace if the matrix verb is intransitive and a lexical NP if it is transitive. This prediction is generally regarded as the most successful aspect of the small-clause analysis.

Consider the examples in (42) against the background of the previous discussion.

(42) a. dat Jan valt
      that John falls

    b. dat Jan in de sloot valt
       that John in/into the ditch falls

The verb **vallen** is intransitive, i.e. it is an unaccusative verb: it selects **zijn** as its perfective auxiliary, its participle can be used as in "een gevallen kind" (a fallen child) and it does not allow impersonal passivization. The sentence in (42b) is ambiguous: in one reading it is asserted that John falls from the bank of a ditch into the ditch, the most natural reading; according to the second reading, John is in a (e.g. dried-out or shallow) ditch when he falls. In order to account for the two readings, (42b) must be assigned two different structures. In the structure that must account for the second reading, the small-clause PP **in de sloot** can be treated as an adjunct. The subject of this PP is then PRO, controlled by the D-structure object of **vallen,** i.e. in this reading we are dealing with the verb **vallen** as it is used in (42a). In the other reading, however, the structure must be different. Consider the sentence in (43) where the phrase **in de sloot** is in postverbal position.

(43) dat Jan valt in de sloot

(43) is no longer ambiguous: it only has the second, rather unnatural reading. This is to be expected if the PP has a PRO subject in the structure representing the second reading (cf. above). However, the absence of the first reading suggests that the subject of the PP in the structure representing that reading must be governed. Since **vallen** is intransitive, this subject must be a trace, therefore. We then arrive at (44a) as representing the less obvious reading and (44b) as representing the natural reading.

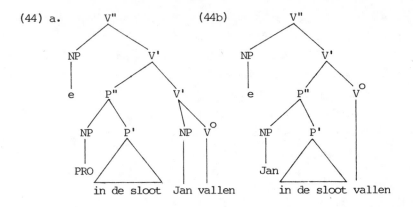

In (44a), then, the small-clause PP is an adjunct with a PRO subject, whereas it is a complement with **Jan** as its subject in (44b). The fact that **vallen** can appear in both contexts requires that **vallen** is associated with two different θ-grids. Before going into this problem, we note that **vallen** as used in (44b) is a member of a class which also has members that belong only to this class. An example is the verb **gaan** 'go'. **Gaan** always selects a PP complement which cannot be moved to postverbal position:

(45) a. dat Jan naar Groningen gaat
　　　　　that John to Groningen goes

　　　b.*dat Jan gaat naar Groningen

It should be noted that the verb **gaan** and the verb **vallen** as used in (44b) are syntactically in fact similar to the copula **zijn,** with the difference that **gaan** and **vallen** select a directional complement. However, the verbs **gaan** and **vallen** are also used in the same kind of constructions as the verbs that are traditionally regarded as copula verbs, although there are all sorts of idiosyncratic selectional restrictions.

    (46) a. die man gaat dood
            that man goes dead
            "that man is dying"

        b.*die man wordt dood
            that man becomes dead

    (47) a.*die man gaat/valt ziek
            that man goes/falls ill

        b. die man wordt ziek
            that man becomes ill

Perhaps such idiosyncratic variation in the choice of copula can be etymological-ly explained, e.g. by pointing at the general idea that someone who dies goes somewhere, but from a synchronic point of view there is just a vast number of irreducible selectional restrictions. Syntactically, however, the verb **gaan** in (46) is identical to the verb **gaan** in (45). Similarly, the verb **vallen** replaces the copula **zijn** in constructions like those in (48).

    (48) dat die sigaret wel te roken is/valt
            that that cigaret well to smoke is/falls
            "that that cigaret is smokable"

Constructions like these are called modal passives in Hoekstra & Moortgat (1979a). Although they show a superficial resemblance to **easy-to-please** con-structions, there are a lot of differences, which suggests that the modal passive is indeed more similar to passive (i.e. involves NP movement). The **easy-to-please** type construction involves the application of WH-movement. An example is given in (49).

    (49) die sigaretten zijn lekker om te roken
            those cigarets are nice for to smoke

For a discussion of these differences, see Hoekstra & Moortgat (1979a) and more recently Van Riemsdijk (1981c).

The fact that the verbs **gaan** and **vallen** can be used as regular copula verbs suggests that the analysis of these verbs presented above is on the right track. It should be observed that not only unaccusative verbs like **vallen** can be mapped into the class of **gaan,** but that this is also possible with unergative verbs like **wandelen**. The relevant data have already been mentioned in chapter two. They are repeated here in (50).

(50) a. dat Jan wandelt

    b. dat Jan gewandeld heeft/*is
       that John walked has/is

    c. dat Jan naar Groningen gewandeld heeft/is
       that John to Groningen walked   has/ is

    d. dat Jan gewandeld heeft/*is naar Groningen

The basic verb **wandelen** is transitive, i.e. assigns a θ-role to its syntactic subject. This is evidenced by the fact that it selects the perfective auxiliary **hebben** as in (50b). In (50c), both **hebben** and **zijn** can be selected. If **hebben** is selected, the PP **naar Groningen** is again an adjunct with a PRO subject. There-fore, the PP may be placed in postverbal position. If **zijn** is selected, on the other hand, placement of the PP in postverbal position is impossible (cf. (50d)). Therefore, if **zijn** is selected, the verb **wandelen** is used as a member of the same class to which **gaan** also belongs. This change in class membership of **wandelen** is paralleled by a change in meaning: in (50a), (50b) and (50c), it is asserted that John is engaged in a certain activity, whereas (50c) specifies a change of position of John if **zijn** is chosen, which happens to result from the process of walking. A similar situation can be described for many verbs of motion.

The analysis of the verbs **gaan, vallen** and **wandelen** presented above meets with a difficult problem, however. The structure assumed for these verbs is as in (51).

(51) $[_{V''}$ [e] $[_{V'}$ $[_{PP''}$ NP P'] V^{o}]]

According to this analysis, then, the S-structure subjects are generated within the small-clause PP at D-structure and moved to their S-structure position by means of MOVE α. At D-structure, then, the matrix subject position must be empty, and this must be due to the property that these verbs do not assign an external θ-role. This conclusion is rather strange, however, since it seems that it would imply that there is no difference in role between the subjects of the sentences in (52), as the θ-role of the subject is in each case determined by the same predicative expression.

(52) a. Jan springt in de sloot
        John jumps into the ditch

     b. Jan valt in de sloot
        John falls into the ditch

     c. John wandelt in de sloot
        John walks into the ditch

However, there are just as many differences in θ-roles between these examples as there are in cases like those in (53), i.e. the action that John is engaged in in getting into the ditch differs in each case in (52).

(53) a. Jan springt "John jumps"
     b. Jan valt "John falls"
     c. Jan wandelt "John walks"

So, whereas our analysis is capable of explaining the selection of the perfective auxiliary and the impossibility of the PP occurring in postverbal position, we face a problem with respect to thematic-role structure. It should be noted, on the other hand that with some of the verbs that are relevant in this discussion, the θ-role of the S-structure subject may be entirely determined by the small clause, while the matrix verb merely specifies some aspect, like ingressive aspect (**gaan, komen**) or duration. So, whereas the notion of motion is present in (54), no such motional aspect is expressed in (55).

(54) Jan komt naar Groningen
     John comes to Groningen

(55) Het werk komt op tijd gereed
     The work comes in time ready

In order to solve this problem, I would like to appeal to the distinction made in Zubizarreta (1982) between argument θ-roles and adjunct θ-roles. An example that she discusses is found in (56).

(56) John intentionally seduced Mary

Here, **John** receives its θ-role from the predicate **seduce Mary,** but it also receives an adjunct θ-role from the adjunct **intentionally.** Therefore, **John** ends up with two θ-roles, one of which is an adjunct θ-role. This situation does not cause a violation of the θ-criterion. According to Zubizarreta, some raising verbs, especially the modals and aspectual verbs may also assign an adjunct θ-role to the subject position that serves as the landing site of the NP subject of their complement (cf. o.c.:chapter two). Accepting the distinction made by Zubizarreta, I would like to argue that the verbs under discussion optionally assign the θ-role that they normally assign to either their object or their subject, as an adjunct θ-role to their subject, which nevertheless remains a θ'-position for the purposes of MOVE α. Whereas the subject- predicate relation that is determined in terms of argument θ-roles may be taken to express the main assertion, the assertion in terms of an adjunct predicate and the category to which it assigns an adjunct θ-role may express a secondary assertion or induce a restriction on the application of the proposition expressed in the main assertion. So, the ambiguity of (57) may be explicated in terms of the two distinct paraphrases in (58) and (59).

(57) Jan wandelt naar Groningen
     John walks to Groningen

(58) John was walking while on his way to Groningen

(59) John ended up being in Groningen by walking there

If (57) is interpreted as (58), its perfect is formed with **hebben:** the main assertion is that John was walking. If (57) is interpreted like (59), on the other hand, its perfect is formed with **zijn.** Then the main assertion is that he ends up in Groningen, with the secondary assertion that he walked there.

While I am aware of the fact that these rather sketchy remarks warrant further research rather than firm conclusions, I trust that the general direction for a solution to the problem that we faced will be clear.

We have shown, then, how certain verbs can become members of the class of raising verbs, i.e. verbs taking a small-clause complement without assigning an argument θ-role to their subject position. They may optionally assign an adjunct θ-role.

There also exists the possibility that verbs are mapped into the class of transitive verbs taking a small-clause complement. An example is the verb **lopen**. (60a) shows that **lopen** is a transitive verb: it selects the perfective auxiliary **hebben**. In (60b), however, it takes a small-clause complement. In that usage, it is syntactically similar to **slaan** as used in (61).

(60) a. dat Jan heeft gelopen
       that John has walked

   b. dat Jan zijn schoenen scheef loopt
      "that John his shoes on one side walks"

(61) dat Jan het metaal plat slaat
     that John the metal flat beats

Other examples are the verbs like **eten** 'eat' and **drinken** 'drink' as used in (62).

(62) a. dat die jongen zich moddervet eet
        that that boy himself mud fat eats
        "that that boy becomes as fat as a pig by gorging himself"

    b. dat hij zich dronken drinkt
       that he himself drunk drinks

Clearly, **zich** in these examples is not the object of **eten** and **drinken**. Rather, it is the subject of the adjectives. A suitable parafrase is "he causes himself to become fat/drunk by eating/drinking too much". I shall not go into the semantics of these expressions (cf. Geis 1973, Dowty 1979). My claim would be, however, that the structure of examples like (60)-(62) is as in (63).

(63) $[_{V''}$ NP $[_{V'}$ $[_{A''}$ NP A'] V^{o}]]

Since the V^{o} assigns a θ-role to its subject, it is transitive and therefore capable of assigning Case to an NP governed by it, in this case to the subject of the small- clause A".

At the end of this section, we return to the claim that for each type of transitive verb there is a corresponding intransitive type. The examples below illustrate this. In (64), examples of transitive verbs are given. (64a) is an example of a verb that assigns only an external θ-role; the verb **doden** 'kill' in (64b) assigns an internal θ-role and an external θ-role; in (64c) an example is provided of a verb that assigns two internal θ-roles and an external θ-role; finally, (64d) is an example of a transitive verb that takes a small-clause complement. Each of these types has an intransitive counterpart. These are listed in the same order in (65). Furthermore, there is a rule that maps predicates from the former type into the latter. These are the passive constructions, which are also given in the same order in (66).

> (64) a. dat Jan lacht
>   that John laughs
>
>   b. dat Jan Piet doodt
>   that John Peter kills
>
>   c. dat Jan Piet een boek geeft
>   that John Peter a book gives
>
>   d. dat Jan Piet vervelend vindt
>   that John Peter boring finds
>
> (65) a. dat het sneeuwt
>   that it snows
>
>   b. dat Piet sterft
>   that Peter dies
>
>   c. dat die fout mij opviel
>   that that mistake me struck
>
>   d. dat Piet vervelend schijnt
>   that Peter boring seems
>
> (66) a. dat er wordt gelachen
>   that there is laughed

   b. dat Piet wordt gedood
      that Peter is killed

   c. dat het boek Piet wordt gegeven
      that the book Peter is given

   d. dat Piet vervelend wordt gevonden
      that Peter boring is found

I have certain doubts as to the correctness of the classification of (65a). The main reason is that the weather verbs in Dutch form their perfect with **hebben,** which suggests that they really are transitive, i.e. belong to the same type as **lachen** in (64a). For discussion, cf. Chomsky (1981). If these verbs are classified as transitives, however, it is expected that they allow an impersonal passive construction, which they do not. I will not discuss the matter any further here, since nothing of importance hinges on it. It will be clear, however, that the list in (64) does not exhaust the entire range of complement types with transitive verbs. Specifically, there are two types which are not mentioned, but which nevertheless must be considered. First, those verbs that take an argument PP, like **wachten** in (67). The other type of transitive verb which is of importance for the present discussion is the control verb. There are two types of transitive verbs taking control complements: those which take subject control, like **hopen** 'hope' in (68) and those that take object control like **dwingen** 'force' in (69).

(67) dat Jan op zijn vader wacht
     that John for his father waits

(68) dat Jan hoopt de wedstrijd te winnen
     that John hopes the game to win

(69) dat Jan Piet dwingt zijn huis te schilderen
     that John Peter forces his home to paint

The absence of an intransitive counterpart to the type in (68) is not surprising. Control complements to verbs always have a specific controller, i.e. they do not allow arbitrary control. Therefore, if there was an intransitive counterpart to (68), there would not be a possible controller and the construction would always be ungrammatical. More relevant to our claim, then, is the fact that there are to

my knowledge no intransitive counterparts to the types illustrated by (67) and
(69). It would seem that there can hardly be a principled reason for this absence,
as the verbs in (67) and (69) do allow an intransitive counterpart generated by
means of a lexical operation, i.e. they have passive counterparts.

(70) dat er op zijn vader werd gewacht
     that there for his father was waited

(71) dat Piet werd gedwongen zijn huis te schilderen
     that Peter was forced his house to paint

The absence of intransitive counterparts to both (67) and (69) might be related
to the same factor. If a verb takes an object- controlled infinitival complement,
this infinitival complement usually alternates with a prepositional argument,
i.e. if the θ-role assigned to the infinitival clause is assigned to another
phrase type, it is a prepositional phrase. This is illustrated by the examples in
(72).

(72) a. dat Jan Piet dwong zijn huis op te ruimen   (=(69))

     b. dat Piet Jan tot overgave dwong
        that Peter John to surrender forced

(73) a. dat Jan Piet overtuigde zijn mond te houden
        that John Peter convinced his mouth to keep

     b. dat Jan Piet van zijn geluk overtuigde
        that John Peter of his luck convinced

This might be taken to suggest that at a more abstract level, the infinitival
complements are argument PP's, thus having a property in common with the verbs of
the type in (67), i.e. both take an argument PP. This similarity suggests that the
absence of an intransitive counterpart should not be considered an accidental
gap, but rather that it must have some principled explanation, which is unfortu-
nately still in the dark. At any rate, there is no theoretical reason to assume
that the claim that we are making, viz. that there is an intransitive counterpart
to each type of transitive verb, is incorrect.

4.3. Verbal compounds and the adjacency requirement on Case assignment

4.3.1. Roeper & Siegel's account of verbal compounds

The subject of synthetic or verbal compounds (henceforth VC's) has received a great deal of attention in recent linguistic literature, some of which will be reviewed in this section. The discussion was initiated by Roeper & Siegel (1978). What all theories on VC's seek to explain is the interpretation of the first member as an argument of the verbal base of the second member. The main points of Roeper & Siegel's analysis can be summarized as follows.

a . VC's are created in the lexicon by means of a lexical transformation. This approach implies that VC's as a phenomenon cannot be reduced to either normal derivation or normal compounding, but must be regarded as a phenomenon **sui generis.**

b. the lexical transformation operates on the subcategorization feature of the verbal base of the second member. Therefore, a distinction can be made between grammatical and ungrammatical VC's on the same basis as the distinction between grammatical and ungrammatical phrases, since both derive from the same source, viz. the subcategorization feature.

c. subcategorization features are ordered lists of complements. This list can be expanded by the addition of optional modifiers by means of redundancy rules. This expansion is optional, but the list of modifiers that can be added is ordered.

d. The left-hand member of an VC corresponds to the first sister of the verbal base in the subcategorization frame of the latter. This is the First-Sister Principle, which is in fact the explanatory core of Roeper & Siegel's system.

e. In order to prevent misgeneration, two additional rules are needed. The function of these rules is to bring the required phrase in first-sister position. The first of these is the rule of variable deletion. This rule may delete material between the verbal base and the required position in the subcategorization frame in order to place the latter in first-sister position. It interacts with two other assumptions: a. that the subcategorization feature is ordered (cf. above) and b. that positions to the right of the first sister are inherited as valency of the newly-created item. Options in the subcategorization frame that are deleted by means of variable deletion can no longer occur in the phrase projected around the newly created item. This rule then accounts for data like those in (74).

(74) a. hand made in a factory   *factory made by hand

    b. well made by Indians   *Indian made well
    c. hand made by Indians   *Indian made by hand
f. The second additional rule is the rule of subcategorization adjustment. Like
variable deletion, it deletes material between the verb and the required position
in the subcategorization frame. The rule is restricted to the affixation of **-ed**.
It deletes two positions to the right of the verb. It thereby accounts for facts
as the following.

    (75) a. truck driver   (=someone who drives trucks)
         b. engine driven   (≠drive the engine, =driven by an engine)

Although the verb **drive** is subcategorized for an object, this object may not
appear in the left-hand position of an VC if **-ed** is attached to the verbal base in
the second member. Thus, in (75b), **engine** cannot be interpreted as the object of
drive. Similarly, the position of predicative complements, prepositional objects
and indirect objects and possibly others as well, is deleted by subcategorization
adjustment to account for such facts as in (76).

    (76) a. *catholic raised
         b. *foolish considered
         c. *theft accused
         d. *girl given   (≠given to a girl)

g. the theory of VC's is restricted to three affixes, **-ed, -ing, -er**. According to
this theory, the affixation rules involving these affixes in the generation of
VC's are different from the affixation rules employing these affixes in simple
derivatives. Therefore, no identity holds between e.g. **-er** in **driver** and **-er** in
truckdriver.

4.3.2. Some problems with Roeper&Siegel's proposal.

The analysis proposed by Roeper and Siegel has been criticized by various
linguists, notably by Allen (1978), Botha (1980,1981) and Selkirk (1981). I shall
not repeat all the arguments here and concentrate on the most principled ones.
    Botha objects to Roeper & Siegel's position that two distinct affixation
rules must be posited that attach the affixes **-ed, -ing** and **-er,** one for simple

derivatives and one for VC's. This leaves unexplained that the simple affixation rules have the same effects as regards meaning, lexical categorization, subcategorization, and allomorphy as the affixation rules for forming VC's. Botha himself stipulates this identity in his affixation hypothesis (Botha 1981: 20 ff.).

Another objection is that there is no justification to restrict the concept of VC's to those formations in which the three affixes -ed, -ing and -er occur. In fact, Botha's affixation hypothesis entails that each affix with which simple derivatives can be formed can be used in the formation of VC's. This essentially follows from Selkirk's and Allen's treatment of VC's in which VC's are structurally non-distinct from regular compounds (cf. Selkirk 1981:267). In fact, the entire content of Botha's affixation hypothesis falls out as an immediate consequence of their hypothesis that there does not exist any structural difference.

A further problem with Roeper & Siegel's approach is that it does not predict that the range of possible categories that can appear as left-hand members in VC's is identical to possible categories of the left-hand member in normal compounds. Again, this disadvantage was pointed out by Selkirk (1981: 268), where she argues that this fact is once more a consequence of her theory that VC's are created by the same rules by which normal compounds are created. It will be evident that those theories of VC's that do not assume a separate morphosyntactic treatment will have to have some semantic mechanism to account for the interpretation of the left-hand member as an argument of the verbal base. I shall not go into other objections against Roeper & Siegel's approach and turn to a discussion of the semantic mechanisms in Allen's (1978) and Selkirk's (1981) theories of VC's.

4.3.3. The semantic approach.

I shall adopt the proposal that VC's have the same structure as normal compounds. There exists a controversy concerning which part of the VC is in fact relevant for the interpretation of the relation between the first member and the second member: the verbal base of the second member or the second member, i.e. the derivative. Selkirk adopts the latter position. It should be observed that the properties of the derivative are not arbitrarily different from the properties of the verbal base; rather they are a function of the properties of the verbal base.

This is dictated by the Projection Principle, which we assume also holds for the lexicon, although in the lexicon specific rules may manipulate thematic information.

An argument in favour of Selkirk's position is the fact that a "functional" interpretation of the first member of a compound is not restricted to compounds with a deverbal second member as shown by the following evidence.

(77) a. gebrek aan geld   geld-gebrek
        lack of money   money lack

     b. kans op succes   succes-kans
        chance of success   success change

(78) a. belust op moord   moord-belust
        eager for murder   murder eager

     b. blind voor kleuren   kleuren-blind
        blind for colours   colour blind

What these examples show is that affixation is not sufficient to justify a special treatment of compounds with a deverbal second member.

In Allen's analysis, it is the verbal base of the second member that determines the interpretation of the first member directly. In her system, there are two filters for the interpretation of verbal compounds. The first filter assigns a direct-object interpretation to the first member if the verbal base of the second member is transitive. The second filter assigns the subject function to the first member if the verb is intransitive. Both filters are optional. If a compound has not received an interpretation from either of these filters, the interpretation is determined by her variable R rule.

Selkirk's semantic interpretive principles can be summarized as follows.
S1: a non-head constituent is optionally assigned a grammatical function by the head constituent.
S2: a non-head may be assigned any grammatical function apart from the SUBJ function
S3: a grammatical function assigned by the head to a non-head must be assigned to a non-head in the first-order-projection of the head
S2. is in sharp contrast with Allen's second filter: whereas Selkirk forbids that the first member receives the SUBJ function, Allen's second filter does assign

the subject function to the first member if the verb is intransitive. It should be noted, however, that this conflict is not really an empirical matter, but rather a terminological one relating to concepts that the terms stand for. To see this, consider the following example.

(79) mule drawn

(79) is cited by Allen as an example where the first member of the compound receives the subject function. In a sense, this is surprising, since the verb **draw** is not intransitive, but that is irrelevant for the point to be made. Indeed, one might say that **mule** is interpreted as the entity that draws, just like **the mule** in "the mule draws the plough". For Selkirk, the verb **draw** itself is not directly relevant: the possible functions that can be assigned to **mule** depend on **drawn**. This is an adjective, derived from the passive lexical form, i.e. Selkirk's proposal is embedded in the theory of Lexical Functional Grammar of Bresnan (1980a). The passive lexical form is related to the active lexical form as in (80).

(80) draw: SUBJ   OBJ   draw$_{pass}$:   SUBJ   (BY OBJ)

         Agent Theme   Theme   Agent

Selkirk's S2 does not allow for **mule** to be assigned the SUBJ function with respect to **drawn**, i.e. **mule** may not be interpreted as the Theme of **draw**. It may be assigned the role of Agent, however, as the function of BY-OBJ may be assigned to it.

Therefore, in the cases of **-ed** derivatives as second members, Selkirk and Allen may be assumed to predict more or less the same range of facts, although within different frameworks. We also see that Selkirk's approach makes the same predictions as Roeper & Siegel's framework, but where Roeper & Siegel need the ad hoc device of subcategorization adjustment, this effect follows without additional cost from Selkirk's analysis.

A real conflict between Selkirk and Allen arises in the case of intransitives: since intransitives do not passivize in English, Selkirk predicts that a first member will never have the interpretation of the subject of the active, whereas Allen predicts precisely the opposite, viz. that the first member may always be interpreted as the subject of the verbal base in the second member.

It turns out that both predictions are wrong. The first member in a compound in **-ing** can in some, but certainly not in all cases receive the interpretation of the subject. It also seems to be the case that Dutch and English differ in this respect. I shall restrict my attention to Dutch.

It seems to me that there is a well-defined class of traditional intransitives that allow nominalizations, mostly in **-ing**[76], to appear as second members in compounds where the first member is interpreted as a subject. (81) provides a list of examples taken from Van Dale.

(81) koraalverstening   coral stone turning   "petrifaction (of coral)"
     kustdeining   coast undulation   "litoral undulation"
     spookverschijning   ghost appearance   "apparition"
     betekeniswijziging   meaning change
     wegsplitsing   road bifurcation
     stroomverzwakking   current weakening
     bodemverzakking   soil subsiding   "subsidence of the soil"
     bloedvatenverkalking   blood vessel hardening
     valutadaling   currency lowering
     kaasrijping   cheese maturation
     gasontsnapping   gas escape
     bomontploffing   bomb explosion
     pupilverwijding   pupil dilation
     celdeling   cell division
     aardverschuiving   earth movement   "landslide"
     prijstijging   price rise

What the verbs in the base of the second member have in common is that they are all unaccusatives. In this respect too, then, the subjects of these unaccusatives pattern like the objects of transitives. In our analysis of intransitives, this fact is automatically explained. The examples above are counterexamples to Selkirk's theory of VC's, unless Selkirk were to adopt the unaccusative analysis in some form or other. In any event, the behaviour of unaccusatives under verbal compound formation/interpretation supports the theory of unaccusativity.

4.3.4. Small clauses and verbal compounds

Most theories of VC's (in particular Botha 1981 and Roeper & Siegel 1978) assume

that there is a permissible VC corresponding to each permissible phrase, unless
there is some particular proviso in the system for VC's that prevents the VC.
Allen(1978:233) points out that this assumption is in fact incorrect. To illustrate this, she presents the following examples.

(82) *worried appearer   to appear worried
      *president becomer   to become president
      *quick elapser   to elapse quickly
      *pale turner   to turn pale

The verbal compounds in (82) obey the First-Sister Principle. Disregarding
quick elapser, we note that the examples all involve predicative complements.
This suggests that Roeper & Siegel's subcategorization adjustment rule, which, as
we mentioned, above deletes the position of predicative complements in the case
of **-ed** affixation, expresses a spurious generalization.

It should be mentioned that the other theories mentioned sofar have no
straightforward explanation for the phenomena that are accounted for by the rule
of subcategorization adjustment, possibly with the exception of Selkirk to which
we return below. Allen (1978:162) notes that the ungrammaticality of the VC's in
(82) can be explained quite straightforwardly within a theory that assigns VC's
the same structure as normal compounds, since the derivatives that appear as
second members are impossible as well: ***appearer,*becomer, *turner.** This explanation is unavailable to Roeper & Siegel, as they posit separate affixation rules
for the formation of VC's. It should be noted, however, that Allen's suggestion
only partially explains the ungrammaticality of these VC's, since there is
nothing within her framework that explains the ungrammaticality of the derivatives.

Returning to the VC's in (76), we note that Selkirk's theory might explain
why they are ungrammatical on the basis of S3, reformulated somewhat in (83).

(83) All non-subject arguments of a lexical category X
      must be satisfied within the first-order projection of X

(cf. Selkirk 1981:259). (83) is the principle that we have assumed to be correct
throughout this book, i.e. we have assumed that all internal θ-roles must be
assigned to phrases that are c-commanded by the head that provides the θ-roles.
(83) is assumed to cut across structures generated by word-formation rules and
syntactic phrase-structure rules. Let us see how this works. (83) accounts for

the difference in grammaticality between (84) and (85).

(84) a. the handing of toys to babies
     b. the putting of books on the table
     c. the giving of books to children

(85) a.*toy handing to babies
     b.*book putting on the table
     c.*book giving to children

Taking **handing** as the X in (83), the first-order projection of **handing** is the
level of the compound in the cases in (85), but it is the level N' in the phrasal
structure in (84). As **handing** takes two complements and a compound can only be
binary branching, no compound can be built with **handing** as its head. So, in (85a),
the indirect-object argument is not within the first-order projection. In (84),
on the other hand, **handing** takes its two non-subject arguments within the first-
order projection and is therefore permissible. The principle in (83) also accounts for the ungrammaticality of such formations as in (86).

(86) a. *tree eater of pasta
     b. *well maker of engines

The object arguments expressed in the phrasal domain N' are outside of the first-
order projection of **eater** and **maker**.

The formulation in (83) would also be capable of explaining the ungrammaticality of the formations in (76) if **raised, accused, considered** and **given** were
assumed to have both a direct-object argument and another argument, corresponding
to **catholic, foolish, theft** and **girl**. We saw earlier, however, that these
participial forms are assumed not to have a direct- object argument, as they are
derived from the passive lexical forms. Therefore, this explanation is unavailable to Selkirk. It turns out, then, that Selkirk's hypothesis in (87) is in fact
too strong.

(87) Optionally, in compounds, (i) a non-head noun may be assigned
     any of the grammatical functions assigned to nominal constituents
     in syntactic structure, and (ii) a non-head adjective may be assigned
     any of the grammatical functions assigned to adjectival
     constituents in syntactic structure.

(87i) is too strong in that it would permit (76c) and (76d), (87ii) is too strong
in permitting (76a) and (76b) as well as the synthetic in (82).

The fact that all kinds of VC's with predicative complements are ungrammatical suggests that the relevant concept to explain this is the notion of small
clause. If it is assumed that these predicative complements are in fact the
predicative part of a small clause, there is no way in which the ungrammatical
examples could be generated. The examples in (82) would be ruled out if it is
assumed that **-er** binds the subject argument. According to the small-clause
analysis, **appear, become, elapse** and **turn** do not have subject arguments, i.e. do
not assign an external θ-role. Moreover, **worried, president** and **pale** are not
arguments of these verbs at all. The same is true for the transitive verbs taking
a small-clause complement. So, the examples in (88) are all ungrammatical.

(88) a. *the genius belief of Mary
     b. *the dangerous assumption of John
     c. *the well-adjusted judgement of John
     d. *the genius consideration of Mary

(cf. (25) above).

It turns out, then, that the small-clause analysis allows an explanation of facts
that are puzzling for other theories of VC's. This may be taken to support the
small-clause analysis. The other theories have no way of excluding the constructions in (89)-(91), which are all forbidded by the proposal that we make.

(89) a. *John's appearance worried
     b. *John's election president
     c. *John's turn pale

(90) a. *the appearance of John worried
     b. *the election of John president
     c. *the turning of John pale

(91) a. *worried appearing
     b. *president elected
     c. *pale turned

4.3.5. Adjacency and Case assignment

It turns out that there is a difference between Dutch and English with respect to the range of permissible VC's. In the previous subsection, it is explained why in English a left-hand member in a compound cannot have the function of predicative complement. In Dutch, on the other hand, such VC's are -perhaps surprisingly- permitted. Some examples are listed in (92).

(92)

opensnijding	open cutting	
kwijtschelding	free scolding	"remission, pardon"
ziekmelding	sick report	
gevangenhouding	prisoner keeping	"detention"
doodbranding	dead burning	
geheimhouding	secret keeping	"secrecy"
geldigverklaring	valid declaration	
drooglegging	dry making	"draining"
fijnmaling	fine grinding	
gelijkschakeling	same connection	"synchonization"
hoogachting	high estimation	"respect, esteem"
priesterwijding	priest ordaining	"ordination"
zaligprijzing	blessed praising	
rijpkeuring	mature inspection	

There is also a small number of this type of VC in **-er**. Some examples are provided in (93).

(93)

plathouder	flat holder
rechthouder	straight holder
doodloper	dead walker
mooimaker	beautiful maker

If our explanation for the impossibility of **(president)becomer** etc. in English is correct, i.e. that there is no external argument to bind for **-er**, it should be expected that such forms are equally impossible in Dutch. This expectation is borne out. However, we do find such VC's as those in (94), which parallel those formations in (91).

(94) bekendwording   known becoming
     bewustwording   aware becoming
     openvalling   open falling
     droogvalling   dry falling
     ensplijting   open splitting

Before we start discussing the question why this difference between Dutch and English should exist, we turn to another type of VC that is unavailable in English. In this case, the left-hand member of the VC exhibits phrase-like characteristics, specifically in that it consists of a preposition and a noun. It should be noted, however, that these left-hand members are not real phrases: no expansion in any direction is possible.

(95) in-gebruik-neming   in use taking
     onder-erf-stelling   under inheritance putting
     onder-water-zetting   under water putting   "inundation"
     ter-aarde-bestelling   to earth ordering   "burial"
     ten-toon-spreiding   to show speading   "display"
     ten-laste-legging   to charge putting   "indictment"

Again, there are no -**er** forms corresponding to these -**ing** forms. The relevance of these examples becomes clear when we realize that we would assign to the corresponding sentential structures an underlying structure with a small-clause complement, i.e. as in (96), where XP is the maximal projection of the head of the small clause.

(96) $[_{V'} [_{XP} NP \ X'] \ V^0]$

The NP is the subject of the small-clause complement and must receive Case from the V^0. The entire phrase must occur in preverbal position to allow for this Case marking. Not only is it impossible to move the P' part over the verb, as we discussed earlier, it is also impossible to place any material between the verb and the small clause. In this connection, structuralist grammars use the label "verbal end group"[77]. Within generative grammar, no satisfactory explanation has been given of the existence of this verbal end group.

It will be recalled that in chapter two, we adopted Stowell's hypothesis that Case assignment is subject to an adjacency requirement. In the structure in (96), the NP that must receive Case from V^0 is not adjacent to the governing verb. If the adjacency requirement is correct, the structure should be ungrammatical, contrary to fact.

The structure in (96) is in fact dictated by the Projection Principle for reasons that we discussed at the beginning of the present chapter. Given the leftward orientation of government in Dutch, D-structures of this form would never give rise to well-formed outputs. What I want to suggest, therefore is that in order to be able to derive well-formed results from a significant class of D-structures, Dutch has developed a rather rigorous way out. The small clause is broken up by a process of reanalysis which forms a complex consisting of the verb and the predicative part of the small clause. The NP subject of the small clause is then assigned Case under adjacency with this verbal complex.

This proposal not only allows us to explain how Case assignment proceeds in these cases, but it explains at the same time why nothing may intervene between the verb and the predicative part of the small clause and why this predicative part may not be moved to postverbal position.

Notice that the reanalysis operation is needed nor possible in English. It is not needed because the NP subject of the small clause is already adjacent to the verb. If adjacency is a prerequisite for reanalysis (cf. Chomsky 1981, Akmajian, Steele & Wasow 1979), restructuring the verb and the predicative part of the small clause would even be impossible as the subject of the small clause will always intervene. Therefore, the VC's discussed in the previous subsection cannot be generated,-at least in English, but they can be generated in Dutch.

If the reanalysis proposal presented here is correct, two important consequences suggest themselves. First, as restructuring applies in the syntax, it must be concluded that some word-formation processes must have access to syntactically generated structures. The phenomenon does not warrant any argument in favour of a reorganization of the model of grammar. For this, the phenomenon is much too parasitic, i.e. not all possible small-clause structures give rise to possible VC s.

A second important consequence is that it leads us to reconsider the conclusion drawn earlier that it should be possible in Dutch to cross maximal projection boundaries for the purposes of Case assignment. If the reanalysis proposal is correct, the possibility of assigning Case to the subject of a sister projection is obtained by the process of restructuring. Again, the phenomenon is much too limited in scope to warrant any firm conclusions.

4.3.6. Conclusion

Our discussion of VC's has demonstrated that current theories of synthetic compounds all leave several things to be desired. Specifically, these theories are incapable of accounting for the possible derivatives and VC's with these derivatives as second member if the verbal base of the second member is an unaccusative verb. Similarly, both transitive and intransitive verbs that take small-clause complements are problematic for all theories of VC's that we discussed above, apart from Roeper & Siegel's theory. However, the mechanism of subcategorization adjustment is not only descriptively incorrect (i.e, it expresses a spurious generalization because it is restricted to -ed affixation), but it does not explain anything. With the concept of small clause, the entire range of impermissible VC's can be explained as far as English is concerned.

In Dutch, however, there are VC's which are predicted to be impossible, but which are in fact permitted. This suggests that various aspects of the small-clause analysis need to be reconsidered.

To a large extent, then, the hypotheses embodied in the unaccusative analysis and the small-clause analysis provide us with an explanatory theory of VC's and both hypotheses are therefore supported by the phenomenon of synthetic compounds.

4.4. The choice of the perfective auxiliary.

In our analysis, we have distinguished between two classes of verbs, those that assign an external θ-role, which we have called transitive, and those that do not assign an external θ-role, which we have called intransitive. One of the criteria used for this distinction is the selection of either **hebben** or **zijn** as the perfective auxiliary. Consequently, we can make the descriptive statement in (97).

(97) Intransitive verbs form their perfect with **zijn**,
     transitive verbs select **hebben**

This descriptive statement seems simple enough, but it is not easy to derive the statement from principled considerations.

The situation in Dutch is more or less identical to the situation in Italian (cf. Burzio 1981, Rizzi 1982:ch.1). In Burzio's and Rizzi's descriptions of auxiliary selection in Italian, the selection is more or less stipulated. Burzio (1981:148) formulates the selection as in (98).

> (98) The AUX will be realized as **essere** if a binding
>   relation exists between the subject and a nominal
>   constituent of the predicate.

The AUX will be realized as **avere** in other cases. Just like Rizzi, Burzio takes the position that **avere** is to be regarded as the unmarked realization of AUX. According to Rizzi, **avere** is changed into **essere** under special circumstances. Rizzi does not make use of the notion "binding relation", but rather formulates the selection in terms of a lexical stipulation in the representation of the verb that may be regarded as the head with respect to auxiliary selection.

This position, then, presupposes the presence of an AUX constituent. Taking the same tack for Dutch, (97) could be reformulated in terms of a context-sensitive rule as in (99).

$$(99) \quad \text{AUX} \rightarrow \textbf{zijn} \; / \; \begin{bmatrix} V^i \\ -\theta \end{bmatrix} \text{--} \; , \; \textbf{hebben} \; \text{otherwise}$$

To flesh out this rule a little bit, we can take AUX to be the sister of some projection of V. Intransitive verbs may be assumed to have a feature $[-\theta]$, which percolates up . The elsewhere statement in (99) may be taken to reflect the unmarked character of this option in Dutch. It will be clear, however, that (99) is basically nothing more than a reformulation of (97). The most central question is whether the distribution of **hebben** and **zijn** could have been the reverse. I think that this is not the case, i.e. I suppose that some more principled explanation should be possible. This will be made clear in the following subsection.

4.4.1. The verbs **hebben** and **zijn** as main verbs

In section 4.1. we have argued that **hebben** and **zijn** can both be used as main verbs taking a small-clause complement. So, we have examples with **zijn** as in (100) and with **hebben** as in (101).

(100) a. dat Jan ziek is
        that John ill is

      b. dat Jan in de tuin is
        that John in the garden is

(101) a. dat Jan zijn werk klaar heeft
        that John his work done has

      b. dat Jan de zon in zijn gezicht heeft
        that John the sun in his face has

The small-clause analysis of these complements leads to an underlying structure for the sentences in (100) as in (102), whereas the sentences in (101) would receive an underlying structure as in (103).

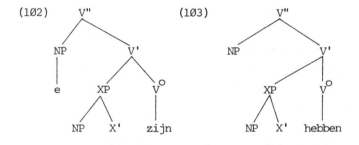

In accordance with the Burzio generalization, the D-structure subject of **zijn** is not assigned a θ-role and the D-structure subject of the XP is not assigned Case, whereas with **hebben,** both Case assignment to the subject of the XP and θ-role assignment to the matrix subject take place. This is to say that **zijn** is itself intransitive, whereas **hebben** is transitive. Therefore, assuming that the perfective auxiliaries **zijn** and **hebben** are at least related to these main verbs, we cannot but conclude that it is not a coincidence that intransitive verbs select the intransitive verb **zijn** to form their perfect, whereas the transitive verbs select the transitive verb **hebben** as their perfective auxiliary.

The origin of the perfective construction can be traced back to structures with small-clause complements. If we assume that participles are categorized as [+V], as we have claimed in the previous chapter, it should not come as a surprise that participial forms can occur in the position of XP, i.e. that participles may function as the head of small-clause complements. The participle originally showed agreement with its subject, as borne out by the Latin sentences in (104).

(104) a. filia amata est
          daughter loved is

      b. habeo filiam amatam
          I-have daughter loved

The "adjectival" participle of both intransitive and transitive verbs, at least of those transitives which are logically two-place predicates, was first found in combination with **worden** (=**become**) and **zijn** (=**be**, OE **beon, wesan**). With transitive verbs, the interpretation of this combination is either perfect or pluperfect, whereas the combination was interpreted as a passive in the case of two-place predicates. Later, a periphrastic active perfect was developed on the analogy of the construction illustrated in (104b). This new perfect, in which **hebben** (=**have, haben, eigan**) is used, is found only with two-place transitives. Finally, the class of one-place transitives came to develop a perfect which is identical to the perfect developed by the other transitives[78]. This final step indicates that the structure of perfects is somehow different from the small-clause complement construction, i.e. whereas one might want to maintain that **hebben** takes a small-clause complement in a sentence like (105a), i.e. assigns it a structure as in (103), this is not possible for a sentence like (105b).

(105) a. dat Jan het boek gelezen heeft
          that John the book read has

      b. dat Jan gelachen heeft
          that John laughed has

That the transitive perfect construction must somehow be different from the small-clause construction, can be demonstrated with the following example.

(106) dat we onderduikers verstopt hadden
        that we fugitives in hiding had
        that we fugitives hidden had

As the two glosses indicate, (106) is ambiguous. Under the first interpretation, it asserts that we just did something, namely hide persons, whereas in the second reading it says that for some time there were persons hiding with us. The ambiguity is resolved if the participle is placed in final position. Then, only the former reading holds.

(107) dat we onderduikers hadden verstopt
      that we fugitives had hidden

Traditionally, this is accounted for by assuming that the participle in the second reading is an adjective, whereas it is verbal in the first reading. Only verbs may occur after the finite verb form. This account is not entirely in accordance with the [+V] hypothesis[79].

A similar distinction between a perfective and an imperfective reading is found with the verb **zijn**. Thus, (108) may mean either that John is a married man or that the wedding ceremony has just been held, whereas (109) only has the latter reading. This is traditionally explained in the same way, i.e. by assuming that the participle is verbal in the perfective reading and adjectival in the imperfective reading.

(108) dat Jan getrouwd is
      that John married is

(109) dat Jan is getrouwd

According to this traditional account, there is not only a distinction between a verbal and an adjectival participle, but also between **hebben** and **zijn** as main verbs and as auxiliary verbs. However, it is not clear whether there are grounds to distinguish between auxiliary verbs and main verbs in Dutch. In Evers' (1975) study of Dutch sentential complementation, the position is taken that there is no distinction in Dutch between main verbs and auxiliaries: the temporal auxiliaries in the traditional sense are considered to be main verbs taking sentential subjects. Evers does not say anything about the difference between **hebben** and **zijn**. Evers' argument not to assume the existence of a separate category AUX in Dutch is that syntactically, the temporal auxiliaries behave just like verbs that are not considered any different from main verbs, i.e. **hebben** and **zijn** are syntactically ordinary verb-raising triggers. Indeed, the kind of motivation that exists in English to distinguish between a class of auxiliaries and a class of main verbs, is typically absent in Dutch. There is no distinct behaviour with repect to processes like inversion, neg.placement etc., where in English the members of one class of items do not trigger **do**-placement, where the members of the other class do. Moreover, modals and temporal auxiliaries in Dutch may be stacked, whereas such stacking is impossible in English (cf. Lightfoot 1979a).

It will be seen below that the assumption that **hebben** and **zijn** are main verbs leads to a problem in accounting for their distribution.

4.4.2. Change of Auxiliary

Sofar we have not raised the question as to the level at which the selection of the auxiliary is to take place. The formulation in (98) suggests that Burzio assumes the level of S-structure as the relevant level, because in the case of passives and unaccusatives, the binding relation which is relevant is established by means of application of MOVE α. Consider, however, the formulation of AUX selection in (110), which is taken from Zubizarreta (1982:156).

(110) A. A verb selects the auxiliary **essere** if
        1. it does not assign an argument θ-role to the subject
        2. the nominal clitic **si** (or the 1st or 2nd person
           counterpart of **si)** is attached to it.
      B. Otherwise, a verb selects the auxiliary **avere**

Whether or not a verb assigns an external θ-role is lexically determined. If it is assumed that **si**-attachment is in fact an affixation rule, operating in the lexicon as has been suggested in various places, the formulation in (110) does not require that AUX selection takes place at S-structure. The same holds for Dutch.

The relevant evidence that AUX selection must take place at S-structure in Italian comes from the rule of restructuring (cf. Rizzi 1982:ch.1). According to Rizzi's analysis of restructuring, there is a class of verbs in Italian that optionally trigger the rule of restructuring, which forms a verbal complex and has the effect of making the complement clause transparent. This transparency can be demonstrated by means of various tests, one of which involves so-called clitic climbing. Consider first the examples in (111): the verb **affermare** is not a restructuring verb. A clitic corresponding to the direct object of the complement verb is attached to the complement verb, as in (111a). The clitic may not climb to the matrix verb, as in (111b). Clitics are attached at the end of infinitival forms, but they are treated as proclitics with finite verbs.

(111) a. Piero affermava di conoscer-la molto bene
        Piero stated   to-know-her very well

b.*Piero la affermava di conoscer molto bene

The verb **affermare** contrasts in this respect with restructuring verbs like **potere** 'be able' or **volere** 'want' **which** allow both for the clitic to remain in the complement clause (cf. (112a)) or to climb to the matrix verb (cf. (112b)).

(112) a. Mario vuole risolver-lo da solo
        Mario wants solve-it by himself

b. Mario lo vuole risolvere da solo

The position of the clitic in (112b) will be taken as evidence that restructuring has applied, whereas restructuring has not applied in (112a). This is corroborated by evidence involving WH-movement, cleft formation, right-node raising and complex NP shift (cf. Rizzi 1982:ch.1).

The relevant phenomenon is the fact that whereas **volere** and **potere** themselves select **avere** (cf. (113), they seem to allow for both **essere** and **avere** if they take a complement clause with a verb that itself selects **essere** (cf. (114)-(115)).

(113) a. Piero ha/*è voluto questo libro
        Piero has/is wanted that book

b. Non ho/*sono proprio potuto
        Not have-I/am-I myself been able

(114) a. Piero è/*ha venuto con noi
        Piero is/has come with us

b. Piero ha/*è telefonato
        Piero has/is telephoned

(115)   a. Piero ha/*è voluto telefonare
           Piero has/is wanted telephone

        b. Piero ha/è voluto venire con noi
           Piero is/has wanted come with us

The dual possibility in (115b) is found only with restructuring verbs.

(116) Piero ha/*è affermato di venire con noi
      Piero has/is stated   to come with us

The evidence in (117) shows that the verb **essere** is selected only if restructuring really has applied and that **avere** is then excluded.

(117) a. Maria ha/*è dovuto venir-ci molte volte
         Maria has/is must   come-here many times

      b. Maria c'è dovuta venire molte volte
         Maria here-is must come many times

      c.*Maria ci-ha dovuto venire molte volte
         Maria here-has must come many times

The placement of the clitic in the complement clause in (117a) indicates that restructuring has not applied: hence, **avere** must be selected. If the clitic has climbed, on the other hand, **essere** must be selected, as in (117b), and **avere** cannot be selected, as shown by (117c).

If Rizzi's claim that restructuring applies in the syntax is correct, the conclusion must be that AUX selection takes place at S-structure in Italian.

Let us now see whether a similar argument can be constructed with verb-raising structures in Dutch. The rule of verb raising resembles the restructuring rule described by Rizzi in a number of non-trivial respects. Most importantly, the classes of V-raising triggers in Dutch and restructuring triggers in Italian are largely coextensive. Secondly, both rules require strict string adjacency between the matrix verb and the embedded verb. From this string-adjacency requirement, some of the differences in membership of the class of triggers of these processes follow, given the positional difference of the verb. So, verbs taking a clear control complement, like **affermare,** never allow restructuring. However,

the notion of real control complement is not entirely clear, as it takes us back
to the question of whether or not there is a class of auxiliaries. So, if **potere**
or **volere** are to be treated as main verbs, they probably take a control complement
(but see the discussion in Zubizarreta 1982). In any event, those verbs that
select a complement introduced by **di** never allow restructuring. This is reminiscent of the fact that V-raising triggers never take complement clauses introduced
by a complementizer either. Following Kayne (1981c), we shall assume that **di** in
Italian is a complementizer, like English **for** and French **de** and unlike English **to**
or French **à**. Given the adjacency requirement, the intervening complementizer
will always block restructuring. Similarly, Italian **sembrare** does not trigger
restructuring, but its Dutch equivalent **schijnen** 'seem' does trigger V-raising.
One might relate this property of **sembrare** to the fact that it has an indirect
object argument that intervenes between **sembrare** and the verb of the embedded
clause. The relevance of string adjacency for the Dutch rule of verb raising is
extensively documented and discussed in Evers (1975), Nieuwenhuysen (1976). It
seems reasonable, given these considerations, that we regard Dutch verb raising
and Italian restructuring as instantiations of one and the same operation MOVE V,
which is itself an instantiation of MOVE α.

If the selection of **essere** vs. **avere** in Italian is more or less the same as
the selection of **zijn** vs. **hebben** in Dutch, we might expect to find a similar
change of auxiliary as demonstrated by (113)-(117). Perhaps surprisingly, it
turns out that Dutch provides some evidence of this phenomenon, although there
are many differences between Dutch and Italian in this respect. It should be
noted first that the phenomenon is extremely limited in Dutch, and perhaps
restricted to some idiolects or dialects[80]. It may be observed with some V-
raising triggers, most easily with **kunnen,** but also with **moeten, mogen** and
possibly, with **proberen.** Sentences in which the phenomenon occurs will be marked
with &. For those speakers that do not accept these sentences, there should be a
marked difference in the degree of unacceptability of the sentences with & and
the sentences with *. Consider the following examples.

(118) a. dat Jan heeft gelachen
        that John has laughed

b. dat Jan heeft kunnen lachen
        that John has been able to laugh

c.*dat Jan is kunnen lachen
        that John is been able to laugh

(119) a. dat Jan is gebleven
          that John is stayed

      b.&dat Jan heeft kunnen blijven
          that John has been able to stay

      c &dat Jan is kunnen blijven
          that John is been able to stay

Thus, whereas (118c) is ungrammatical for all speakers, (119b) is preferred by some speakers, whereas other people prefer (119c). The verb **kunnen** itself selects **hebben**.

(120) dat Jan het heeft/*is gekund
      that John it has/is been able to

Interestingly, the use of **zijn** is the only possibility in the perfect of constructions with a passive embedded under a modal. Speakers that do not allow the "change of auxiliary", i.e. speakers that do not allow (121b) and (122b) do not have any possibility of constructing a perfective counterpart of the a-examples.

(121) a. de auto kon gelukkig nog op tijd gerepareerd worden
          the car could fortunately still in time repaired be

      b.&de auto is gelukkig nog op tijd gerepareerd kunnen worden
          the car is fortunately still in time repaired can become

(122) a. zij moest onder narcose geopereerd worden
          she had under anaesthesia operated to become

      b.&zij is onder narcose geopereerd moeten worden
          she is under anaesthesia operated must become

It is a puzzling fact that replacement of the present forms of **zijn** in these examples by past forms renders them much less acceptable. I have no explanation for this observation.

The fact that **kunnen** and **moeten** give better results than other traditional auxiliary verbs (**willen**) suggests that the distinction between root and epistemic

modality is at issue here. There is indeed a slight semantic difference between
(119b) and (119c) which points in this direction: the possibility of remaining
would be more under John's control in (119b) than in (119c). This idea is
strengthened by the fact that selection of **zijn** is obligatory if a passive
complement is embedded under the verbs **kunnen** and **moeten**. The epistemic interpretation of these verbs is also obligatory in those cases. Furthermore, the
difference in grammaticality of (123) and (124) suggests that the verb **kunnen** in
(121) is indeed more of an auxiliary than **kunnen** as used in (123).

(123)   dat Piet kon voetballen en Jan dat ook kon
        that Peter could play football and John that also could

(124) *dat deze auto nog op tijd gerepareerd kon worden en die auto
        that this car yet in time repaired could become and that car

        dat ook kon
        that also could

Aspectual verbs like **gaan** behave just like **kunnen** in (124):

(125) *dat Piet ging voetballen en Jan dat ook ging
        that Peter went play football and John that also went

If it is true that what is relevant for the phenomenon of "auxiliary change" is
the difference between a root and an epistemic modal, and if epistemic modals are
considered to be subject-raising triggers, whereas root modals are considered to
be transitive verbs, it should be expected that **zijn** is always selected with
these epistemic modals. Therefore, the variation in judgement would constitute a
problem under this approach as well. Moreover, the phenomenon of "auxiliary
change" can also be observed with verbs other than **kunnen** and **moeten**. An example
is the verb **proberen**. The difference between (126a) and (126b) shows that it
would be difficult to maintain the position that only the epistemic-root distinction is relevant.

(126) a.&dat hij nog een tijdje is proberen te blijven
        that he yet some time is tried   to stay

      b.*dat hij om die grap is proberen te lachen
        that he for that joke is tried to laugh

Incidentally, the verb **proberen** can be used to demonstrate that the possibility of selecting **zijn** as a function of the embedded verb indeed depends on prior restructuring. It has been noted above that **proberen** can either trigger V-raising or take a postverbal complement. The difference can be seen in the form taken by the embedded verb: if verb raising has applied, this verb appears in the form of the infinitive (infinitive pro participio) whereas it takes the expected participial form if V-raising has not applied.

(127) a. dat Jan de krant heeft proberen te lezen
        that John the paper has try to read

b. dat Jan heeft geprobeerd de krant te lezen
        that John has tried the paper to read

If verb raising has not applied, only **hebben** can be selected. This is clear from the contrast between (126a) and (128).

(128) *dat Jan is geprobeerd nog een tijdje te blijven
        that John is tried   yet a while   to stay

A further difference concerning the phenomenon of auxiliary change in Italian and Dutch is that in Italian it is always the last verb in a cluster of restructured verbs that determines the choice of the auxiliary, no matter what other verbs in the complex may require. (cf. Rizzi 1982:22). Therefore, we might say that in a verbal cluster, it is the most deeply embedded verb in Italian that functions as the head of the cluster with respect to the selection of the perfective auxiliary. This is certainly not true for Dutch. If an aspectual verb such as **komen, gaan** or **blijven** intervenes between the perfective auxiliary and the main verb, the auxiliary must take a form of **zijn**.

(129) a. Jan heeft gezwommen
        John has swum

b. Jan is/*heeft gaan zwemmen
        John is/has   go   swim

(130) a. Jan heeft meegedaan
        John has   joined

   b. Jan is/*heeft komen meedoen
      John is/has come   join

(131) a. Jan heeft gewacht
         John has waited

      b. Jan is/*heeft blijven wachten
         John is/has   stay   wait

That these aspectuals themselves select **zijn** will not cause much surprise: these
verbs would be analyzed as raising verbs taking a small-clause complement. Therefore, they select **zijn** in accordance with (79). However, in order to ensure that a
form of **zijn** is selected in (129)-(131) we have to devise an analysis according to
which the aspectuals rather than the embedded verbs function as the head with
respect to the selection of the temporal auxiliary.

4.4.3. **Hebben** and **zijn** as perfective auxiliaries taking small-clause complements.

Turning back to Evers' position that temporal auxiliaries are in fact main verbs
taking a clausal complement, we shall now sketch the kind of problems this
approach leads to. It will be noted that the idea has an initial intuitive appeal,
since the verbs **hebben** and **zijn** are also used as main verbs taking a small-clause
complement. Moreover these verbs combine with verbs of their own type, i.e.
hebben with transitive predicates and **zijn** with intransitive predicates. If we
formalize the idea that the temporal auxiliary **zijn** is also a main verb taking a
small-clause complement, we arrive at an underlying structure as in (132).

(132)

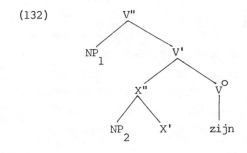

Since **zijn** does not assign a θ-role to its subject NP_1, it will not assign Case
to NP_2, the subject of te X" complement, and therefore induce subject raising
This is entirely as expected. In fact, the structure in (132) is identical in al
relevant respects to the structure in (102), which was envisaged for small-claus
complements. The only question that remains for (132) is what the value of X is
Before this matter is discussed, we turn to **hebben**. The idea that **hebben** is also
main verb when it functions as a temporal auxiliary would yield a structure whic
is in all respects identical to (132). Since **Jan** has the role of laugher in "Ja
heeft gelachen" (John has laughed), and **lachen** assigns a thematic role to th
specifier of its projection, **hebben** as a temporal auxiliary should also induc
subject raising, unlike the verb **hebben** that we find with a small-clause comple
ment as in (101). Therefore, it must be concluded that **hebben** as a tempora
auxiliary is different from **hebben** as main verb. Moreover, if **hebben** as a
auxiliary is treated as a verb taking a small-clause complement from which i
induces subject raising, the theory does not provide any insight into th
distribution of **hebben** vs. **zijn,** since they are treated alike. In fact, th
structure in (132) is misguided in certain respects. This brings us to th
question of what the label X is taken to stand for in (132).

In many accounts of the perfective construction, the fact that the main ver
appears in its participial form is regarded as a consequence of some sort o
selectional or subcategorizational requirement of the auxiliary verb (cf. Ever
1975). Within such accounts, then, the participial form is regarded as a mer
coincidence. In keeping with the analysis in section 3.3.3.1., I would like t
maintain the position that a participle has its own lexical representation. It i
categorized as [+V] and is consequently unable to assign Case to a governed NP
nor is it capable of assigning a θ-role to the subject by itself, even if the
verb with which it corresponds does assign an external θ-role. It would be
desirable, therefore, if we could argue that X in (132) is in fact [+V]
Therefore, the head of X" in (132) is unable to assign Case to a governed NP and t
provide a θ-role for NP_2, i.e. NP_2 is a θ'-position. **Zijn** as a temporal
auxiliary must then be sensitive to this aspect of the NP_2 position.

We noted before that this analysis of the participle in these perfectiv
constructions comes into conflict with the small-clause analysis for thos
constructions with **hebben** and **zijn** which have an imperfective interpretation (cf
(106) and (108)). If the participles in these examples are treated as [+V]'s i
both the perfective and the imperfective reading and if the verbs **hebben** and **zij**
are regarded as main verbs in both cases, it is hard to see how a distinctic
between the perfective and imperfective reading can be accounted for. Nor doe

there seem to be a basis for explaining why inversion of the finite verb and the
participle is only possible if the structure has a perfective interpretation.
There is yet another difference between the constructions with a perfective and
an imperfective reading. In the latter, the verb **hebben** can be used twice, as in
(133). The same is true for constructions with **zijn**, cf. (134). Since inversion
is only possible if the construction has a perfective reading, it is predicted
that two occurrences of **hebben** can never be found if the participle is in final
position. This prediction is correct.

(133) a. dat we een onderduiker verstopt hebben gehad
         that we a fugitive in hiding have had

      b.*dat we een onderduiker hebben gehad verstopt

(134) a. dat Fons getrouwd is geweest
         that Fons married is been

      b.*dat Fons is geweest getrouwd

For all these reasons, the idea that **hebben** and **zijn** as perfective auxiliaries
are identical to the main verbs **hebben** and **zijn** must be given up.

4.4.4. The perfective auxiliaries in verbal clusters

From the preceding discussion the conclusion may be drawn that the perfective
auxiliaries **hebben** and **zijn** should be treated as categories in their own right.
Let us first reconsider the notion of transitivity which is crucial in the
account of the distribution of these auxiliary items. Until now, the transitive
character of a verb has been represented in its lexical representation by means
of a θ-role which was not associated with any complement. It was assumed that
this "dangling" θ-role is assigned to the syntactic subject position (or rather
to its content) by convention. This convention could be specified in the following way. Let verbs which have a "dangling" θ-role be assigned the feature [+θ
], whereas unaccusative or intransitive verbs have a negative value for this
feature. This feature is percolated up along the projection line and thus

provides a route along which the "dangling" θ-role can be transported to the syntactic subject. A projection which is specified with the [+θ] feature is then fit to convey a θ-role, but if it is specified as [-θ], it is unfit for this purpose. This convention is in itself rather insignificant as it is just a formalization of the way in which the external θ-role is assigned.

I shall assume furthermore that participles are derived by means of a rule of word formation, which adds the affix **ge-d** at the morphophonological level and which eliminates the [-N] feature at the level of the categorial specification. It also changes the positive value of the θ-feature into a zero value. Therefore, these participles retain their external θ-role, but they are unable by themselves to project a route along which this θ-role can be transported. The external θ-role may be expressed by a **door (by)** phrase. In this respect, this rule of word formation differs from the rule which relates such pairs as causative and non-causative **break,** since the latter rule eliminates the external θ-role, cf. the contrast in (135).

(135) a. the ship was sunk by the enemy
      b. the ship sank (*by the enemy)

We may assume that the rule of participle formation not only neutralizes the positive value for the θ-feature, but also the negative value. It will be seen that this has no effect.

The above remarks are irrelevant for the analysis of participles in prenominal position and in other constructions that we discussed in section 3.3.3.1. Let us assume furthermore that the items **hebben** and **zijn** may be combined with a participle in a verbal cluster. In a sense, they may be regarded as added to these participles by means that are more similar to rules of word formation than to rules of syntax. So, we find clusters like (136), which may be the head of a phrase as determined by the Projection Principle.

(136)

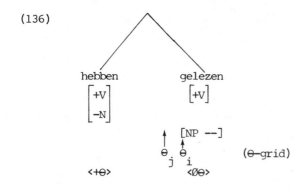

What are the features of the entire cluster? As usual, these are determined by the constituting parts. What I would like to argue is that the feature-percolation conventions needed to provide the combination with the right features are already available, i.e. these conventions are independently motivated in the field of word formation.

The relevant rules of word formation to illustrate the operation of the required feature-percolation conventions may be called deverbalization, i.e. rules that derive nouns from verbs and adjectives. Consider the following examples.

(137) a. dat Jan naar vrede hunkert
          that John after peace hankers

      b. gehunker naar vrede
         hankering after peace

(138) a. gehoorzaam aan de wet
         obedient to the law

      b. gehoorzaamheid aan de wet
         obedience to the law

These examples show that the specific subcategorization of the verb in (137a) and of the adjective in (138a) is inherited by the nominal derivatives in the b-examples. The derivatives themselves consist of two parts, the base and the affix. One could ask, then, which of these two parts is the head. In syntax, the head of a construction is the element that determines the categorial value of the construction. If this criterion for head status is also adopted in morphology, the base in the examples (137b) and (138b) cannot be considered the head. Therefore, we assign head status to the affixes, which we assume to have categorial features as well. These features are percolated to the top of the construction. In the representations below, the integers o and −1 denote free, resp. bound forms. As is clear from these examples, the morphology is symmetric, there are both prefixal heads and suffixal heads. (cf. Hoekstra, Van der Hulst & Moortgat 1980a, Lieber 1980). An asymmetric morphology is presented in Williams (1981b).

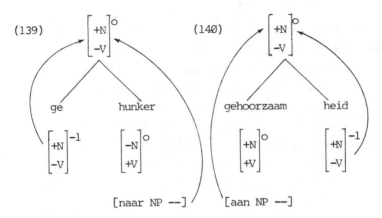

A derived word not only needs to have categorial features, it must also possess contextual features. These can be supplied by the affix as well. This is the case for example with the affixes **en–** and **–ize** as in **enrich** and **industrialize**. Both affixes uniquely impose a transitive subcategorization on their derivatives, irrespective of the contextual properties of the base. In the cases under discussion, however, the contextual property of the derivative is not determined by the affixes **ge–** and **–heid,** but rather by the base. Let us adopt the following convention to account for this situation (cf. Lieber 1980).

(141) The product of combining an affix and a base receives its features
       from the head, unless the head has no value for a particular feature.
       Then, the feature is determined by the non-head.

The way in which this convention operates can be seen in (139)-(140). The affixes supply the categorial specification, but since they lack a subcategorial feature, this is provided by the base. The affixes like **en–** and **–ize,** on the other hand, would not only provide the categorial features, but also the contextual feature.

Returning now to the cluster in (136), we see that the convention in (141) determines the feature composition of the cluster so that it will have the categorial features of **hebben,** as well as the [+θ] feature. Therefore, the external θ-role in the representation of **gelezen** may be transported to the syntactic subject position. Hence, a cluster like in (136) appears in sentences like (142).

(142) dat Jan het boek gelezen heeft
       that John the book read has

Let us assume that the representation of the perfective auxiliary **zijn** differs from **hebben** in that it is marked as [-θ]. If **zijn** replaces **hebben** in (136), then, no route will be projected to transport the external θ-role to the subject position. Accordingly, no Case will be assigned to the object. Therefore, this cluster will appear in sentences like (143).

(143) dat het boek door Jan gelezen is
      that the book by John read is

What is relevant here is that the participle **gelezen** has the same features in all its uses, i.e. we do not have to assume the existence of a perfective participle and a passive participle. This is a desirable state of affairs.

The only case left is the perfect of unaccusatives. What we have to account for is that the participle **gesneuveld** 'perished' may not be combined with **hebben,** but only with **zijn**. Notice what would happen if **gesneuveld** is combined with **hebben**. Since **hebben** supplies the cluster with the feature [+θ], it provides a projection along which a θ-role can be transported to the syntactic subject position. **Gesneuveld** and participles of other unaccusatives do not have an external θ-role. This conflict yields an ungrammatical result[81].

I consider it less than optimal that the analysis presented here has to treat **hebben** and **zijn** in their perfective usage as different from their use as main verbs. However, in the present analysis, the differences are in fact as minimal as possible. Therefore, we may conclude that the descriptive statement with which we opened this section (cf. (97)) could not be reversed for principled reasons. To see this, consider (144), which gives the representation of the main verbs **hebben** and **zijn** taking small-clause complements, and (145) where these verbs are represented in their function of perfective auxiliaries.

(144)   hebben   zijn

$$\begin{bmatrix} +V \\ -N \end{bmatrix}^{\circ} \qquad\qquad \begin{bmatrix} +V \\ -N \end{bmatrix}^{\circ}$$

     [XP --]   [XP --]

  ↑ ↑   ↑

  θ θ   θ   (θ-grid)

    <+θ>   <-θ>

(145)   hebben   zijn

$$\begin{bmatrix} +V \\ -N \end{bmatrix}^O \qquad\qquad \begin{bmatrix} +V \\ -N \end{bmatrix}^O$$

<+Θ>   <-Θ>

The verbs in (145) differ from those in (144) in having no subcategorization feature and no associated Θ-grid. Therefore, they do not project any structure around themselves, unlike the verbs in (144). In this sense, they may be regarded as non-main verbs, i.e. whereas main verbs determine a projection, the verbs in (145) may only occur in a structure in combination with a main verb which supplies thematic information. Therefore, they are inserted in verbal clusters such as (136). We may of course call them auxiliaries, but it should be kept in mind that they differ in important respects from those items that are called auxiliaries in English.

Summarizing the main points of the analysis, we have seen that under the assumption that temporal auxiliaries are ordinary main verbs, there arise various problems. First, there is no basis to account for the relative distribution of **hebben** and **zijn**. Second, the fact that the embedded clause must be headed by a verb with participial form must be stipulated. Third, there is no basis to explain the differences with real small-clause complements which take a participial head and perfective constructions. It was shown that there is no way in which the position can be maintained that the verbs **hebben** and **zijn** in their use as perfective auxiliaries are in fact the same as the main verbs **hebben** and **zijn** that appear in constructions with small clauses. The present analysis recognizes this fact by treating the verbs **hebben** and **zijn** in their perfective usage as categories in their own right. However, the difference with the main verbs is minimal: only the subcategorization and associated Θ-grid of the main verbs **hebben** and **zijn** are absent in the representation of these forms in their use as perfective auxiliaries. It was demonstrated that this assumption allows us to keep the feature composition of the participles constant. An independently motivated convention for feature percolation ensures that only the right structures are generated. Therefore, the present analysis may be regarded as an improvement on the analysis that assumes that these perfective auxiliaries are main verbs.

4.5. Concluding remarks

In this chapter, we have provided several considerations that argue in favour of the small-clause analysis. On the one hand, conceptual considerations have been offered such as the fact that the small-clause analysis allows us to assign structures to various types of constructions that are in accordance with the unambiguous-path requirement. Similarly, many constructions can be filtered out by the independently motivated theories of Case assignment and ECP if the small-clause analysis is assumed. Specifically, these subtheories account for the lack of nominal constructions corresponding to verbal constructions with small-clause complements, given the notion of structural government, which is a property of verbs but not of nouns. Another general consideration which favours the small-clause analysis is the Projection Principle in combination with the assumption that thematic roles are assigned to configurationally defined positions.

On the other hand, it has been demonstrated that there is empirical evidence that strongly supports the small-clause analysis. It allows us to account in a principled manner for the possibility of placing PP's in postverbal position in Dutch. The small-clause analysis also provides the basis for explaining the range of possible synthetic compounds in English. It was shown that the range of synthetic compounds in Dutch is significantly different from that in English, which can be related to the positional difference of the verb and to the adjacency requirement on Case assignment.

In the final subsection, we have argued that the verbs **hebben** and **zijn** when used as perfective auxiliaries cannot be considered to be main verbs taking small-clause complements, but have to be treated as distinct from normal main verbs. A feature system was developed that can account for the relative distribution of **hebben** and **zijn** as perfective auxiliaries with transitives and intransitives, respectively.

Notes

1. Actually, I have the impression that a truth claim is implicitly accepted in all linguistic discussions, even in the works of those who, like the Bloomfieldians, denied such a truth claim in their more theoretically-oriented discussions. This point has been noted by Chomsky on several occasions. At present, there seems to be quite general agreement as to the mental reality of theoretical constructs in linguistics. What divides the minds is the matter of autonomy of any linguistic mental reality, i.e. whereas most generativists are inclined to assume that linguistic knowledge is autonomous, others take the reductionist position, according to which our linguistic abilities are determined by mental capacities that are not unique to linguistic behaviour. My position is that considerations of modesty as well as our present knowledge of the functioning of the brain, specifically its modularity suggest that in fact the weaker position taken by generativists should be maintained, until sufficient evidence is produced for the adoption of the more far-reaching claim that our linguistic behaviour is a specific instantiation of an undivided mental reality, which is responsible for other forms of behaviour as well.

2. Cf. Johnson (1974: chapter 5) who cites Morgan and Postal for having established a rule typology along these lines.

3. MOVE WH subsumes processes previously dealt with by rules like topicalization, cleft formation, tough-movement, question formation etc. Chomsky (1977) argues that all construction types which display a number of specific properties involve the rule of MOVE WH. Similarly, processes like passive and subject-to-subject raising are subsumed under the rule of NP-movement. The development leading to this reduction is sketched in some detail in chapter 3.

4. The standard analysis of processes like question formation, topicalization etc. (cf. Chomsky 1973,1977) assumes that the long distance that may exist between the gap and the landing site is not created by means of unbounded movement, but that successive cyclic application of MOVE WH can bridge this long distance.

5. This is also clear from such notions as grammatical subject, psychological subject and logical subject which refer to quite different entities. It is not clear to me what justifies the common term subject in these cases. More or less the same is true of the notion of initial subject, final subject etc. as used in RG. I assume that it is this aspect of grammatical relations that Chomsky (1981:10) has in mind when he states that grammatical relations are not suitable candidates for the status of primitives of the theory from the point of view of language acquisition.

6. Chung uses the earlier spelling **jang** instead of the now common **yang**.

7. It is of course conceivable that semantic or pragmatic factors make some sentences sound deviant which are structurally completely identical to entirely grammatical sentences. Consider for example the contrast between (i) and (ii):
　　(i) This bed was slept in

(ii)?New York was slept in

It would seem that the oddity of (ii) cannot be determined by a structural factor. I would claim that (i) and (ii) are structurally on a par, and both grammatical from that point of view. There is a general pragmatic requirement, however, that the predicate must make a relevant predication over the subject. It is rather obvious that New York is less readily affected by someone's sleeping in it than a bed. A little imagination would suffice, however, to think of a situation in which (ii) makes perfect sense.

8. The semantic representation may he equated with the level of LF' which is presently being referred to or it may be conceived of as a representation derived from it.

9. PS-rules for Dutch are also presented in Koster (1978a:11 ff) and Van Riemsdijk (1978a:33).

10. The examples in (5) and (7) as well as many other Dutch examples instantiate subordinate clauses rather than main clauses. The reason for this is familiar. It is generally assumed that the order of constituents in embedded clauses in Dutch and German represents the basis word order. The second position of the finite verb in main clauses is then accounted for by means of a Verb Second rule (cf. Koster 1976).

11. De Haan (1979) adopts the opposite view that embedded clauses are to be generated in postverbal position. We return to his motivation for this position below.

12. Partitive constructions like "een emmer bramen" (a bucket blackberries) are potential counterexamples. We return to those constructions in section 2.7.2.1. See also footnote 15.

13. For more extensive discussion of this feature system and some consideration of alternatives, see Van Riemsdijk (1978a) and Jackendoff (1977).

14. This can be dealt with by PS rules in a system such as the one envisaged in the framework of General Phrase Structure Grammar, developed by Gazdar (1980, 1981) and Gazdar & Pullum (1982). In their system, each rule bears an index which percolates down to the head of the phrase and is shared as a feature in all lexical representations of the items that may function as the head of this phrase. For each subcategory of a particular category, then, a specific PS-rule with its own index is employed.

15. Consequently, lexical insertion in this system is context sensitive. In the system of GPSG (cf. 14), lexical insertion is context free, however. We shall argue below that, given the principles of GB-theory, lexical insertion can be regarded as a context-free operation within the GB-framework as well.

16. The requirement that there is at most a single unassociated θ-role in the θ-grid need not be stipulated, but follows as an immediate consequence from the fact that there can only be a single subject for the domain of a phrase to express the unassociated θ-role. If there were two unassociated θ-roles and both were assigned to the expression in subject position, a violation of the θ-criterion would result.

17. In chapter 3, we shall review the development of this reduction process in some detail.

18. Rizzi (1983) argues for some empirical differences between these two posi-

tions, viz. actual movement vs. movement as a metaphor. He concludes that the non-movement interpretation is superior. Kayne (1983b) provides an illustration of the effect of Rizzi's proposal. At present, I am not quite convinced by these illustrations and will therefore attach no specific value to this issue.

19. Bold face is used in most examples to indicate intended coreference. In more complicated examples I make use of indices as in (23c).

20. The notions A-bound (argument bound) and A'-bound (non-argument bound) are to be understood as: bound by an antecedent in an argument position and bound by an antecedent in a non-argument position, respectively. COMP and positions created by adjunction in general are non-argument positions. The label variable is reminiscent of predicate logic. This label will be clear if one considers (ii) as the LF-representation of (i) (cf. Chomsky 1977).
(i) Who did you see?
(ii) for which x, x a person, you saw x
    where x is a variable bound by the WH-quantifier.

21. In spite of this rather uncontroversial fact, Chomsky (1981:80) maintains that sentences of this type are ungrammatical because they violate subjacency. In fact, he uses this type of sentence as an argument in favour of subjacency as an independent principle.

22. The assumption that the embedded subject position is governed by the matrix verb is problematic in that it would lead to a Case conflict, the empty category being marked with Nominative Case by TENSE in the embedded clause and with Objective Case by the matrix verb under the assumed government relation. We are forced to assume, therefore, that this Case conflict is resolved in some way or other.

23. This problem could be solved, then, by assuming that the embedded COMP is present at the moment of application of MOVE WH and that it is deleted only afterwards. However, the same problem arises in the case of Dutch V-raising complements if one assumes that these are of the category S' as well. In those cases, one must assume that S'-deletion also applies (cf. Vat 1980). However, although this would solve the problem with respect to leftward movement (WH-movement), rightward movements are not constrained by the structure of the V-raising complement either, as Evers (1975) has convincingly shown. Since rightward movements cannot make use of an escape hatch like COMP, it must be concluded that there is no bounding node to the right of the V-raising complement. We shall adopt Evers' conclusion that the projection of the V-raising complement is pruned after V-raising.

24. The subject of extraction from NP has received much attention in Dutch linguistic literature (cf. Kooij & Wiers 1978, Klein & Van den Toorn 1978, De Haan 1978). In this discussion, no firm conclusions have been established, however.

25. Burzio (1981) argues that some specific complements (in the case of the causative construction) may be taken to be VP's. If our claim that S is the maximal projection of V is correct, one might want to adapt Burzio's conclusion to the effect that the complements which he regards as VP's are really S's without a subject.

26. In the published version of these lectures (Chomsky 1981), he adopts the definition of government given by Aoun & Sportiche.

27. The reason for this assumption is that these prepositions allow for a small-clause complement in so-called absolute constructions (cf. Ruwet 1982 for the

avec-construction in French and the discussion of the **met**-construction below).

28. VSO-languages do not present the same problem as SVO languages. We can assume that VSO languages have a structure identical to Dutch with the single difference that INFL precedes V". This assumption would solve the problem with the VP in VSO languages at the same time, if we also assume that the VSO order is derived from the order INFL NP VP by means of a rule that merges INFL and V. VSO languages always allow for the order SVO in some types of construction, as Greenberg has observed. This would suggest that our claim is correct that VSO languages are actually SVO languages with a sentence-initial INFL which attracts the verb.

29. The claim that the head of S might differ for various language types has also been made by Platzack (1983) and Taraldsen (1981a).

30. See Koster (1978b) for more arguments against the expansion of NP to S'.

31. The change from **het** 'it' to **er** 'there' and the change of position with respect to the preposition has been described by Van Riemsdijk (1978a) in terms of a R-suppletion rule and the rule of R-movement, to which we shall return below.

32. One might wish to formalize this hypothesis in terms of the mechanism of co-superscripting in the sense of Rouveret & Vergnaud (1980).

33. It should be noted that both the Case Filter and Stowell's Case Resistance Principle and Kayne's hypotheses make predictions beyond the predictions made by the UCC, in spite of a large amount of overlap. Whether the UCC should be extended so as to cover the other predictions made by the principles that it generalizes is a matter that I shall not discuss here.

34. See Bennis (1978) who argues for this level of attachment for appositives.

35. The nominal complements in partitives were marked with genitive Case in Middle Dutch. This brings us to a further class of potential counterexamples to te UCC, viz. the class of postnominal genitival complements in languages like German, as in (i).
   (i) Der Ankunft des Zuges
       the arrival the-(Gen) train (Gen)
If these genitival complements are considered ordinary NP's, they will violate the UCC. They also violate condition (ii) in Kayne mentioned above. We have to assume therefore that the genitive marker shields the NP off from being governed by the head noun. My suggestion would be that these complements have the same structure as the corresponding postnominal PP complements in English, the genitive marker spreading out in the NP in the left branch of the grammar.

36. Although the examples in (112) are counterexamples to the UCC as it stands, something more can be said about these constructions. In Van Riemsdijk (1978a), an analysis is proposed for the combination of a preposition with a non-human pronoun in its complement (cf. note 31). The obligatory effect of R-movement, changing (ii) into (iii) after the rule of R-suppletion has changed (i) into (ii), is derived from the filter in (iv).
   (i) *op het   (on it)
   (ii) *op er   (on there)
   (iii) er op   (there on)
   (iv) *P - [+PRO, +R]   (Van Riemsdijk 1978a:87)
Note first of all that the filter in (iv) becomes superfluous if **er** is analyzed as an intransitive preposition itself. The effect of the filter would then follow from the UCC, as a PP occurs in the position governed by a preposition. The assumption that **er** is a preposition is quite plausible as it can satisfy the PP

subcategorization of other lexical elements, cf. (v)-(vi).

(v) dat ik de boot in de tuin leg
     that I the boat in the garden lay

(iv) dat ik de boot er leg
     that I the boat there lay

Interestingly, those prepositions that allow a PP complement, also allow **er** to occur on their right, in violation of the filter in (iv), cf.

(vii) voor er bij   (for there with)
(viii) voor er na   (for there after)
(ix) van er voor   (from there before)

In any event, therefore, these prepositions (which are limited to **van**, **voor** and **tot**, apart from the prepositions **met** and **zonder** that occur in absolute construc- tions) are exceptional. The reduction of the rather ad hoc filter in (iv) to a more general principle like the UCC is at least an improvement. Another filter that has been proposed in the recent literature and that seems to be a good candidate to be reduced to the UCC is the double infinitive filter of Longobardi (1980), which is formulated in (x).

(x) $^*V_{inf\ 1}$ $[_{VP}$ $V_{inf\ 2}$ (= Longobardi (92))
     Condition: $V_{inf\ 1}$ c-commands $V_{inf\ 2}$

If c-command is replaced by government in this condition, the filter is exactly an instantiation of the UCC. Yet another example that comes to mind as a possible candidate for reduction to the UCC is Ross' (1972) "Double-ing" filter. I have not investigated whether this reduction is indeed possible.

37. Rizzi (1982:ch. 4) presents strong evidence in support of this claim. In section 2.6. above (cf. 55), it was pointed out that the clitic **ne** can only cooccur with objects and not with subjects. This is not exactly accurate: in fact, **ne** is required with postverbal subjects in the case of so-called ergative or unaccusative verbs, as Belleti & Rizzi (1981) point out. So, (i) is grammati- cal, unlike (ii) and (iii)

(i) Ne sono cadute alcune
      Of-them are fallen down some
(ii) *Alcune ne sono cadute
(iii) *Ne hanno telefonato due
      Of-them have telephoned two

Given the process of free inversion, it cannot be decided whether **Quante pietre** in (iv) is extracted from preverbal or postverbal position. However, the obliga- tory presence of **ne** in (v) demonstrates that extraction must have taken place from postverbal position.

(iv) *Quante pietre hai detto che sono cadute?
      How many stones have-you said that are fallen?
(v) Quante hai detto che ne sono cadute?
      How many have-you said that are fallen?

The reason for this is that **ne** can only cooccur with subjects in postverbal position.

38. Cf. Hoekstra (1983) for further discussion and motivation of this assumption.

39. It appears that the **mit**-construction in German is much more restricted than the equivalent **met**-construction in Dutch. There is apparently much variation among speakers in their acceptance of these constructions.

40. The change of order of main and embedded verb does not seem to be the most relevant part of the V-raising operation. First, in German the order is not changed, whereas the effects of V-raising hold there as well as in Dutch and second, even in Dutch the order of verbs can remain the same for some verbs (cf.

Hoekstra & Moortgat 1979a), whereas many speakers also accept the order as in
(141) for almost all V-raising triggers.
41. The absence of such a lexixal pronominal anaphor is of course explained in a
principled fashion: a pronominal anaphor must occur in an ungoverned position.
Lexical NP's must be Case marked. Case is assigned under government. The point
here is, however, that the assumption that PRO, as an invisible category, is
different from each logically possible type of lexical NP is rather unattractive
from the point of view of language acquisition, as the properties of this
invisible element cannot be detected on the basis of correspondences with any
overt element.

42. A very interesting recent reanalysis of this pruning process is presented in
Huybregts (1983). He argues that this pruning is an automatic consequence of an
analysis of these V-raising structures in terms of a dual simultaneous syntactic
representation. Under this analysis, the issue of the subject in cases such as
(147) vanishes.

43. This analysis is due to Den Besten (1977) and is quite generally accepted.

44. This fact might be accounted for on the following assumptions:
   (i) **er** must bind the empty head of NP in quantitative constructions
  (ii) an adjective in an NP without a nominal head is itself the head of
      the NP.
If (ii) is correct, **er** may nog be combined with a quantitative NP with an
adjective in the position of the head because of line (i). Obviously, there is a
difference between Dutch and English in this respect to the extent that in
English an adjective may not occupy an N position, i.e. not function as a noun, as
can be deduced from the obligatoriness of using **one** in sentences such as (164).
With respect to quantifiers, the situation seems to be the reverse, i.e. they
seem to function as nouns in English, but not in Dutch. Therefore, (iii) is
grammatical, unlike its Dutch counterpart in (iv). In Dutch, **er** has to be
inserted to make the sentence grammatical.
   (iii) John has four books and Peter has five
   (iv) *Jan heeft vier boeken en Piet heeft vijf
   (v) Jan heeft vier boeken en Piet heeft **er** vijf
If the above assumptions are correct, this situation can be explained in the
following way. The object position is governed. Therefore, an empty nominal head
may not be PRO. So, if there is a nominal head, it must either be filled with an
adjective, functioning as a noun as in (vi), or **one** is inserted as in (vii), or
the position is occupied by a quantifier as in (vii), or it is a variable, i.e. an
A'-anaphor as in (v), bound by a suitable quantifier in an A'-position.
   (vi) Jan kocht twee blauwe truien en Piet kocht drie rode
   (vii) John bought two blue sweaters and Peter bought three red **ones**
I have no insights to offer as to why these differences between Dutch and English
exist.

45. The sentence in (169b) is ungrammatical under the intended interpretation
according to which the property of being drunk is attributed to the guests, as
indicated by the bold face printing.

46. Stowell cites Perlmutter (1972) who also suggests that the fixed order of
clitics "may be but a special case of the fixed order of morphemes within the
word" (Perlmutter 1972:65).

47. Cf. Katz & Postal (1964).

48. R. Lakoff (1971:150) points out that "it is wrong to tie the occurrence of
passivization to a manner-adverbial node in deep structure: counterexamples have

been presented showing that passivization can occur with verbs that cannot take manner adverbs; and that passive does not occur with some verbs that do take manner adverbs".

49. Williams (1981a:104) argues that optional subcategorization, e.g. a lexical specification like [— (NP)] for pseudo-transitive verbs like **eat**, is superior to a lexical detransitivization rule to handle the same phenomenon. This argument is very surprising, since optional subcategorization and lexical detransitivization are two mechanisms that can hardly be compared. As pointed out in the text, the notation [— (NP)] basically collapses two different subcategorization frames, viz. [— NP] and [—]. Oehrle (1981:206) notes that no verb is actually followed by an optional NP. It is an entirely independent matter whether or not one postulates a lexical redundancy rule to state the relation between two different subcategorization frames of one and the same verb to express a regularity over a subdomain of the lexicon. If one does so, the redundancy is factored out in a direct way. An alternative would be to describe this redundancy by means of a meaning postulate. See Dowty (1981) for discussion.

50. Fiengo notes further that there is a considerable amount of idiosyncracy. Consider the following contrast:
  (i) Cuba's recognition by the US
  (ii) *John's recognition by Fred
One could of course stipulate that there are two nouns **recognition,** one of which is subcategorized for an NP complement, and therefore allows NP-preposing (or **of**-insertion alternatively, whereas the second **recognition** would be subcategorized for a PP which happens to be headed by **of**, thus accounting for the contrast between (i) and (ii). However, Fiengo (1981:46) suggests that a semantic or pragmatic factor is involved here, depending on extragrammatical knowledge. I think that his observation is correct (see also note 7).

51. The distinction between major and minor rules is originally due to Lakoff (1970).

52. A characterization of the notion Theme is given in Anderson (1977). See also Gruber (1965) and Jackendoff (1976). Hust & Brame (1976), in their discussion of the efforts by Jackendoff, convincingly argue that these efforts have not led to achieve the requisite level of precision.

53. The rule of **en-**avant is proposed in Ruwet (1972:ch.2). For further discussion, see Kayne (1975:section 2.19) and Couquaux (1981).

54. The notion of idiomaticity as used here harks back to the Saussurean notion of conventionality and arbitrariness of the form-meaning relation within words. Complex expressions come in two varieties: morphologically and syntactically complex. Given the word status of morphologically complex words, the compositional meaning is not fixed, but dynamic, as word meanings generally are.

55. It should be noted that in this respect the category verb differs from the other categories, i.e. derived nominals corresponding to verbs that take obligatory control and that are therefore subject to Visser's generalization can take infinitival complements without there being a suitable controller. Thus, the NP's in (i)-(iii) are grammatical whereas their sentential counterparts must include the argument that functions as the controller of the complement.
  (i) de vrees om daarheen te gaan
      the fear for there to go
  (ii) de belofte om het hek te schilderen
      the promise for the fence to paint
  (iii) de wens naar het strand te gaan

        the desire to the beach to go
(ia) *er werd gevreesd om daarheen te gaan
        there was feared for there   to go
(iia)*er werd beloofd om het hek te schilderen
        there was promised for the fence to paint
(iiia)*er werd gewenst naar het strand te gaan
        there was wished to the beach to go

I have no explanation to offer for this asymmetry between verbs and other
categories. It should be noted, however, that this is probably related to the
fact that, whereas complements to verbs are often obligatory, they are invariably
optional with nouns. Clearly, this issue warrants future research.

56. The formation of this brace is accounted for by Bach's (1979) Right Wrap
operation.

57. Actually, this formulation requires some modification. The order of finite
and non-finite verb forms is subject to dialectal variation. It is not always
possible to have the finite verb preceding the non-finite forms. Secondly,
adjectives that happen to have a participial form, even the so-called pseudo-
participles (i.e. adjectives having a participial form without there being a
corresponding verb) may follow the finite verb in many cases as well. The
criterion seems to make a clear distinction in the cases of simple adjectives
like **sick** only (cf. Sassen 1963).

58. The rule in (68) is found in Chomsky (1976). The partial factor Y is meant to
factorize idiom chunks and prepositions in constructions like (i) and (ii),
respectively.
    (i) Joe was taken **advantage of**
    (ii) the boat was decided **on**

59. Actually, there is a proverb in which **menen** is used in an active construction
with an AcI-complement, viz. "elk meent zijn uil een valk te zijn" (everyone
thinks his owl a falcon to be). This proverb is probably built on a non-native
pattern. It is not clear how this proverb would be used in an embedded clause and
passivization seems excluded. I would like to dismiss this example as irrelevant,
therefore. For some speakers, some near-synonymous verbs can replace **achten** in
(71), e.g. **verwachten** (expect) as in (i). Personally, I do not accept (i). In any
event, other verbs used in (71) are subject to the same restriction that there is
no corresponding active, cf. (ii).
    (i) De gasten worden verwacht op tijd te komen
        the guests are expected in time to come
    (ii)*Men verwacht de gasten op tijd te komen
        One expects the guests in time to come

60. Some verbs of the unaccusative class fall within the class of accomplish-
ments, whereas others would be classified as activities, and still others as
statives according to Dowty's criteria. Similarly, none of the classes of predication types distinguished by Dik subsumes the class of unaccusatives. The
possibility of subsuming this class of verbs under any semantic classification
becomes even more problematic if we are right in our claim, made below, that so-
called inversion predicates form one class with the unaccusatives.

61. The notion auxiliary is used here in a pretheoretical sense. The status of
these elements is further discussed in section 4.4.

62. There are some transitives verbs which may select both **hebben** and **zijn**.
Examples are **vergeten** and **volgen**. It is traditionally claimed that a difference
in meaning determines the choice between **hebben** and **zijn**. **Vergeten hebben** is

argued to mean 'have failed to do', whereas **vergeten zijn** would mean 'not know anymore'. In spite of explicit instruction concerning this distinction in schools, the actual use of this distinction does not reflect this. The alleged meaning difference in the case of **volgen** 'follow' is even less clear.

63. Many people do not accept these nominalizations with **aan**.

64. I have seen only one proposal that involves a rule which demotes a direct object to indirect object, viz. the so-called 2-3 retreat presented in Perlmutter & Postal (to appear a:62). However, it seems to me that the only motivation for this rule of retreat is to save the Stratal Uniqueness Law from being violated by the kind of structures in Kinyrwanda discussed in Keenan & Gary (1977). Keenan & Gary argue that Kinyrwanda allows a doubling of the direct object. If they are right, a violation of the Stratal Uniqueless Law would result, which requires that no two nominals bear the same relation to a particular predicate at the same level or stratum. Since Perlmutter & Postal do not present independent evidence for their 2-3 retreat, I shall assume that there is in fact no need for such a rule and that therefore the "law" in (135) is correct.

65. It is in fact not necessary to arrive at this conclusion. Alternatively, one might assume that **it** is really a referential expression which therefore must occupy a θ-position at D-structure, if one also assumes that the clausal complement is in fact not in an argument position, but attached at a higher level of structure in a non-argument position. An argument in favour of this position has been pointed out to me by Bob Rigter, who notes that **it** in (i) must be regarded as a referential expression, since it functions as the antecedent of a reflexive (**itself**).
    (i) it suggested itself that this solution should be rejected.
The clause in A'-position would then receive a θ-role by virtue of being coindexed with **it**. We shall return to this possibility below (see also note 81).

66. Many people have noted that the Burzio-generalization is somewhat odd in that it expresses a correlation between two conceptually unrelated aspects: Case assignment and θ-role assignment. It seems desirable, therefore, to seek a deeper explanation for this correlation. We return to this issue in note 81.

67. There are some well-known counterexamples to this claim, cf. **struck/ stricken, proved/proven, sunk/sunken, melted/molten** etc.

68. There is an interesting counterexample to the HFF in (i). Here, **goed** is the nucleus of the prenominal modifier, but it is nevertheless followed by the degree modifier **mogelijke**, which is in fact part of an embracing modifier **zo...mogelijke**.
    (i) een zo goed mogelijke oplossing
       a   so good possible solution
       "the best possible solution"
What is interesting is that the adverb **mogelijk** can also occur as an adjective, as in (ii), and hence can be inflected. In fact, in (i) the adverb **mogelijk** is inflected.
    (ii) een mogelijke oplossing
       a   possible solution
This might be the reason for the acceptability of (i): the final element in the prenominal modifier can take on the inflection. It seems to me that this yields some perspective on a more fundamental understanding of the HFF. What is relevant is that **genoeg** can never be inflected. This accounts for the difference between (i) and (160). It should be noted that Dutch adjectival inflection is very limited: the paradigm comprises two forms: **goed-goede**. The first form can be analyzed as uninflected or as having a zero inflection marker. This may give rise

to the variation in speakers' judgements concerning constructions of the form in
(iii), if the modifier is not required to appear in the form with the -e
inflection.
    (iii) [$_{AP}$ Adj Adv] N
Therefore, some speakers find examples such as in (iv) marginally acceptable.
    (iv) een groot genoeg bos   (cf. een groot/*grote bos)
         a   big   enough forest

69. Erica García points out to me that (176b) is in fact not completely
ungrammatical. This supports our explanation given above, since the "Theme"
argument of **tell** can more readily be left out than the Theme argument of **give** or
promise, i.e. not only is (176b) better than (175b), but (i) is better than (ii)
and (iii) is better than (180).
    (i) I told the people
    (ii) I promised the people
    (iii) The people were told

70. See also note 37 and 44.

71. This hypothesis is in need of further refinement. Below we shall see that an
alleged θ'-position can also be filled by **het**. The question then arises what
determines the choice between **het** and **er**. A suggestion might be that **het** actually
is a referential expression (see note 65), which must therefore occur in a θ-
chain. **Er** on the other hand may be regarded as a non-referential expression. This
suggestion will be further elaborated on in note 81.

72. Gazdar (1980:25,26) argues that there are strong reasons to reject the claim
that transitivity can be represented by the subcategorization feature [-- NP]. He
states that this representation fails to generalize over languages with different
word orders. Above we have argued that the elements of a subcategorization frame
need not be considered to be ordered. Therefore, this argument is no longer
valid. Gazdar also cites Comrie (1979) and Amritavalli (1979), who argue that
there are situations in which a verb has an adjacent NP within its VP without
being transitive. Amritavalli (1979:91) concludes therefore "that verbs should
be marked both for transitivity and for strict subcategorization features and
that these features are independent of each other". It should be observed that
this is especially true in the case of inversion constructions. In this chapter a
different interpretation of the notion transitivity is presented which solves the
kinds of problems discussed by Amritavalli.

73. Although the arguments presented in Stowell (1981) and in this chapter
strongly support the claim that AP's and PP's have subjects as well, this
conclusion brings with it a problem with respect to the subject of NP, for which
we have no satisfactory solution as yet. Since Chomsky (1970), a genitival NP
specifier of nouns has been considered to be the subject of the NP. There are two
main reasons for this assumption. On the one hand, the semantic parallel between
(i) and (ii) would be structurally expressed in this way. On the other hand, the
identification of genitives with subjects is supported by the SSC (and later the
Binding Theory), given the fact that these genitival NP's make the NP they
specify opaque for an outside binder, as is illustrated by the contrast in (iii)-
(iv).
    (i) The enemy destroyed the city
    (ii) The enemy's destruction of the city
    (iii) **Mary** saw a picture of **herself**
    (iv)***Mary** saw John's picture of **herself**
The small-clause analysis forces us to assume, however, that **John** in (v) is the
subject of a small-clause NP, just as **John** in (1b) is the subject of a small-
clause AP headed by **ill**. But this conclusion is at odds with the assumption that a

genitival NP specifier is the subject of NP is such constructions as (vi).
   (v) John is a scholar
   (vi) John is Peter's friend
In (vi), then, we would end up having two subjects for the NP in predicate
position. It should be observed, however, that in a framework which dispenses
with PS-rules, the actual structure of a particular phrase is determined by the
thematic properties of the head. On this basis, we made a distinction between
argument PP's, which do not have a subject, and predicative PP's, which do assign
a thematic role to an external argument. Let us assume, therefore, that NP's can
also be either arguments, in which case they may have a genitival NP subject, or
predicative NP's. Nouns heading a predicative NP would have an extra θ-role,
e.g. the θ-role R as suggested by Williams (1981a). The problem would then be
solved if this role R is assigned by convention to an NP at a level of projection
above the structure of the argument NP. Further investigation is needed to
explore the consequences of this proposal, e.g. with respect to the Binding
Theory.

74. This proposal would reject the distinction between the main verb **zijn** and the
copula verb **zijn** which is made in traditional grammar. Apparent counterexamples
are expressions like "God is" (God is) and "Wat niet is kan komen" (What not is
may come). I put these examples aside, given their idiomatic character, i.e. it
is impossible to say "Jan is" (John is) or "Dit is niet" (This is not). From my
point of view, these examples are ungrammatical.

75. In keeping with our discussion of examples like (36c) in section 2.6., I
assume that the proper governor in these cases is not a trace in the intermediate
COMP, but the matrix verb (see also note 22).

76. It should be noted that Dutch nominalizations in **-ing** are more like the
English derived nominals in **-ion** than the English nominalizations in **-ing**.

77. See especially Paardekooper (undated).

78. These remarks on the history of the perfective construction are based on Kern
(1912).

79. A similar situation, though not quite the same, is found with the verb **krijgen**
'get', which is sometimes argued to be the auxiliary of the indirect object
passive as in (i).
   (i) dat ik het pakje toegestuurd krijg/krijg toegestuurd
       that I the package sent   get / get   sent
In the case of participles of bitransitive verbs in the **krijgen** construction, the
order of participle and finite verb is free. If the participle belongs to a
transitive verb, however, the obligatory order is that the participle precedes
the finite verb, cf. (ii).
   (ii) dat Reagan zijn voorstel nooit aanvaard krijgt/*krijgt aanvaard
        that Reagan his proposal never accepted gets / gets accepted
At present, I have no insights to offer for this discrepancy between participles
of transitive and bitransitive verbs.

80. The phenomenon of change of auxiliary has never received any attention in the
linguistic literature, apart from a dialectal study by Hofmans (1981).

81. This is good point to say something more about the Burzio-generalization. As
we mentioned earlier, the status of the generalization is a little strane, as it
expresses a cooccurrence between two in principle unrelated phenomena, as has
been observed many times. If we consider the effect of the Burzio-generalization
for constructions which only involve NP's, it turns out that the subject is

always part of a thematic chain, i.e. a chain to which a Θ-role is assigned.
Either it is a Θ-position itself, or it serves as the landing site for an
argument NP which fails to receive Case at its original position. Therefore,
Burzio's generalization might be reduced to the principle in (i), which is in
fact much more natural, and might also be related to the Extended Projection
Principle.

(i) The subject must be part of a Θ-chain

Te most obvious counterexamples that come to mind are those involving complement
sentences. In this respect, there is a difference between Dutch and English in
that in English the subject position in these constructions is invariably filled
by **it**, whereas there is a choice between **het** and **er** (and Ø) in Dutch. Restricting
our attention to English, we refer to note 65 where we mentioned a possible
alternative according to which the complement clause occupies an A'-position,
while **it** occupies the argument position, either the object position, from which
it is moved to subject position, or the subject position itself. In either case,
the subject is part of a Θ-chain and the complement clause receives a Θ-role by
virtue of being coindexed with **it**. Therefore, principle (i) would not be violated
by these constructions. It should be noted that Stowell (1981) presents evidence
for the position of the complement clause outside of the head domain.

Turning to Dutch, now, we could assume that the analysis of constructions with
het in subject position is identical to the analysis of the English constructions. If we assume that **het** is a referential expression, we are in fact forced to
adopt this analysis. **Er**, however, is not a referential expression. Therefore,
there is no need to assume that the complement clause is in an A'-position if the
subject is filled by **er**, but rather we may assume that the complement clause is in
the head domain of the verb. This distinction between the position of the
complement clause with **het** and **er**, as depicted in (ii) is made in Hoekstra (1983).

(ii)

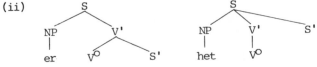

It should be observed that the idea that a Θ'-position in Dutch can be filled by
het, just like it can be filled by **it** in English, runs into problems in relation
to the other possibility of filling the Θ'-subject position with **er**. The
question then arises as to the distribution of **het** vs. **er**. Thus, the subject
position with so-called raising verbs taking a tensed complement must be occupied
by **het**, i.e. **er** is impossible:

(iii) **het**/*er schijnt/lijkt dat Piet ziek is
      it /there seems/appears that Peter ill is

If (i) is correct and if the idea that **er** is a non-referential expression is
correct as well, we have a principled account for the obligatoriness of **het** in
these cases. A further problem, then, relates to those constructions in which **er**
does occupy the subject position. This possibility is restricted to passives as
in (iv), with one exception, namely **blijken**, to which return below.

(iv) er werd beweerd dat Maria Callas een aria zong
     there was said that Maria Callas an aria sang

Er is never possible with adjectives taking a sentential complement (cf. (v)),
nor with the raising predicates, with the exception of **blijken** 'turn out' as in
(vi).

(v) *er was leuk/mogelijk/wenselijk dat Jan mee ging
      there was funny/possible/desirable that John with went

(vi) er bleek dat niemand daaraan gedacht had
      there turned out that nobody there-of thought had

Apparently, therefore, it cannot be claimed that **er** may occupy a Θ'-position in
Dutch. The question is, therefore, how the context for the use of **er** must be

characterized. The answer to this question is dependent on the difference between **blijken** on the one hand and the other raising verbs on the other. It turns out that, unlike the other subject-raising triggers, **blijken** can take a single nominal argument as in (vii). Therefore, the similarity between **blijken** and passives is that both can take a θ-subject. **Er** can be regarded as signalling the absence of this θ-role (cf. Kirsner 1979).

    (vii) Zijn onnozelheid bleek alras
          His simplicity turned out soon

Let us assume therefore that **er** may occupy dethematized positions, i.e. positions that could receive a θ-role in other constructions. Such a position could not be correctly characterized as a θ'-position, but rather we should say that the θ-role 'absorbed' is assigned to the position taken by **er**. The same could be said of **er** in existential constructions. In Hoekstra (1983), a piece of corroborating evidence is presented for the distinction made in (ii): whereas extraction out of complement clauses is possible if the subject position is occupied by **er**, this is impossible if the subject position is occupied by **het**:

    (ix) ***Wat** was het essentieel dat Piet e vergeten was?
          What was it essential that Peter forgotten had
    (x) **Wat** werd er beweerd dat Maria Callas e gezongen had
          What was there asserted that Maria Callas sung had

The difference in extraction possibilities is accounted for in Hoekstra (1983) on the assumption that traces in COMP must be governed by the matrix verb, which is possible if the complement clause is in the head domain, but not otherwise. Kayne (1983b) presents a different account, which is consistent with the assumptions made above. It turns out, then, that there are no cases that seem to violate the requirement in (i).

References

Lg= Language   TLR= The Linguistic Review
LI= Linguistic Inquiry   SPEK= Spektator
LA= Linguistic Analysis   FdL= Forum der Letteren
UWPL= Utrecht Working Papers in Linguistics
IULC= Indiana University Linguistics Club
LAUT= Linguistic Agency at Trier
BLS= Papers from the Annual Meeting of the Berkeley Linguistic Society
SPIL= Stellenbosch Papers in Linguistics

Akmajian, A., S.Steele & T.Wasow
1979   The Category AUX in Universal Grammar. In: **LI** 10,
                       p. 1-64.
Allen, M.R.
1978   **Morphological Investigations.** diss. University of
                       Connecticut
Amritavalli,R.
1979   The Representation of Transitivity in the Lexicon. In:
                       LA 5, p. 71-92.
Anderson, S.R.
1977   Comments on Wasow 1977. In: Culicover, Wasow &
                       Akmajian (eds.), p.361-377.
Anderson, S.R. & P. Kiparsky (eds.)
1973   **A Festschrift for Morris Halle.** New York: Holt,
                       Rinehart & Winston.
Aoun, J.
1981   **The formal nature of anaphoric relations.** diss. MIT.
Aoun, J. & D.Sportiche
1981   On the formal theory of government. mimeo MIT,
                       to appear in **TLR.**
Aronoff, M.
1976   **Word formation in generative Grammar.** Cambridge (Mass.):
                       MIT Press.
Bach, E.
1979   Control in Montague Grammar. In: **LI** 10, p.515-532.
1980   In defense of passive. In: **Linguistics and Philosophy** 3,
                       p. 297-342.
Bach, E. & G.M. Horn
1976   Remarks on "Conditions on transformations". In: **LI** 7,
                       p. 265-300.
Baker, C.L.
1970   Notes on the description of English questions: the role of
                       an abstract question morpheme. In: **Foundations of Language**
                       6, p. 197-219.
1979   Syntactic theory and the projection problem. In: **LI** 10,
                       p. 533-581.
Barwise, J. & R.Cooper
1980   Generalized quantifiers and natural language. In:

Linguistics and Philosophy 4, p. 159-219.
Belletti, A, L. Brandi & L. Rizzi (eds.)
1981   **Theory of Markedness in Generative Grammar.** Pisa: Scuola
                     Normale Superiore.
Belletti, A & L.Rizzi
1981   The syntax of "ne": some theoretical implications. In: **TLR**
                     1, p. 117-154.
Bennis, H.
1978   Appositie en de interne struktuur van NP. In: **SPEK** 8,
                     p. 209-228.
Besten, H.den
1977   **On the interaction of Root Transformations and Lexical
                     Deletive Rules.** mimeo, University of Amsterdam.
1979   A Case Filter for Passives. published in Belletti,
                     Brandi & Rizzi (eds.), 1981.
1980   Government, Syntaktische Struktur und Kasus. In: M. Kohrt
                     & J. Lenerz (eds.), **Sprache, Formen und Strukturen.**
                     Tubingen: Max Niemeyer Verlag.
Beukema, F. & T.Hoekstra
1983a   **Met** met PRO of **met** zonder PRO. to appear in **De Nieuwe
                     Taalgids.**
1983b   Extractions out of **with** constructions. to appear in **LI.**
Blom, A.
1977   Het kwantitatieve **er.** In: SPEK 6, p. 387-395
Bolkestein, A.M. et al.
1981   **Predication and expression in Functional Grammar.** London:
                     Academic Press.
Botha, R.P.
1980   Roeper and Siegel's theory of verbal compounding:
                     a critical appraisal. In: **SPIL** 4, p. 1-45.
1981   A Base Rule Theory of Afrikaans Synthetic
                     Compounding. In: Moortgat, Van der Hulst & Hoekstra
                     (eds.), p. 1-77.
Brame, M.A.K.
1975   **Conjectures and refutations in syntax and semantics.**
                     Amsterdam: North Holland Publ. Comp.
1979   **Essays toward realistic syntax.** Seattle: Noit Amrofer.
Bree, C.van
1981   Hebben-**constructies en datiefconstructies binnen het
                     Nederlandse Taalgebied.** diss. Leiden.
Bresnan, J.W.
1978   A realistic transformational grammar. In: Halle, Bresnan &
                     Miller (eds.), p.1-59.
1980a   **Passive in Lexical Theory.** paper MIT.
1980b   Polyadicity. In: Hoekstra, Van der Hulst & Moortgat
                     (eds.), p. 97-121.
Burzio, L.
1981   **Intransitive verbs and Italian auxiliaries.** diss. MIT.
Chomsky, N.A.
1955   **The Logical Structure of Linguistic Theory.** published
                     in 1975, New York: Plenum.
1957   **Syntactic Structures.** Den Haag: Mouton.
1965   **Aspects of the Theory of Syntax.** Cambridge (Mass.):
                     MIT Press.
1970   Remarks on Nominalization. In: Jacobs & Rosenbaum (eds.).
1973   Conditions on Transformations. In: Anderson &
                     Kiparsky (eds.).

1975   **Reflections on Language**. New York: Pantheon.
1976   Conditions on Rules of Grammar. In: **Essays on Form
                and Interpretation**. Amsterdam: North Holland Publ. Comp.
1977   On WH-Movement. In: Culicover, Wasow & Akmajian (eds.),
                p.71-132.
1980   On Binding. In: LI 11, p. 1-46.
1981   **Lectures on Government and Binding**. Dordrecht: Foris
                Publications.
1982   **Some Concepts and Consequences of the Theory of
                Government and Binding**. Cambridge (Mass.): MIT Press.
Chomsky, N.A. & H.Lasnik
1977   Filters and Control. In: **LI** 8, p. 425-504.
Chung, S.
1976   An object-creating rule in Bahasa Indonesia. In: **LI** 7,
                p.41-87.
Cinque, G.
1980   On extraction from NP in Italian. In: **Journal of Italian
                Linguistics** 5, p. 47-99.
1981   On Keenan & Comrie's Primary Relativization Constraint.
                In: **LI** 12, p. 293-308.
Cole, P. & J. M. Sadock (eds.)
1977   **Syntax and Semantics** 8. New York: Academic Press
Comrie, B.
1979   The languages of Micronesia. In: **Linguistics** 17:
                p. 1057-1071.
Couquaux, D.
1981   French Predication and Linguistic Theory. In: May &
                Koster (eds.), p. 33-64.
Culicover, P., T.Wasow & A.Akmajian (eds.)
1977   **Formal Syntax**. New York: Academic Press.
Dik, S.C.
1978   **Functional Grammar**. Amsterdam: North Holland Publ. Comp.
1981   **Studies in Functional Grammar**. London: Academic Press.
1983   (ed.) **Advances in Functional Grammar**. Dordrecht:
                Foris Publications.
Dik, S.C. & Gvozdanović, J.
1981   Subject and Object in Serbo-Croatian. In: Hoekstra, Van
                der Hulst & Moortgat (eds.), 1981.
Dougherty, R.
1975   Harris and Chomsky at the syntax-semantics boundary.
                In: Hockney et al. (eds.), **Contemporary Research in Philo-
                sophical Logic and Linguistic Semantics**. Dordrecht:
                Reidel.
Dowty, D.R.
1978   Governed Transformations as Lexical Rules in a Montague
                Grammar. In: LI 9, p. 393-426.
1979   **Word Meaning and Montague Grammar**. Dordrecht: Reidel.
1981   Quantification and the lexicon. In: Moortgat, Van der
                Hulst & Hoekstra (eds.). p.79-106.
Drachmann, G.
1981   On explaining "All the explicanda of the previous theo-
                ry": Popper and the growth of linguistics. In: **Folia
                Linguistica** XV/3-4, p. 345-361.
Dresher, E. & N.Hornstein
1979   Trace Theory and NP movement rules. In: **LI** 10, p. 65-82.
Emonds, J.E.
1969   **Root and Structure Preserving Transformations**.diss. MIT.
1972   Evidence that Indirect Object Movement is a Structure
                Preserving Rule. In: **Foundations of Language** 8,

p. 546-561.

1976   A transformational Approach to English Syntax. New
                       York: Academic Press.
Engdahl, E.
1980   WH-constructions in Swedish and the Relevance
                       of Subjacency. In: NELS X (T.Jensen (ed.),
                       Cahiers de Linguistiques d'Ottawe).
Erteschik, N.
1973   On the nature of island constraints. diss.MIT.
Everaert, M.
1982   A syntactic passive in Dutch. In: UWPL 11, p. 37-73.
Evers, Arn.
1975   The transformational Cycle in Dutch and German.
                       distributed by IULC.
1982   Twee functionele principes voor de regel "verschuif
                       het werkwoord". In: GLOT 5, p.11-30.
Fiengo, R.
1974   Semantic Conditions on Surface Structure. diss. MIT.
1981   Surface Structure. Cambridge (Mass.): Harvard
                       University Press.
Finer, D. & T.Roeper
1982   The Projection Principle and the Lexicon. mimeo
                       University of Mass. at Amherst.
Fillmore, C.J.
1965   Indirect Object Constructions in English and the Orde-
                       ring of Transformations. Den Haag: Mouton.
1968   The Case for Case. In: E.Bach & R.T.Harms (eds.),
                       Universals in Linguistic Theory. New York:
                       Holt, Rinehart & Winston. p. 1-88.
Freidin, R.
1975   The Analysis of Passives. In: Lg 51, p. 384-405.
Freidin, R. & H. Lasnik
1981   Disjoint Reference and WH-trace. In: LI 12: p. 39-53.
Gazdar, G.
1980   Phrase Structure Grammar. paper University of Sussex.
                       Appeared in G.Pullum & P. Jacobson (eds.), The Nature
                       of Syntactic Representation. Dordrecht: Reidel. 1981
1981   Unbounded Dependencies and Coordinate Structure.
                       In: LI 12, p. 155-183.
Gazdar, G. & G.K. Pullum
1981   Subcategorization, constituent order and the notion
                       "head". In: Moortgat, Van der Hulst & Hoekstra (eds.),
                       p. 107-124.
1982   Generalized Phrase Structure Grammar. A theoretical
                       Synopsis. distributed by IULC.
Gazdar, G. & I.Sag
1981   Passive and reflexive in phrase structure grammar. In:
                       J.A.G. Groenendijk, T.M.V. Janssen & M.B.J. Stokhof
                       (eds.), Formal Methods in the Study of Language. Amster-
                       dam: Mathematical Centre Tracts 135. p. 131-152.
Geis, J.E.
1973   Subject complementation with causative verbs. In:
                       B.Kachru et al. (eds.), Issues in Linguistics: Papers
                       in honor of Henry and Renee Kahane. Urbana: University
                       of Illinois Press. p. 210-230.
Geest, W.de
1973   Complementaire Constructies bij verba sentiendi.
                       Utrecht: HES Publ.

Greeenberg, J.H.
1963   Some Universals of Language with specific reference to
               the order of meaningful elements. In: id. (ed.), **Univer-
               sals of Language.** Cambridge (Mass.): MIT Press.
               2nd. printing 1966.

Grimshaw, J.
1979   Complement selection and the lexicon. In: **LI** 10,
               p. 279-325.

Groot, C. de
1981   The structure of predicates and verb agreement
               in Hungarian. In: Daalder, S. & M.Gerritsen (eds.),
               Linguistics in the Netherlands 1981. Amsterdam:
               Elsevier. p. 149-158.

Gruber, J.
1965   **Studies in Lexical Relations.** diss. MIT.

Guéron, J.
1980   On the syntax and semantics of PP extraposition. In:
               LI 11, p. 637-678.
1983   **Inalienable possession, Pronoun-inclusion and Lexical
               Chains.** lecture GLOW conference in York, March 1983.

Haan, G. de
1978   Onafhankelijke PP-complementen van Nomina. In: **SPEK** 8,
               p. 330-339.
1979   **Conditions on Rules.** Dordrecht: Foris Publications.

Halle, M. &   J.Bresnan & G. Miller (eds.)
1978   **Linguistic Theory and Psychological Reality.** Cambridge
               (Mass.): MIT Press.

Halle, M. & J-R. Vergnaud
1978   **Metrical Structures in Phonology.** mimeo MIT.

Heny, F.
1979   Review of Noam Chomsky "The Logical Structure of
               Linguistic Theory". In: **Synthese** 40, p. 317-352.
1981   Introduction. In: id. (ed.), **Binding and Filtering**
               London: Croom Helm, p. 1-45.

Hoek, T.van den
1970   Opmerkingen over zinscomplementatie. In: **Studia
               Neerlandica** 1970.

Hoeksema, J.
1980   Verbale verstrengeling ontstrengeld. In: **SPEK** 10,
               p. 221-249.

Hoekstra, T.A.
1978a   De Status en Plaats van het Indirekt Objekt. In: Kooij
               (ed.), **Aspekten van Woordvolgorde in het Nederlands.**
               Leiden. p. 40-69.
1978b   Waarom niet niet NEG is. In: **GLOT** 1, p. 93-119.
1981a   De theorie van functie-argument struktuur. In: **Studies
               voor Damsteegt.** Leiden.
1981b   The Base and the Lexicon in Lexical Grammar. In:
               S.Daalder & M.Gerritsen (eds.), **Linguistics in the
               Netherlands** 1981. Amsterdam: Elsevier. p. 93-101.
1983   The distribution of sentential complements. In:
               H.Bennis & W.U.S. van Lessen Kloeke (eds.), **Linguistics
               in the Netherlands** 1983. Dordrecht: Foris Publica-
               tions.

Hoekstra, T.A. & G.Dimmendaal
1983   An alternative approach to Swahili grammar. In: **Lingua**
               60, p. 53-86.

Hoekstra, T.A., H.van der Hulst & M.Moortgat

1980a   Introduction. In: ids.(eds.) 1980c. p. 1-48.
1980b   Het lexicon en de klasse van mogelijke grammatica's.
                             In: **FdL** 21, p. 177-195.
1980c   (eds.), **Lexical Grammar**. Dordrecht: Foris Publications.
1981   (eds.), **Perspectives on Functional Grammar**. Dordrecht:
                             Foris Publications.

Hoekstra, T.A. & M.Moortgat
1979a   Passief en het lexicon. In: **FdL** 20, p. 137-161.
1979b   Review of Van Riemsdijk "A Case Study in Syntactic
                             Markedness". In: **GLOT** 2, p. 181-194.

1979c   Review of Koster "Locality Principles in Syntax". In:
                             GLOT 2, p. 195-214.

Hofmans, M. 1980   Hebben en zijn en de deverbalisering van de modale
                             werkwoorden in het Nederlands. In: M. Dominicy (ed.),
                             Linguistics in Belgium 5. Brussel: Didier Hatier.
                             p. 91-108.

Horn, G.
1974   **The Noun Phrase Constraint**. diss. University of Mass.
                             at Amherst.

Hornstein, N.
1977   S and the X' convention. In: **LA** 3.
Hornstein, N. & D.Lightfoot
1981   Introduction. In: ids. (eds.), **Explanation in**
                             Linguistics. London: Longman. p. 1-31.
Hornstein, N. & A. Weinberg
1981   Case Theory and Preposition Stranding. In: **LI** 12,
                             p. 55-94.

Hust, J. & M. Brame
1976   Jackendoff on interpretive semantics. In: **LA** 2.
Huybregts, M.A.K.
1983   **Cross-serial dependencies** & **the form of   syntactic**
                             structure. Lecture at the Brussels International
                             Conference on Sentential Complementation, June 1983.

Jackendoff, R.S.
1972   **Semantic interpretation in generative grammar**.
                             Cambridge (Mass.): MIT Press.
1973   The Base Rules for Prepositional Phrases. In: Anderson &
                             Kiparsky (eds.)
1975   Morphological and semantic regularities in the lexicon.
                             In: **Lg** 51, p. 639-671.
1976   Toward an explanatory semantic representation. In:
                             LI 7, p. 89-150.
1977   **X'-syntax**: A study of Phrase Structure. Cambridge
                             (Mass.): MIT Press.
Jackendoff, R.S. & P. Culicover
1971   A reconsideration of dative movements. In: **Founda-**
                             tions of Language 7, p. 397-412.
Jacobs, R.A. & P. Rosenbaum (eds.)
1970   **Readings in English Transformational Grammar**. New
                             York: Ginn & Comp.

Jesperson, O.
1940   **A modern English grammar** vol. 5. Copenhagen:
                             Munksgaard.

Johnson, D.
1974   **Towards a theory of relationally-based grammar**. diss.
                             University of Illinois.
1977   On Relational Constraints on Grammar. In: Cole &
                             Sadock (eds.), p. 151-178.

Sadock (eds.), p. 151-178.

Katz, J.J. & P.M. Postal
1964   **An integrated theory of linguistic description.** Cambridge (Mass.): MIT Press.

Kayne, R.S.
1975   **French Syntax: The transformational cycle.** Cambridge (Mass.): MIT Press.
1980   Extensions of binding and case marking. In: LI 11, p. 75-96.
1981a   ECP extensions. In: LI 12, p. 93-134.
1981b   Unambiguous paths. In: May & Koster (eds.),p. 143-184.
1981c   On certain differences between French and English. In: LI 12, p. 349-372.
1981d   Two notes on the NIC. In: Belletti, Brandi & Rizzi (eds.), p. 317-346.
1982a   **Nouns and verbs, predicates and arguments.** Lecture GLOW conference in Paris, March 1982.
1982b   **Le datif en Francais et en Anglais.** mimeo Université de Paris VIII.
1983a   Connectedness. In: LI 14, p. 223-249.
1983b   untitled. Lecture at the Brussels International Conference on Sentential Complementation, june 1983.

Keenan, E.L.
1979   **On surface form and logical form.** paper distributed by LAUT.
1980   Passive is phrasal (not sentential or lexical). In: Hoekstra, Van der Hulst & Moortgat (eds.) 1980c. p. 181-213.

Keenan, E.L. & B.Comrie
1977   Noun phrase accessibility and universal grammar. In: LI 8, p. 63-100.
1979   Data on the noun phrase accessibility hierarchy. In: Lg 55. p. 333-351.

Keenan, E.L. & J.Olmsted Gary
1977   On collapsing grammatical relations in universal grammar. In: P.Cole & J.M. Sadock (eds.), p. 83-120.

Kern, J.H.
1912   **De met het Participium Praeteriti omschreven werkwoordsvormen in 't Nederlands.** Amsterdam: Johannes Muller.

Keyser, S.J. (ed.)
1978   **Recent transformational studies in European languages.** Cambridge (Mass.): MIT Press.

Keyser, S.J. & T. Roeper
1981   **On middle verbs in English.** mimeo MIT and the University of Mass. at Amherst.

Klein, M. & M.C. van de Toorn
1978   Vooropplaatsing van PP's. In: SPEK 7, p.423-433.

Kirsner, R.S.
1979   **The problem of presentative sentences in Modern Dutch.** Amsterdam: North-Holland Publ.Comp.

Kooij, J.G. & E. Wiers
1978   Vooropplaatsing, verplaatsingsregels en de interne struktuur van nominale groepen. In: J.G. Kooij (ed.), **Aspekten van woordvolgorde in het Nederlands.** Leiden.

Koster, J.
1973   PP over V en de theorie van J.Emonds. In: SPEK 2, p. 294-311.

1976   Dutch as an SOV language. In: **LA** 1, p. 111-136.
1978a   **Locality Principles in Syntax.** Dordrecht: Foris
                        Publications.
1978b   Why subject sentences don't exist. In: Keyser (ed.),
                        p. 53-65.
1981   **On binding and control.** paper University of Tilburg.
1982   **Do syntactic representations contain variables?**
                        paper University of Tilburg.
Kraak, A. & W. Klooster
1968   **Syntaxis.** Culemborg: Stam-Robijn.
Kuno, S.
1973   Constraints on internal clauses and sentential
                        subjects. In: **LI** 4, p. 363-385.

Lakoff, G.
1970   **Irregularity in Syntax.** New York: Holt, Rinehart &
                        Winston.

Lakoff, R.
1971   Pasive resistance. In: **CLS** 7, p. 149-162.
Lasnik, H. & J. Kupin
1976   A restrictive theory of transformational grammar.
                        In: **Theoretical Linguistics** 4.

Lawler, J.
1977   A agrees with B in Achenese: A problem for Relational
                        Grammar. In: P.Cole & J.M. Sadock (eds.),   p. 219-248.

Lehmann W.P.
1978   The great underlying ground plans. In: id. (ed.),
                        Syntactic Typology. Sussex: The Harvester Press. p. 3-56.

Lieber, R.
1980   **On the organization of the lexicon.** diss. MIT.
Lightfoot, D.W.
1979a   **Principles of diachronic syntax.** Cambridge:
                        Cambridge University Press.
1979b   Rule classes and syntactic change. In: **LI** 10, p.
                        83-108.
1980   The history of NP movement. In: Hoekstra, Van der
                        Hulst & Moortgat (eds.) 1980c, p. 255-284.
1983   **The Language Lottery.** Cambridge (Mass.): MIT Press.
Longobardi, G.
1980   Remarks on infinitives: a case for a filter.
                        In: **Journal of Italian Linguistics** 5, p. 101-155.

Marantz, A.
1980   **On the nature of grammatical relations.** diss. MIT.
May, R.
1977   **The Grammar of Quantification.** diss. MIT.
May, R. & J. Koster (eds.)
1981   **Levels of syntactic representation.** Dordrecht:
                        Foris Publications.

McCawley, J.
1983   What's with **with.** In: **Lg** 59, p.271-287.
Moortgat, M.
1980   Conditions on rules in Lexical Grammar. In:
                        S.Daalder & M.Gerritsen (eds.), **Linguistics in the
                        Netherlands** 1980. Amsterdam: Elsevier. p. 110-119.
Moortgat, M., H.van der Hulst & T.Hoekstra (eds.)
1981   **The Scope of Lexical Rules.** Dordrecht: Foris
                        Publications.
Nanni, D.
1980   On the surface syntax of constructions with easy-type

adjectives. In: **Lg** 56, p. 568–581.

Newmeyer, F.
1980   **Linguistic Theory in America.** New York: Academic
                    Press.
Nieuwenhuysen, P.
1976   Evers' V-raising. In: **SPEK** 5, p. 589–602.
Oehrle, R.
1976   **The grammatical status of the English Dative
                    Alternation.** diss. MIT.
1981   Lexical Justification. In: Moortgat, Van der
                    Hulst & Hoekstra (eds.), p.201–228
Paardekooper, P.C.
undated   **De beknopte ABN-syntaxis.** Den Bosch, 5th imp.
Perlmutter, D.
1972   **Deep and surface constraints in syntax.** New York:
                    Holt, Rinehart & Winston.
1978   Impersonal passives and the unaccusative hypothesis.
                    In: **BLS** 4, p. 157–189.
1979   Working 1's and inversion in Italian, Japanese and
                    Quechua. In: **BLS** 5.
1981   Functional Grammar and Relational Grammar: Points of
                    Convergence and Divergence. In: Hoekstra, Van der
                    Hulst & Moortgat (eds.) 1981. p. 319–352.
Perlmutter, D. & P.M. Postal
1977   Toward a universal characterization of passive.
                    In: **BLS** 3, p. 394–417.
to appear a   Some proposed laws of basic clause structure. In:
                    D. Perlmutter (ed.), **Studies in Relational Grammar.**
                    Chicago: The Chicago University Press.
to appear b   The 1-advancement exclusiveness law. In: D. Perlmutter
                    (ed.) **Studies in Relational Grammar.** Chicago: The
                    Chicago University Press.
Perlmutter, D. & A. Zaenen
to appear   **The indefinite extraposition construction in Dutch and
                    German.**
Pesetsky, D.
1982   Complementizer-trace phenomena and the Nominative
                    Island Condition. In: **TLR** 1, p. 297–344.
Platzack, C.
1983   Germanic word order and the COMP/INFL parameter. In:
                    Working papers in Scandinavian syntax 2.
Postal, P.M.
1974   **On Raising.** Cambridge (Mass.): MIT Press.
Reinhart, T.
1976   **The syntactic domain of anaphora.** diss. MIT.
1979   A second COMP position. In: Belletti, Brandi &
                    Rizzi (eds.).
Riemsdijk, H.C. van
1978a   **A Case Study in Syntactic Markedness.** Lisse:
                    The Peter de Ridder Press.
1978b   On the diagnosis of WH-movement. In: Keyser (ed.),
                    p. 189–206.
1981a   **The Case of the German adjective.** paper University
                    of Tilburg.
1981b   **Derivational vs. representational grammar.** paper read
                    at the Seoul International Conference on Linguistics.
1981c   **A note on Case Absorption.** paper University of Tilburg.
Riemsdijk, H.C. van & E.S.Williams

1981   NP-Structure. In: **TLR** 1, p. 171-218.
Rizzi, L.
1982   **Issues in Italian Syntax.** Dordrecht: Foris Publications.
1983   **On chain formation.** Lecture GLOW conference in York,
                           March 1983.
Roeper, T. & M. Siegel
1978   A lexical transformation for verbal compounds. In:
                           LI 9, p. 199-260.

Rosenbaum, P.S.
1967   **The grammar of English Predicate Complement
                           Constructions.** Cambridge (Mass.): MIT Press.
1970   A principle governing deletion in English sentential
                           complements. In: Jacobs & Rosenbaum (eds.).

Ross, J.R.
1967   **Constraints on variables in syntax.** diss. MIT.
1972   Doubl-ing. In: **LI** 3, p. 61-86.
Rouveret, A. & J-R. Vergnaud
1980   Specifying reference to the subject: French causatives
                           and conditions on representations. In: **LI** 11,
                           p. 97-202.

Ruwet, N.
1972   La syntaxe du pronomen **en** et la transformation
                           de "montée du sujet". In: **Theorie syntaxique
                           et syntaxe du francais.** Paris: Editions du Seuil.
1982   Une construction absolue. In: **Grammaire des insultes
                           et autres études.** Paris: Editions du Seuil.

Sadock, J.M.
1977   In defense of spontaneous demotion. In: P. Cole &
                           J.M. Sadock (eds.), p. 47-58.

Safir, K.
1982   Inflection government and inversion. In: **TLR** 1,
                           p. 417-467.

Sassen, A.
1963   Endogeen en exogeen taalgebruik. In: **De Nieuwe
                           Taalgids** 56, p. 10-21.

Selkirk, E.O.
1977   Noun phrase structure. In: Culicover, Wasow &
                           Akmajian (eds.), p. 285-325.
1981   English compounding and the theory of word structure.
                           In: Moortgat, Van der Hulst & Hoekstra (eds.),
                           p. 229-277.

Siegel, M.E.A.
1983   Problems in preposition stranding. In: **LI**
                           14, p. 184-188.

Stoett, F.
1923³   **Middelnederlandsche Spraakkunst. Syntaxis.** Den Haag.
Stowell, T.
1981   **Origins of phrase structure.** diss. MIT.
Taraldsen, K.T.
1978a   **On the NIC, vacuous application and the that-trace
                           filter.** distributed by IULC.
1978b   The scope of WH-movement in Norwegian. In:
                           LI 9, p. 623-640.
1981a   The head of S in Germanic and Romance. In:
                           T.Fretheim & L. Hellan (eds.), **Proceedings of
                           the Sixth Scandinavian Conference on Linguistics.**
                           Trondheim: Tapir.
1981b   The theoretical interpretation of a class of marked

extractions. In: Belletti, Brandi & Rizzi (eds.).

Tiersch, C.
1978   **Topics in German Syntax.** diss. MIT.
Thomason, R.
1976   Some extensions of Montague Grammar. In:
                    E. Partee (ed.), **Montague Grammar.** New York: Academic
                    Press.

Vat, Jan
1980   Zich en zichzelf. In: S.Daalder & M. Gerritsen
                    (eds.), **Linguistics in the Netherlands** 1980.
                    Amsterdam: Elsevier Publishing Com. p. 127-138.

Vendler, Z.
1967   **Linguistics and philosophy.** Ithaca: Cornell
                    University Press.

Vennemann, T.
1974   Topics, Subjects and Word Order: From SXV to SVX via
                    TVS. In: J.M. Anderson & C. Jones (eds.) **Historical
                    Linguistics.** Amsterdam: North-Holland Publ. Comp.
                    p. 339-376.
1976   An explanation of drift. In: C.N. Li (ed.), **Word
                    order and word order change.** Austin: University
                    of Texas Press. p. 269-305.

Verhagen, A.
1979   Fokusbepalingen en grammatikale theorie. In:
                    SPEK 8, p. 372-402.
1981   Koncepties in grammatika-onderzoek. In: **SPEK** 10,
                    p.340-368.

Vooijs, C.G.N. de
1947   **Nederlandse Spraakkunst.** Groningen: Wolters.
Wasow, T.
1972   **Anaphoric Relations in English.** diss. MIT.
1977   Transformations and the lexicon. In: Culicover,
                    Wasow & Akmajian (eds.), p. 327-360.
1980   Major and minor rules. In: Hoekstra, Van der Hulst
                    & Moortgat (eds.) 1980c. p. 285-312.

Wiers, E.
1978   Kleins appositionele constructies. In: **SPEK** 8,
                    p. 62-80.

Williams, E.S.
1980   Predication. In: **LI** 11, p. 203-237.
1981a   Argument structure and morphology. In: **TLR** 1,
                    p. 81-114.
1981b   On the notions "lexically related" and "head
                    of a word". In: **LI** 12, p. 245-273.
1982   Another argument that passive is transformational.
                    In: **LI** 13, p. 160-163.
1983   Against small clauses. In: **LI** 14, p. 287-307.
Zubizarreta, M.L.
1982   **On the relationship of the lexicon to syntax.**
                    diss. MIT.

Curriculum Vitae

Teun Hoekstra werd geboren op 24 januari 1953 te Ridderkerk. In 1972 behaalde hij het diploma gymnasium alfa en begon hij zijn studie Nederlandse Taal- en Letterkunde aan de Rijksuniversiteit te Leiden. Daar behaalde hij in 1974 zijn kandidaats. Van 1974 tot 1976 was hij als leraar Nederlands verbonden aan de Sg. Hugo de Groot te Rotterdam. In 1978 behaalde hij cum laude het doktoraal diploma met Nederlandse Taalkunde als hoofdrichting en Algemene Taalwetenschap als bijvak. Sindsdien is hij in verschillende aanstellingsvormen werkzaam geweest bij de Faculteit der Letteren in Leiden. Thans is hij medewerker aan de Vakgroep Nederlands en belast met de verzorging van onderwijs en het verrichten van onderzoek op het terrein van de moderne taalkunde. Van 1977 tot augustus 1983 was hij tevens als docent moderne taalkunde verbonden aan de MO-opleiding Nederlands van de School voor Taal- en Letterkunde (thans Haagse Leergangen) te Den Haag. Hij is als redacteur verbonden aan de tijdschriften voor taalwetenschap GLOT en Lingua en de linguistische reeks Linguistic Models.
Hij is sinds 1974 getrouwd met Sonja en vader van Menno (6 jaar) en Femke (3 jaar).